THE WORD AND THE CHRIST

THE WORD
AND THE CHRIST

An Essay in Analytic Christology

RICHARD STURCH

CLARENDON PRESS · OXFORD
1991

Oxford University Press, Walton Street, Oxford OX2 6DP

Oxford New York Toronto
Delhi Bombay Calcutta Madras Karachi
Petaling Jaya Singapore Hong Kong Tokyo
Nairobi Dar es Salaam Cape Town
Melbourne Auckland
and associated companies in
Berlin Ibadan

Oxford is a trade mark of Oxford University Press

Published in the United States
by Oxford University Press, New York

© *R. L. Sturch* 1991

British Library Cataloguing in Publication Data
Sturch, Richard L.
The word and the Christ.
1. Christology
I. Title
232
ISBN 0–19–826198–5

Library of Congress Cataloging in Publication Data
Data available.

Typeset by BP Integraphics, Bath, Avon

Printed in Great Britain by
Bookcraft (Bath) Ltd
Midsomer Norton, Avon

Acknowledgements

I should like to record here my gratitude to Mr A. N. S. Lane, of the London Bible College, and to the Revd Dr Alan Padgett, of Oriel College, Oxford, discussions with whom improved what follows in several places. I should also like to thank Professor John Hick for very kindly lending me a copy of his article on 'The Logic of God Incarnate' (*Religious Studies*, 25, December 1989) in advance of publication.

Contents

Abbreviations

ET	English translation
par.	and parallels
p/b	paperback edition
PG	Patrologia Graeca, ed. J. P. Migne (Paris, 1857–66)
PL	Patrologia Latina, ed. J. P. Migne (Paris, 1844–64)
PO	Patrologia Orientalis, ed. R. Graffin, F. Nau, and F. Graffin (Paris, 1907–)
v.l.	varia lectio (variant reading)

Introduction

Distinctions within Christology

I HAVE called this a study in 'analytic Christology', and, having begun so inauspiciously, had better try to justify myself as quickly as possible. Christology, the study from a theological standpoint of Jesus of Nazareth who was called 'the Christ', covers in fact quite a range of different topics. There is, for example, the field of New Testament Christology, that is, the attempt to understand and explain how the writers of the New Testament thought about Jesus. This is of course in a sense a 'second-order' field of study; it is not trying to study Jesus Himself directly, but only what certain people said and thought about Him (though nearly all writers on this topic have also supposed that what these particular people said and thought was of quite special importance and authority). Other fields of study coming under the general heading of 'Christology' are however more a matter of trying to state truths about Jesus directly: and among them I would suggest that we may distinguish three in particular, which may be labelled 'analytic', 'proclamatory', and 'revisionist'.

Analytic Christology takes something about Jesus for granted. What this something is may vary from one theologian to another. Some may use the biblical assertions about Him as a basis; others, a particular formulation such as the decree of the Council of Chalcedon, or a denominational confession; others a more vaguely expressed 'tradition of the Church'. Or the theologians may draw up their own starting-points, perhaps with a view to committing themselves as little as possible at so early a stage, so as to let almost anyone feel free to participate as reader and mental commentator. Schillebeeckx, for example, defines Christology as starting by 'identifying Jesus of Nazareth as someone who on behalf of God brings definitive and decisive salvation to men'.[1] Some would doubtless

---

[1] Schillebeeckx (1979), p. 741.

feel this was asserting too much; perhaps we should omit 'definitive and decisive' until we have established (if we do) that what Jesus brings really is definitive and decisive.

However, having explained the basis from which they are going to start, analytic Christologists seek to work out what sort of states of affairs must hold, what propositions about Jesus Himself, about God, and about the human race must be true, if their 'basis' is to make sense. They are setting out to analyse the implications of their own starting-points; aware that these starting-points, however true they may be, are only true because certain other things are true as well, they seek to work out what these latter may be. A good deal of patristic Christology was 'analytic' in this sense. The starting-point of nearly all the Fathers was that Jesus Christ was their Saviour and the proper object of faith and worship, as declared in the Bible: but whether this could only be true if He were one in substance with the Father, or whether some less close relationship to the Father would also justify this starting-point, that became a matter for debate. So also at a later date did the question of whether the starting-point could be true if in Jesus the eternal Word took the place of a human spirit; or if He had two distinct wills, a divine and a human; and so on. In each case the question was (if I may be allowed a complex mixture of metaphors) about what lay behind a starting-point that was common ground to everyone.

Proclamatory Christology seeks rather to move *forward* from the starting-point. It too asks about the starting-point's implications, but not so much about what must have been true to enable the starting-point to be true also, as about what *new* truths the starting-point itself leads us to discover. The analytic Christologist, finding himself or herself a Christian believer, asks 'Why am I here? How is it that this faith is true?'; the proclamatory Christologist (who may of course be the same person) asks 'Where do I go from here? What is this faith pointing me to?' Much of the 'large type' in Karl Barth's *Church Dogmatics*, Volume IV, is in this sense proclamatory (the analytical material being more in the 'small type'); indeed, one is tempted to say that the best way to understand his treatment there of the Person of Christ is to see it as a gigantic three-point sermon, proclaiming not just the truth of the Incarnation but also its implications and consequences.[2] But of course modern procla-

---

[2] Barth (1956–8).

matory Christology was being written before Barth. For instance, the closing sections of P. T. Forsyth's *The Person and Place of Jesus Christ*[3] could well be seen as proclamatory (and indeed, in their depiction of Christ's *kenosis* and *plerosis*, not unlike the first two parts of Barth's treatment). Nor have such Christologies ceased; a more recent example would be that of the Roman Catholic writer Dom Sebastian Moore, *The Fire and the Rose are One*.[4] Proclamatory Christology is theology all right; its appeal is first of all to the intellect: its aim, however, is not to satisfy the intellect with the feeling of a difficulty solved (as in analytic Christology) but to enable the intellect to understand better what great things the Lord has done for us, and through this to affect the reader's whole personality.

One particular brand of proclamatory Christology—maybe it should even be regarded as a separate type on its own ('contextual Christology', perhaps?)—is that which seeks to relate the figure of Christ to changes in other fields of human thought and knowledge. How (if at all) is our understanding of Christ to be affected by, shall we say, theories of evolution, or the rise of psychoanalysis, or advances in biblical criticism, or the possibility of life on other planets? Examples could be cited: Illingworth's essay in *Lux Mundi*[5] on 'The Incarnation and Development', or Mascall's discussion of multiple incarnations in his *Christian Theology and Natural Science.*[6] W. R. Matthews, in a book[7] which is itself a good example of this kind of work, summed up the approach in the words: 'If we really believe in the Incarnation, we must hold that it will illuminate all fresh discoveries and in turn be illuminated by them.' 'All' may be a little sweeping, but basically Matthews was right; and in thus setting the figure of our Lord in the context of new discoveries, contextual Christology is in effect helping to proclaim Him.

'Revisionist' Christology, like the others, takes a starting-point which is in some sense given it by Scripture or general Christian consensus; but it does so in order to *correct* it. Previous understanding of the person of Jesus has been in some way mistaken and needs

---

[3] Forsyth (1909).   [4] Moore (1980).   [5] In Gore (1889), ch. 5.
[6] Mascall (1956), pp. 38ff.   [7] Matthews (1950), p.84.

to be set right. I suppose the classic example of this was in the work of Ritschl, with his criticism of formulae which belong to the 'sphere of disinterested scientific knowledge' in which 'the religious conception of Christ finds no place', by contrast with a revised approach; 'If Christ by what he has done and suffered for my salvation is my Lord, and if, by trusting for my salvation to the power of what he has done for me, I honour him as my God, then that is a value-judgment of a direct kind', and quite different from the traditional doctrine of the Two Natures.[8] The result, affirmation of Christ's Deity, may be very similar—indeed, it is meant to be—but the approach is clearly very different, and the orthodox as a result felt a certain (understandable) doubt about whether the content of the affirmation could really be the same. And far more drastic 'revisions' have been known of course—among some of the Hegelian theologians of the nineteenth century, for example. Thus we find Biedermann praising Strauss for having 'hit negatively on the right point, the one on which everything depends, that a *person* is not the subject for the predicates of Christology'.[9] Clearly a revision which eliminates the person of Jesus from Christology is so drastic that one wonders whether 'revision' is a strong enough word to describe it; it leaves much recent 'radical' Christologizing in books like *The Myth of God Incarnate*[10] far behind.

Obviously these types of Christology can overlap, and the boundaries between them cannot always be precisely drawn. What to one reader may be analytic or proclamatory may strike another as revisionist. Notoriously, something very like this happened in the great Christological controversies of the fourth, fifth, and sixth centuries: what to Nestorius (let us say) was a straightforward attempt to understand better the mystery of the Lord's Incarnation was to Cyril a revision, or rather an undermining, of the whole idea of that Incarnation—and vice versa. An analysis may not be an *accurate* analysis (for centuries people 'analysed' dawn and evening in terms of a literally rising and setting sun), and to have one's analysis challenged by a more accurate rival, or even a less accurate one, may be most disturbing. More seriously, a given essay in Christ-

---

[8] Ritschl (1900), pp. 398–9.   [9] In Welch (1965), p. 334.   [10] Hick (1977*b*).

ology may come under more than one classification. Writers may begin by seeking to analyse and find that they want to revise instead, because no analysis that they can contrive seems satisfactory; or they may move from revision to the proclamation of their new ideas, or of Christ seen in terms of them; or they may be trying to put Christology into a contemporary context and find that in order to do so they must first analyse just what this Christology is. The present essay is intended to be one in analysis; yet it may well be that we have to bring in the context, and so perhaps move a little closer to proclamation, or even that it will conflict with ideas held by its readers, and appear to them (what it certainly does not set out to be) revisionist in its results. I can only ask the reader to persevere and find out.

The plan of the present work is as follows: to consider first of all the possibility that analytic Christology is not needed, simply because revision is. Serious questions have been raised about the tenability of traditional doctrines of the Person of Christ, and this however we understand the word 'traditional' here. We begin therefore by seeing how strong a case can be made out for abandoning any attempt at analysis. It should, however, be pointed out in advance that the objections that will be raised come from many different sources. Some critics of traditional Christology are atheists. Some are theists, indeed professed Christians, who wish to reject the idea of incarnation. Some again do believe in the Incarnation, but regard the traditional forms of the doctrine as in some way objectionable or misleadingly expressed. The fact that a particular objection is raised to traditional Christology by someone does not mean that that someone rejects the Incarnation.

The next step might naturally be supposed to be to try and answer these questions and objections. But since analysis of the doctrine may help us to answer them, the pattern used by St Thomas Aquinas in the *Summa Theologiae* will be used instead: that is, we proceed to try our hand at analysis first, setting aside (though keeping in mind) the arguments which suggested that this might be a waste of time. Only when the analysis has been carried out can we turn back to the earlier arguments and see whether they will still hold good in the light of what we have since worked out. This book is of course intended for professing Christians, and in this section some minimal form of Christianity will have to be assumed—that in some way God is known, and people are redeemed, in Jesus

Christ. I have also included after the main body of the book some short excursuses, attempts to handle problems that seem relevant but do not fit easily into the general pattern. I think they may in the end further the aims of the present study.

I

The 'Obsolescence'
of Traditional Views

'THE Son', begins the second of the Thirty-Nine Articles of the
Church of England, 'which is the Word of the Father, begotten
from everlasting of the Father, the very and eternal God, of one
substance with the Father, took man's nature in the womb of the
blessed Virgin, of her substance: so that two whole and perfect
natures, that is to say, the Godhead and Manhood were joined
together in one Person.' Perhaps that will do as a place to begin.
'Any attempt', it has been remarked, 'to describe [the generally
accepted position in Christology] is inevitably going to give the
impression of being ill-informed, of generalizing unjustly and of
distorting current theology',[1] so it is probably best to ignore current
theology altogether for the moment and take a formula from the
past. As a matter of fact, criticisms of orthodoxy, where they are
specific in their selection of the position to be criticized,[2] usually
choose the definition of the Council of Chalcedon; but that is con-
siderably longer. Moreover, the Monophysite Churches of the East
do not accept the Council of Chalcedon, but would certainly
find their own positions as much under attack in most of the criticism
that follows as the position of the Chalcedonians.[3] Also, the
Anglican formula avoids the use of one of Chalcedon's key terms,

[1] Rahner (1961), p. 152.
[2] Lack of specificity is not a defect in these criticisms. Even the orthodox do
not always use the same formulae, so their critics need not do so either; indeed,
the wider the range of positions attacked, the more effective a successful attack
will be.
[3] Incidentally, there has been a good deal of agreement in recent years among
both Monophysite and Chalcedonian theologians that the differences between the
two sides are more verbal than real, another good reason for not starting with a
formula which Monophysites find verbally unacceptable. Thus Mascall (1977),
pp. 146–7, 243, cites *St Vladimir's Theological Quarterly*, 11 (1967), 150ff., and 14
(1970), 222ff., and the *Acta Apostolicae Sedis*, 73 (1971), 814. Cf. also Samuel (1973).
(I owe this reference to Dr Alan Padgett.)

the word 'hypostasis', which is notoriously difficult to understand, and as far as I can make out was so even in the fifth century.[4] (Reference to the Chalcedonian formula will, however, appear with considerable frequency; it is impossible to pretend to forget it.) The main thing is that throughout the greater part of her history nearly all the Church has agreed on three things: that Jesus Christ was truly human, that He was truly divine, and that He was truly one person. And it has normally used the language of 'two natures', human and divine, though Monophysite Christians would say that these two were joined together so as to form a single nature after the Incarnation. It is this position that has been subjected to a great deal of criticism in more recent years; and it is at this criticism that we must now look. As it comes from such different sources, which are under no obligation to be consistent with one another, we shall need to look at it under a number of different heads.

Of course, there is a sense in which any revisionist Christology must, if it is correct, render previous views obsolete, and even if it is mistaken must *claim* that they are obsolete. We are concerned here, however, with the contention that traditional ideas about Christ can be seen to be obsolete even before we begin to revise them. A cobbler will no doubt be able to mend my shoes before I realize that there is anything wrong with them, but that does not mean to say that I cannot realize that they are letting the water in, even before I take them to him for repair.

One particular form the charge of obsolescence might take will, however, be ignored here, because to state it in detail and answer or discuss it later would take us so far from Christology and into such fundamental problems that another book altogether would be required. This is the charge that the approach of earlier generations to Christology (and indeed to most theological questions) has been by way of appeal to the Bible, supplemented perhaps by appeal to authoritative pronouncements by the Church's authorities (such as the Council of Chalcedon)—and that this kind of approach is itself obsolete. Neither Bible nor Church can, according to this criticism, be treated as an independent source of knowledge any longer: the principles, therefore, which guided the Fathers, the

---

[4] See Excursus VI, below.

Schoolmen, or the Reformers cannot be ours; and no more can their Christologies.

A certain amount of what will be said later on in the (I hope) more constructive part of this essay will in fact be relevant to this contention, though, as I have said, there will not be enough room to deal with the whole problem of authority in theology. For the moment it may suffice to say that even if the criticism were justified, it would not show that traditional Christology was mistaken, only that the methods by which it was arrived at were not reliable ones. The detective in a whodunit may jump to conclusions, but that does not mean that he or she is necessarily suspecting the wrong person. All it means is that other evidence will be needed to back up any such suspicions; and all *this* charge of obsolescence would mean, even if it were justified, would be that defenders of traditional Christology will need to look more carefully at their proofs. Other 'obsolescence' charges, however, do strike directly at traditional formulae. We may begin with the charge that the vocabulary of Christology is obsolete.

This objection is summed up by Hans Küng as follows: 'The two-natures doctrine, using terms and ideas which bear the imprint of Hellenistic language and mentality, is no longer understood today.'[5] The questions of *ideas* (as opposed to *terms*) and of Hellenistic imprint we shall come to later on; for the moment our concern is with the question of terms or language that cannot be understood today. If the charge is justified, then at the very least we must accept what Küng says elsewhere: 'The truths taught by the ancient Christological councils ... must constantly be taken out of the sociocultural Hellenistic context and transferred to the mental climate of our own time.'[6] But actually things may be in worse case than that. For vocabulary may become obsolete because it has been realized that there never was anything to which it referred. The 'Philosopher's Stone', for example, has vanished from the chemist's vocabulary because of the realization that no stone, nor anything like one, could ever transmute base metals into gold; and it may be that the old Christological vocabulary has become obsolete for the same sort of reason, and never did teach a truth that could be transferred to the mental climate of our own time.

Even if this is not so, the charge of obsolete language is obviously

---

[5] Küng (1976), p. 131.   [6] p. 450.

a serious one. I said earlier on that we might take the formula of the Thirty-Nine Articles to begin with, and not that of Chalcedon, because of the difficulty of one of the terms used by the latter, namely 'hypostasis'. But the Article used quite freely another of Chalcedon's terms, 'nature', and this Küng evidently finds as objectionable as the other. And is he not right? 'Nature' in present-day English refers as a rule to the animals and plants of this planet, and some features of its minerals like, wind, cloud, river, lake and hill, as contrasted with what the human race has done to or with them. The brook is Nature, and so are the trees by its banks and the birds that sing in them; the cigarette-ends and soft-drink cans that litter the banks, and even the bridge that crosses from one to the other, are not Nature. But this clearly has nothing to do with the Person of our Lord. 'Two Natures' makes no sense if this is what we mean by 'Nature'—and normally it is.

Of course, occasionally we do use 'nature' in a very different way. 'It is not in my nature to love much', says the central character in William Golding's *Pincher Martin*; 'Let bears and lions growl and fight, For 'tis their nature to', wrote Isaac Watts, in language which is not indeed contemporary but is still comprehensible. Yet this use of the word is not much help to us either. It seems to suggest factors in our life—or the lives of bears and lions—which are beyond our or their control. (Hence of course the understandable annoyance of many homosexuals at reference to 'unnatural' sexual relationships; for them, they feel, homosexual relationships are, in this sense, *natural*.) But what has this got to do with the Incarnation? Is the Article suggesting that whereas for most of us there are some elements in our life that are beyond our control, Jesus Christ had extra things beyond His, the 'divine nature' which is presumably beyond even God's control? Surely not! 'Individual nature' is no more help to us than the 'nature' of the countryside. Even the word with which the extract from the Article closed, 'Person', is liable to much the same accusation of obsolescence. This may seem odd at first. 'A person' means simply 'a human being' (except perhaps in science fiction and the like); it is quite normal English, and indeed has recently become rather commoner than it used to be, as an alternative to 'man'. And Jesus certainly was a person in this sense, as the Article says He was. So why talk of obsolescence? Simply because this is *not* what the Article was trying to say. That Jesus was a human being it had already said, with its references to 'taking man's nature' and 'Manhood'; the 'Person' it now speaks of is meant to refer to Jesus as *God* as well as man. The word does not mean 'human being' in the Article; it is meant to cope with the fact that Jesus was more than just a human being; and *a fortiori* its Greek equivalent, πρόσωπον, does not mean 'human being' in the formula of Chalcedon. Quite clearly the vocabularies of the Article and the Council are obsolete to the extent of being positively misleading; Küng's 'no longer understood today' is really something of an under-statement. 'Liable to be misunderstood today' would be more like it.

Our second charge will be that the concepts embodied in the vocabulary are obsolete too. It is at least a possibility, as was said just now, that the vocabulary of traditional Christology is obsolete because the concepts used in it referred to nothing in reality, like the concept of the Philosopher's Stone. The criticism we are to con-sider now is perhaps a less provocative way of making the same point. In Küng's words, not only the terms but also the *ideas* of the 'two-nature' doctrine are dated and no longer understood.

We may illustrate this with a parallel example from the doctrine of the sacraments, suggested by Dr Frances Young.[7]

At the Reformation controversy raged over the exact way in which the eucharistic bread and wine is the body and blood of Jesus Christ. One side wanted to see it as symbolic, the other as literal. An account of the literal meaning according to the 'science' of the time was offered: the under-lying *substance* became the body and blood of Christ, while the *accidents* remained those of bread and wine. Such an explanation of the literal mean-ing ceases to have any value when we think in terms not of substance and accidents, but of molecules, atoms, electrons and nuclei.

The words 'substance' and 'accident' have of course changed their meanings over the years; we should use them today chiefly in phrases like 'a green substance of the consistency of chalk' or 'an accident on the MI motorway', and anyone introducing a newcomer to the debates of the Reformation era would have a lot of explaining to do before the words could be used safely. But, more important, the explanation would probably take the form of saying something like this: 'In those days, they thought of things as composed of two elements, the substance, which did not change as long as the bread remained bread and the wine remained wine, and the

---

[7] In Hick (1977*b*), p. 35.

accidents, which could change when, say, the bread became stale or the wine was heated.' The very concepts with which both sides operated in the sixteenth century have become obsolete; they require explanation, and explanation in terms of what used to be supposed the case but is supposed no longer.[8] The same seems to be true of the concepts used in the Article or the definition of Chalcedon. The very fact that the words 'nature' and 'person' have changed their meanings and that no equivalents have taken their place implies that the concepts they used to represent are obsolete. It is not like the words 'sore' and 'let', which have certainly changed their meaning since Cranmer wrote 'We are sore let and hindered in running the race that is set before us', but whose work has been taken over without serious loss by (say) 'severely' and 'hampered'. *No* words have arisen to do what 'nature' and 'person' did in the sixteenth century, any more than with 'substance' and 'accident', because we no longer have any task for them to do. Strictly speaking, there never was a task for them to do; they never were correlated with anything in reality: only, in those days this was not realized, and now it is. Of course, there is no reason to suppose that our own vocabulary, or our own conceptual apparatus, is final or incapable of improvement; future generations may some day be saying much the same sort of thing about the twentieth century as we have been saying about the sixteenth. But it is most unlikely that future generations will ever reinstate the old language and the old concepts: and in any case our own concepts are by definition all we have with which to do our thinking, and our own language all we have with which to express it; we have got to treat our present equipment as if it were adequate, because there is nothing else we can do. Certainly we cannot allow that obsolete concepts will do just as well simply because our present ones may possibly one day be obsolete too. The thoughts embodied in the old formulae are as out of date as the words in which they were expressed.

Again, other ideas, not embodied in language, have also surely become obsolete. It is fairly easy to detect obsolescence in a concept like that of 'nature' or 'person', because of the change in vocabulary.

---

[8] I know of course that some do still defend the validity of concepts like 'substance' and 'accident'. But not only are these in a minority; they themselves realize that they have to defend the use of these concepts and show how they can still be used—if indeed they can. In other words, even if these concepts are not really obsolete, they certainly give that impression. Nobody feels the need to defend the concept of a scientific law, for example.

But not all our ideas are simply concepts, nor are all reflected in the dictionaries. There are many beliefs that people take more or less for granted at one time and ignore or positively disbelieve at another. One obvious example has already been referred to. For thousands of years everyone took it for granted that the sun really did move around the world, rising and setting in the most literal sense of those words. No educated person supposes this nowadays. But religious ideas are just as subject to this kind of change as scientific ones are, and it may be that some of these changes have rendered obsolete ideas that once made the idea of an Incarnation plausible. Thus in New Testament times, to quote Professor Maurice Wiles, 'the idea of supernatural divine intervention was a natural category of thought and faith, in a way that is no longer true even of the main body of convinced believers today. It was within the context of such a general belief in divine intervention that belief in the specific form of divine intervention which we know as the incarnation grew up.'[9] Of course, this is in no way evidence against the idea of incarnation, and Wiles is, naturally, aware of this; his point is not so much that it makes belief in the Incarnation impossible as that it makes it easier to believe the doctrine to be (in his words) 'an interpretation of Jesus appropriate to the age in which it arose than to treat it as an unalterable truth binding upon all generations'. In a feudal age it was easy to see the Church as a feudal structure with authority delegated by the Pope to bishops, and by them to priests, with lay people simply as their subjects; in a democratic society it is easier to see her as a structure where the whole people of God are the 'authority' and the clergy are 'enablers' rather than lords. This does not mean that the second view is right and the first wrong; but it does make more plausible the idea that both were perhaps produced by their times and neither a definitive, God-given truth. So also with the idea of divine intervention. That one age believed readily in such interventions, and ours does not, in no way entails that they are impossible, but it does make a bit more plausible the idea that perhaps the doctrine of *the* great Divine Intervention was a product of first-century habits of thought rather than revelation from above.

Another contributor to the same symposium takes a similar line when discussing the 'kenotic' Christologies of the nineteenth and

[9] In Hick (1977*b*), p. 4.

earlier twentieth centuries.[10] 'The idea of kenosis in bourgeois Christian thought', writes Mr Donald Cupitt,[11] 'is clearly socially-conditioned. In a class society . . . there was a need for christological validation of the duty to "condescend to men of low estate". The change in the connotations of the word "condescend" since those days gives us a revealing glimpse of theology's cultural relativity, and makes clear the hopeless inappropriateness of the idea of kenosis today.' Cupitt is not, I think, saying that Kenoticist divines (he has Gore, who was both an aristocrat and a socialist, particularly in mind) were consciously devising a Christology to justify a particular social attitude, though his language may suggest this. The point is rather that religious concepts change together with social ones, and that if a social concept, in this case that of a superior class lowering itself to familiarity with an inferior, becomes out of date or even objectionable, then any religious concept which shares its approach will become out of date or objectionable too. (Conversely, of course, useful new concepts may come into theology which could not be used before; but that is not our concern at the present moment.)

There is also the problem of historical relativism. The principle of historical relativism is not a source of criticism of traditional Christology alone, but raises a more general query about any attempt to produce an 'unchanging faith' 'once delivered to the saints', whether Christological or not, and indeed whether Christian or not. That there is a historical continuity between Christians of the present day and those of New Testament times is obvious and indisputable, but does it make sense to talk of *doctrinal* continuity, even in cases where we use the same words? The use of time-honoured expressions may conceal an almost total disagreement over meanings. Take the famous Christological title 'Son of Man'. To some this has been a statement of our Lord's full humanity, and more particularly of His *representative* humanity; as the hymn says,

> 'Son of God, eternal Saviour,
> Source of life and truth and grace,
> Son of Man, whose birth incarnate
> Hallows all our human race.'[12]

---

[10] Cf. Excursus III, below.   [11] Hick (1977*b*), p. 137.
[12] S. C. Lowry (*Hymns Ancient and Modern*, 677).

To others, seeking to share the apocalyptic frame of mind common in the first century, it is the title of a supernatural figure derived ultimately from the visions of the Book of Daniel. While to others it is simply a periphrasis for 'I', a phrase Jesus was in the habit of using to allude to Himself, but with little or no theological significance. All these ideas can be found among modern English Christians, sharing a common culture. How much greater must be the differences between any of them and the people who originally used the expression! We are to a great extent creatures of our time and our surroundings. So were they; and this holds for our theologies as well. As it has been well put,[13]

a theologian setting about his task in, for example, the seventeenth century does not simply place a little more material on top of a pile whose contents and composition he has painstakingly examined and grasped. Even if he ... wishes to assert no originality, his debt will be, albeit unconsciously, at least as great to the movements of thought and sensibility, the priorities of concern, in the society around him, as to the past which is the avowed object of his loyalty ... From this point of view, he stands not on the shoulders of Paul (and the rest, as in some huge gymnastic pyramid), but in a circle with him, looking inwards at that from which both derive.

And, inevitably, seeing it rather differently!

It is not, then, simply a matter of an obsolete vocabulary or conceptual framework; the difficulty is a more fundamental one even than these. The ideas of past generations are to a great extent inaccessible to us; if we seek to repeat them, or even to understand them, we bring to our endeavours such a load of our own generation's ideas that those endeavours are sure to fail, even if they seem to succeed. Of course, we are not *completely* cut off from our past. We are twentieth-century *Christians*, not twentieth-century Hindus, Muslims, Sikhs, or agnostics. Our beliefs are affected by those of past Christian ages as well as by those of the present day. But this does not affect the fact that the Christologies of those days cannot be held today: not because they are false, but because, true or false (if indeed those terms can be applied at all once one has realized the full force of historical relativism), we cannot hold them; it is literally not within our power to do so. The most we can say is something on the lines of 'My way of experiencing God and clothing that experience in words is then along a path initiated by Jesus,

[13] Houlden (1977), p. 15.

with the impulse given by the New Testament, but it is related to him and is in a way formed by what in the world demands my belief and adherence'.[14] Within these limits there can and will be considerable variation, from the would-be 'orthodox' to the defiantly 'radical'; but the limits are inescapable.

[14] Houlden (1977) p. 82.

2

The 'Logical Incoherence'
of Traditional Views

WE are now moving from linguistic and what one might call socio-logical considerations to more philosophical ones. The charge is that any statement of the doctrine of the Incarnation that is reasonably 'orthodox' is also in some sense self-contradictory or logically incoherent, like asserting that something is a round square. And those who make this charge have, interestingly enough, a number of less 'radical' writers and thinkers on their side—not because these others wish to deny the Incarnation, but because, while admitting that it is paradoxical, they do not see anything wrong with paradox. The idea of paradox is not easily distinguished from self-contradiction. We might suppose that the difference is this, that a paradox is only an *apparent* self-contradiction. Frederick is twenty-one years old, yet if you go by birthdays he is 'a little boy of five'. Why? because he was born on 29 February, and therefore has no birthdays except in leap years.[1] There is no contradiction; only 'a most ingenious paradox'. But there are a few who will have none of this 'apparent' stuff. 'When the Reason takes pity on the Paradox, and wishes to help it to an explanation, the Paradox does not indeed acquiesce, but nevertheless finds it quite natural that the Reason should do this, for why do we have our philosophers, if not to make supernatural things trivial or commonplace?'[2] Less vividly, Dietrich Bonhoeffer said of the formula of Chalcedon that in it 'an unequivocally positive, direct statement about Jesus Christ is superseded and split into two expressions which stand over against one another in contradiction'.[3]

This will not do. A contradiction is by definition untrue; it differs

[1] See W. S. Gilbert, *The Pirates of Penzance.*   [2] Kierkegaard (1967), p. 66.
[3] Bonhoeffer (1978), p. 102.

from other falsehoods only in that it is something which never was, never will be, and never could be true. If the doctrine of the Incarnation involves a contradiction, there is no more to be said. 'Contradicting oneself', to quote Sir Peter Strawson, 'is like writing something down and then erasing it ... A contradiction cancels itself and leaves nothing'.[4] We cannot take the line that Kierkegaard took; either the doctrine of the Incarnation, however mysterious, is in the end logically coherent after all or it is to be abandoned. But which?

We may perhaps feel doubts about the extreme assertion of Professor John Knox that 'it is impossible, by definition, that God should become a man'.[5] The logician will be almost as unhappy with this as with Kierkegaard. If one element of the definition of 'God' as Professor Knox uses the word is 'incapable of becoming a man', then what is to prevent someone more orthodox from using a definition which is otherwise identical with Knox's but does not include this one particular element? In which case no impossibility would arise. Of course, almost certainly what Knox really meant was that the common understanding or definition of the word 'divine' contains elements which are incompatible with elements in the corresponding definition of the word 'human'. The question is, what are these elements?

And surely there are a great many. God is infinite, without beginning in time or location in space, incapable of death, 'without body, parts or passions'. People are finite, born at particular times and in particular places, mortal, embodied, with many parts and many passions (both in the modern sense of the word and in the older one of 'being passive, being acted on by other things'). Surely here we have quite enough to say that the definitions of 'divine' and 'human' are such as to make it impossible for anyone to be both.

However, this is not quite fair to the traditional theories. The people who thought them up were not fools; they were well aware of these differences. The elaborate Christological theories of the Church Fathers were, after all, in large part intended precisely to explain just how Jesus *could* be both God and Man despite such apparent difficulties and contradictions, and we cannot simply pro-

---

[4] Strawson (1952), p. 3. Interestingly, Bonhoeffer uses similar language of Chalcedon ('the Definition cancels itself out') without comment (1978, p. 88).

[5] Knox (1967), p. 67.

duce those difficulties all over again as evidence that the theories
were mistaken. They are only evidence that the theories were *needed*.

But such theories have relied, as a rule, on distinguishing between
qualities that belong to Christ's divine nature and qualities that
belong to His human. The fact that He is infinite in His Godhead
does not, it is argued, affect His being finite in His humanity, any
more than Janet's competence as a computer programmer prevents
her from being incompetent at golf. But there are two queries to
be raised here. First, this applies well enough to notions like 'competence'. For you have to be competent *at something*; there is no
such thing as competence 'by itself'. What we are talking about
in Janet is the presence or absence of two quite different properties,
competence-at-programming and competence-at-golf. Does this
apply when we are talking about such things as createdness or
infinity? Surely not. And second, are there not qualities which would
affect Christ's *human* life only, but affect it in contradictory ways?
This, I think, is the force of an argument advanced some years
back by Professor C. B. Martin.[6] Christians have of course always
maintained that Jesus was perfectly good, and have agreed that
if *per impossibile* it were shown that He was not good it would
follow that He was not God. But, Martin argued, it is not merely
true that God is good, it is also true that He could not *conceivably*
be anything but good. Of Jesus of Nazareth, however, good though
he may have been in actual fact, we could at least *conceive* him
not to have been good. 'The contradiction is that Christ can be
conceived to have been other than he was, that is, not good, yet
as God it is inconceivable that he should not have been good.'

It is perhaps a little unfortunate that Martin preferred to use
the word 'conceivable' here; it suggests that it is perhaps our imaginative powers that are really in question. But I think his point can
be expressed equally well in terms of *possibilities*. If Jesus Christ
was truly a human being, 'consubstantial with us' as Chalcedon
put it, then He must have been *able* to sin, it must have been *possible*
for Him to sin, even if in fact He never did. But if He was truly
God, then He cannot have been able to sin; it is not *possible* for
God to sin. This is one area where we cannot ascribe one quality
to God the Word and another to Jesus of Nazareth; if Jesus was

---

[6] Martin (1959), p. 61; cf. Flew and MacIntyre (1955), p. 225.

God incarnate, His sinning here on earth was an impossibility, whereas if He was truly human, it was not.

Similarly, what are we to make of Christ's temptations? If He was human, then the temptations were really tempting; He might have succumbed. But if He was divine, He could not possibly have succumbed, and the temptations were not real at all. If He was God incarnate, both these 'ifs' were true; but the consequents obviously *cannot* both be true. Therefore either He was never tempted at all, or He was not God incarnate.

A rather different charge of 'mystification', which is perhaps related to the charge of obsolescence mentioned earlier, was made by Dr Michael Goulder.[7] He argued that modern defenders of traditional views, such as C. F. D. Moule, who allow that there is an element of paradox in the idea of the Incarnation, are propounding not a genuine paradox but a 'mystification', a pseudo-paradox. A genuine paradox, like that of Frederick's birthday or the combining of wave and particle theories of light, is capable of being resolved, at least in theory. A mystification or pseudo-paradox, on the other hand, is 'in some radical sense unclear, and upon probing is found not to be capable of being stated at all'. Mystifications need not begin as such. The phlogiston theory of combustion began as a perfectly normal scientific theory: but when it turned out, after experiments, to involve the consequence that phlogiston had negative mass, it had become a pseudo-paradox. 'Negative mass' is a notion apparently defying comprehension. Now seeming contradictions are bound to turn up in religious discourse; there is a limit to what we know about God and man, just as there is a limit to what we know about electrons, and these limits may be indicated by the emergence of a seeming contradiction. But there is no justification for seeming *nonsense* in our discourse. 'The religious man cannot allow that under probing his assertions melt away into apparent nonsense, that he has no idea what he is saying'.[8]

Now the doctrine of the Incarnation requires that there be some kind of continuity between the pre-existing Logos or Word and the man Jesus. Some suggestions have been made as to what this continuity might be; but some have been implausible, or even condemned as heresy, and others are simply vacuous. And unless some

---

[7] Goulder (1979), pp. 51ff.   [8] p. 53.

continuity is asserted, the incarnationists' doctrine is 'not a paradox but a mystification, not an apparent contradiction but apparent nonsense.'

Why 'vacuous'? Because if the implausible and heretical kinds of continuity—such as Apollinarius' suggestion that the Logos took the place of Jesus' mind or spirit—are eliminated, all that is left is an unspecified claim that while there is nothing continuous or in common between Jesus of Nazareth and God, nevertheless 'metaphysically' he is the Word of God. And this amounts to about as much as saying 'He is the Word in a purely Pickwickian sense' would.

I said that the charge of mystification was related in a way to the charge of obsolescence. For, as we have seen, a theory that began as a perfectly sound specimen, capable of being proved right or wrong, can be modified till it becomes only a mystification. And this is more or less what happened with Christology. The conceptual apparatus with which the Fathers tackled the problem, and which some theologians still have a weakness for (Goulder cited Mascall as an example) seemed to be required by what the Bible said about Jesus. But our views of the Bible, and of the implications of what it says, have changed, and such notions as 'the human nature assumed by the Word' are no longer part of our conceptual apparatus. The result is that incarnation is now a pseudo-paradox which it is not possible to defend—nor even state.

I think that perhaps we should include under the heading of 'incoherence' another objection of a rather different sort, first raised I believe by Schleiermacher.[9] The doctrine of the Incarnation is customarily expressed in terms of 'two natures'—the divine and the human. But while it may make sense, or may have made sense at one time, to talk about 'human nature' as if it were something which all men and women had in common, it has never made sense, in the Christian Church at least, to talk about the *divine* nature. Polytheists might do so, meaning a mysterious something which Zeus, Hera, Ares, and Apollo had in common; but with us, who are monotheists, this simply will not do. 'How', asked Schleiermacher, 'can divine and human be thus brought together under any single conception, as if they could both be more exact determinations, co-ordinated to each other, of one and the same universal?

---

[9] Schleiermacher (1928), pp. 392ff.

... In one sense [of the word 'nature'] we actually oppose God and nature to one another, and hence in this sense cannot attribute a nature to God. Nature in this sense is for us the summary of all finite existence.' And if we use it instead in the sense of 'animal' and 'vegetable' 'natures', or the sense in which we say that a person has a noble or an ignoble 'nature', still 'we use it solely of a limited existence, standing in opposition to something else, an existence in which active and passive are bound up together, and which is revealed in a variety of appearances'. Note that we are not concerned here with the argument of (for example) Bishop Montefiore, that 'the nature of God is beyond our human comprehension ... If we had really known the nature of God, there would have been no need of an Incarnation to reveal Him to us.'[10] It is not that we do not or cannot understand the nature of God properly; it is that to ascribe a 'nature' to God at all is wholly illegitimate, and therefore it is also illegitimate to say that in Jesus God's nature and human nature were 'joined together in one Person'. If we are going to have any sort of doctrine of Incarnation, it must be of a kind which avoids this language—such as, perhaps, Schleiermacher's own Christology of 'God-consciousness'.

Next, we may take up and develop a point raised by Mr Cupitt.[11] Christians are often thought to believe that 'Jesus is God' (though, as he points out, theologians tend to be wary of this way of putting it). Now what type of 'is' do we have here? There are many different kinds. Mr Cupitt mentions two, the 'is' of *predication* (as in 'Smith is dark-haired') and the 'is' of *identity* (as in 'Smith is the mechanic who mended my car last week'). (A third which he suggests, an 'is' of acclamation, as in 'Great is Diana of the Ephesians!', is an error; it is the whole sentence which is acclamatory, as may be seen by recalling such acclamations as 'Elvis lives!' and the fact that 'Diana of the Ephesians is great' is clearly an 'is' of predication.) There are others he does not mention. There is the 'is' of *existence* (as in 'There is the "is" of existence'!); the 'is' of *class-inclusion* ('A Nigerian is an African'); an 'is' of *representation* (as in 'This is the High Street' said while pointing to a line on a map); an 'is' of *causal explanation* (as when, seeing fireworks in the distance,

---

[10] In Vidler (1962), pp. 153ff.
[11] In Goulder (1979), pp. 31ff., esp. p. 36. Cupitt's beliefs have changed frequently over the years, and it should not be assumed that points cited from his writings necessarily represent his later views (or, as the case may be, his earlier ones).

I say 'That is the Rotary Club celebrating Guy Fawkes Night'); and an 'is' of *part-inclusion* ('Advocating revolution is Marxism!'). No doubt others exist as well.

Now some of these clearly are not used in 'Jesus is God'. Not that of existence, obviously. Nor that of class-inclusion, for that would mean 'Jesus is a god'. Representation and causality could be correct in some Christologies of a revisionist kind. Thus, someone who believed that Jesus never existed might see in His story an allegory of the divine love and say 'Jesus is God' in the representative sense, rather as a reader of C. S. Lewis's 'Narnia' stories might say 'Aslan is Christ'. And someone feeling God at work in the life of Jesus might say 'This is God!', meaning 'God is at work here!' But certainly traditional orthodoxy would want to say more than this. Part-inclusion? No: this could be wanted for Trinitarian doctrine ('The Father is God, the Son is God, and the Holy Ghost is God: and yet they are not three Gods, but one God'[12]), but not for Christology, for the human Jesus of Nazareth is not part of God. We are really left with Cupitt's original two, predication and identity.

But is the 'is' of 'Jesus is God' one of identity? If so, it ought to be *reversible*. The detective in the whodunit can conclude either 'Sikes is the guilty party' or 'The guilty party is Sikes': the two expressions of identity have the same meaning, and if one is true then the other is also. But can we really say 'God is Jesus'? 'God is *in* Jesus', yes. But 'God is Jesus' by itself suggests that there is no more to God over and above the man Jesus, which is not true.

Reversibility is no problem where predication is concerned. 'Smith is dark-haired' cannot be reversed so as to make 'dark-haired' the subject of the verb 'is'. So presumably our 'is' is one of predication. And yet—is not 'God' a proper name? And how can a proper name follow the 'is' of predication? Predication ascribes a quality or relationship to something ('My hair is greying', 'Abraham is the father of Isaac', and so on), and a proper name picks out an individual, not a quality or relationship. A proper name can follow the 'is' of identity all right ('The guilty party is Sikes') but not that of predication; it can only be its *subject*, preceding it.[13]

However, perhaps 'God' is not a proper name after all. We

---

[12] The '*Quicunque Vult*' ('Athanasian Creed').
[13] Inverted sentences like 'Great is Diana' are of course not real exceptions.

remember Elijah's words on Mount Carmel: 'If the LORD is God, follow him; but if Baal, then follow him.'[14] 'God' seems here to be a descriptive term, equivalent to (say) 'the Supreme Being' or 'the proper object of our worship'. This is fair enough; but unfortunately it is no help to orthodoxy. For such phrases as those we have suggested as equivalent to 'God', beginning as they do with the definite article 'the', pick out individuals just as proper names do, and therefore can no more follow the 'is' of predication than proper names can. In Elijah's sentence, the 'is' is one of identity: 'if the LORD is identical with the Supreme Being/proper object of our worship, then follow him.' Certainly if we miss out the 'the' we can then use 'God' as a predicate, but at the cost of saying 'Jesus' (or 'the LORD') is *a* god' (or '*a* proper object of our worship') which says something quite different, and not what we want to say at all (nor what Elijah wanted to say, either). Of course, a polytheist might accept such an assertion. I have seen a Hindu shrine which, among the images of Krishna and Śiva, included one of Christ on the Cross; and doubtless the worshippers there would have agreed that 'Jesus is a god' in the predicative sense of 'is'. But this is not open to us who are monotheists.

It follows, then, that there is a radical incoherence in the assertion 'Jesus is God'. It looks like an assertion that can be made, truly or falsely; but in fact it cannot. And since traditional orthodoxy is surely committed to saying that Jesus *is* God, it is committed to asserting nonsense, and we had better look elsewhere.

A more radical kind of doubt yet is expressed by Professor Schubert Ogden in his Sarum Lectures for 1980, *The Point of Christology*.[15] Almost all Christologies, traditional or revisionist, have (he thinks) been asking the wrong question. They have asked 'Who is Jesus?' and given what seemed to them appropriate replies; they have asked 'about the being of Jesus in himself, as distinct from asking about the meaning of Jesus for us'.[16] This does not do justice to such Christological passages in the Gospels as Matthew 16: 13ff., let alone much of John. Jesus' question that elicited Peter's confession was 'But who do you say that I am?'—not simple but complex. 'Calling as it does for a personal confession, and a confession, moreover, that can be made only with the revelation of God, it

---

[14] 1 Kings 18: 21.　　　[15] Ogden (1982), esp. pp. 15–40.　　　[16] p. 16.

confronts me with the same three questions: not only who Jesus is but also, and inescapably, who I am and who God is.'[17] 'The question christology asks is not simply a question about Jesus, but also, and at the same time, a question about the meaning of ultimate reality for us ... As a consequence, it asks about the meaning of Jesus for us here and now, not about the being of Jesus in himself there and then in the past.'[18] And even this question can only be answered—or indeed asked—given logically prior (Ogden's term[19]) questions about the meaning of our own existence and about the ultimate reality by which our existence is determined.

By tackling only the question 'Who is Jesus?', revisionists have involved themselves in discussing *Jesus'* existence as determined by ultimate reality, not ours. They also go wrong—though this must be discussed later[20]—in identifying the Jesus who is said to be Christ with the so-called historical Jesus, and in supposing that in calling him the Christ (or the like) we are saying something about his perfect actualization of the possibility of authentic self-understanding (or the like). The result is that most revisionist Christologies are inadequate. Traditional ones share at least the first two of these drawbacks, besides others of their own, and though no doubt they can still be defended 'by those who are concerned and resourceful enough', their difficulties seem intractable. But that is by the way; the point is that 'Christology' as usually understood is misguided from the outset. We must begin with Jesus for us here and now; we should have to do so even if the 'Jesus of history' were not inaccessible, as he is. And naturally from a new starting-point we shall find ourselves on a different journey.

[17] p. 28.   [18] p. 41.   [19] p. 29.   [20] See below, p. 49.

3

The 'Insoluble Problems'
Arising from Traditional Views

A BELIEF may be expressed in what seems quite comprehensible language, and may contain no obvious self-contradiction, and yet may, when its implications are worked out, and other facts which cannot be disputed taken into account, land us in quite impossible difficulties. The idea of the Incarnation, as traditionally understood, looks like rather a good example of this. That the Son of God became man may sound intelligible, may even *be* intelligible if taken on its own, and yet may turn out to raise problems that cannot be solved. There are three areas in which such problems seem to arise: Jesus' own self-consciousness, His relationship to God, and His relationship to humankind.

To attempt to describe, or even to conceive, the mental life or self-consciousness of an incarnate God has always seemed hard. The main problem, as past generations saw it, was over Jesus' *knowledge*. God is omniscient; Jesus was God; did it not follow that Jesus was omniscient? But this ran up against serious difficulties, as was recognized at a very early stage. The human brain can only hold a limited amount of information; and did not Jesus, according to Luke 2: 52, 'increase in wisdom', like one of us acquiring more information and skill? Most notoriously of all, did not Jesus on one occasion actually *deny* being omniscient: 'About that day or that hour no one knows, not even the angels in heaven, not even the Son; only the Father.'[1] Some of the Western Fathers in particular simply rejected the plain meaning of this saying. 'He was ignorant in this sense', wrote Augustine,[2] 'that He made sure others were ignorant—that is, He did not know in a way that would enable Him to tell His disciples just then.' (In Aquinas even this peculiar

---

[1] Mark 13: 32 par.   [2] *De Trinitate*, I. 12 (PL 42, 637a).

form of 'not knowing' has gone; 'He is said not to know because He does not make it known.'³) This was *not* a satisfactory solution of the problem; it appeared to save the Lord's omniscience at the expense of His truthfulness. 'Truth tells a lie!' exclaimed Theodoret with justified indignation.⁴ Various other solutions were proposed in the course of time, perhaps the most startling being one advanced by Eulogius of Alexandria in a letter to Pope Gregory the Great⁵ and approved by him, that the Son who was ignorant was not He who is the Head of the Church but His Body—that is, the Church itself; and perhaps the most plausible being Duns Scotus' suggestion⁶ that Christ's soul could not indeed receive all truths at the same time, but could know any item singly, and thus could be aware of any fact He turned His attention to throughout an infinite range of truths. He therefore could have known the time of His Return, had He chosen, but He did not so choose, and therefore did not know it. But even this might not account for what seem to be actual slips on our Lord's part, like making Abiathar High Priest during the lifetime of his father Abimelech.⁷ Hence (in part at least) the attraction of 'kenotic' theories of the Incarnation, according to which the eternal Word really did 'empty Himself' in becoming human and ceased to be omniscient. But this itself leads to hideous problems. Is it remotely conceivable that the infinite knowledge and power of God should suddenly become the dim semiconsciousness of an unborn baby, and yet somehow the same person be the subject of both? 'If you want to get the hang of it,' wrote C. S. Lewis, 'think how you would like to become a slug or a crab.'⁸ But while it is possible to imagine becoming a crab in the sense of finding oneself in a crab's body, to imagine a complete 'kenotic' transformation is really to imagine oneself ceasing to exist and being *replaced* by a crab.⁹ Moreover, as has often been pointed out, Christ is not supposed to have laid aside His humanity at the Ascension, but to have remained both human and divine to this day and for ever. Are we to suppose, then, that never again will God the Son have His original knowledge and power? This seems ridiculous.

---

³ *Summa Theologiae*, 3, q. 10, art. 3 ad 1.
⁴ *In anathemata Cyrilli*, 4 (PG 76, 411a).
⁵ Gregory the Great, *Epistles*, 10. 39 (PL 77, 1097a).
⁶ *Opus Oxoniense (Ordinatio)*, 1. 3, dist. 14, q. 2, n. 20.
⁷ Mark 2: 26.   ⁸ Lewis (1955), p. 151.
⁹ Cf. Goulder (1979), p. 54. Cf. also below, Excursus III.

Kenosis, then, will not help us. Christ must have been omniscient if He was really God, and He cannot possibly have been omniscient, if He was really human.

But while it may just be conceivable that the problem of Christ's knowledge could be resolved (on Scotus' lines, perhaps?), the problem of His *will* is even more intractable. Again this is a problem that was raised in patristic times. The Monothelites argued that a single hypostasis (and it was agreed, except by Nestorians, that there was only one hypostasis in Christ) could only have one will. Their opponents argued that this could only be the case either if Christ's were somehow a new hybrid kind of nature (which would be a weird new form of Monophysitism) or if no human will existed in Him, which would be a form of Apollinarianism, denying His real humanity. And they could quote St Athanasius in their support; describing the prayer of Christ in Gethsemane, he had said: 'He manifests two wills here, the human, which belongs to the flesh, and the divine, which belongs to God.'[10]

The debate is by no means ended, even in the twentieth century. For example, on the 'Monothelite' side we find H. R. Mackintosh writing: 'We cannot predicate of Him two consciousnesses or two wills; the New Testament indicates nothing of the kind, nor indeed is it congruous with an intelligible psychology.'[11] (We might remark in passing that as far as Gethsemane is concerned, Mackintosh is surely right and Athanasius wrong: that strange and tremendous prayer was that of a human will desiring indeed to avoid the cup but submitting without reservation to the will of the Father.) On the other side we find that W. R. Matthews,[12] after agreeing that in order to maintain the unity of Christ's person it might appear that there must be a single will, goes on: 'The conception of either the divine or human nature as devoid of will is paradoxical in the extreme and would evacuate the Incarnation, if thought out, of all meaning. Monothelitism then must be wrong. But the conception of two wills in one person which are always in harmony, that is to say have identical contents, is a conception which many of us will find hard to entertain.' For all that, it is a conception to which he eventually returns.[13] The life of Jesus can be seen as a 'moving

---

[10] *De Incarnatione contra Arianos* (PG 26, 1021b).
[11] Mackintosh (1913), p. 470.   [12] Matthews (1950), pp. 29–30.
[13] pp. 69–71.

pattern of behaviour-events, which means primarily of willed actions'; and we must also think of the Will of God (from the standpoint of time) as a 'perfectly coherent moving pattern of acts of will'. In the Incarnation we have this second pattern manifested on a smaller, human scale; 'the pattern of the Father's will, on this hypothesis, is the essential reality of the temporal personality of the Son.'

But it is to be noted that Matthews, unconsciously perhaps, has moved away from orthodox Dyothelitism; it is the pattern of the *Father's* will that is manifested in Jesus, not that of the will of God the Son. Has he perhaps found it as hard as Mackintosh did to swallow two wills in the Son alone? If so, we have here strong testimony to the unworkability of a two-wills Christology. Here is a distinguished theologian, anxious to maintain such a Christology, indeed believing that he has actually done so, who has in reality conceded that it cannot be done. On the other hand, he is surely right in his criticism of Monothelitism. There can be no such thing as a mixed will—the expression has no meaning—and yet neither the divine nature nor the human can be thought of as lacking a will. We can assert neither one will nor two in Christ if a traditional doctrine of the Incarnation is accepted; consequently the only possible conclusion is that we ought not to accept it.

And we have not finished yet. Suppose Christ did indeed have a human will. Was that will *free*? This question is clearly related to the one we discussed earlier, where we saw that there appeared to be a flat contradiction between the propositions that Christ could sin (being human) and that He could not sin (being divine). But here it is not so much a matter of formal contradictions as of the implications for theology of asserting either that Christ's will was free or that it was not. It is surely vital to modern Christian understandings of ethics and of the 'problem of evil' that people should be free to choose between right and wrong. If not, the whole idea of moral obligation seems to collapse, and, moreover, God is made the ultimate author of sin. Certainly this freedom is not absolute, nor anywhere near that. It is miserably hampered and vitiated by original sin; and, more happily, it is aided, enlightened, guided, and inspired by the grace of God: but it retains some measure of the independence God has given it.

But can we say this of Christ? Surely not. Christ was without sin, the Bible tells us, and indeed it is inconceivable that God should be united to a sinner, that is, to a rebel against Himself. But in that case it is inconceivable that Christ was free to sin; for had He had that freedom, He could have used it, and so unmade the Incarnation after it happened—a wholly impossible idea. Either by the very fact of being God incarnate He was incapable of sinning, and therefore was not free, or His human will was at all times guarded and ruled by the divine, and therefore once again was not free.

Yet if He was not free, are we not landed again with a variety of Apollinarianism—His humanity lacking our free will? And what meaning can we ascribe to the stories of the Temptation or of the Agony in the Garden? None, it would seem. Being unable to sin, He *could* not be 'tempted in every respect as we are';[14] nor could He really have wished the cup of the crucifixion to pass from Him, His human will being at all times subject to the divine. Indeed, might we not go further still and doubt whether we can even call Him good? He Himself rejected the address 'Good Master', on the grounds that One alone was good, namely God. Was the reason for this reply perhaps the fact that He Himself was not, strictly speaking, 'good', never having had any choice in the matter? Schleiermacher ascribed to Jesus 'a spiritual power which is far removed from anything we call virtue'[15] on precisely these grounds: there never could have been any inner conflict within Jesus, and therefore there could not have been in Him goodness of the sort we meet with (occasionally) in other people. And does not this in effect destroy the 'consubstantiality' with us on which Chalcedon insisted so strongly? And, still more important, does it not overthrow the splendid assurance of the Letter to the Hebrews that 'because he has suffered and been tempted, he is able to help those who are tempted'[16] and that 'we have not a high priest who is unable to sympathize with our weaknesses'?[17]

Moreover, the doctrine of the Incarnation requires a breach in the continuity of God's life which is at variance equally with modern and with traditional views of the nature of God. In former times it was possible—indeed, it was common—for people to see the hand of God, or of one of the gods, directly intervening in all sorts of

---

[14] Heb. 4: 15.   [15] Quoted by Matthews (1950), p. 35.
[16] Heb. 2: 18.   [17] Heb. 4: 15.

events. He parted the Red Sea before Moses and the Israelites; He gave the Law on Mount Sinai amid cloud and fire; He made Gideon's fleece wet with dew when the ground about it was dry; He made the shadow on the dial of Ahaz move back; and so on. And He might be expected to do so again at any moment. The 1662 Book of Common Prayer seems to take this for granted in many places. To give only one example: in the Prayer for Fair Weather it is assumed that the 'plague of rain and waters' from which we need rescue was sent as a punishment for our iniquities, and the corresponding Thanksgiving, echoing this, goes on to say that God in His mercy has 'relieved and comforted our souls by this seasonable and blessed change'. Rain and sunshine alike were specially sent by God.

It is safe to say that this is no longer a natural way of looking at things. We see the world more as a continuous web of events governed by laws of nature, as a pattern of causes and effects. The words of Schoonenberg, that 'God never works by intervention, in the stead of creatures, that on the contrary he realizes all through making his world realize itself';[18] or of Wiles, that 'talk of God's activity is to be understood as a way of speaking about those events within the natural order or within human history in which God's purpose finds clear expression or special opportunity';[19] these are surely quite representative. The conversion of a sinner is God at work in a way in which the same sinner's coming to prefer coffee to tea for breakfast is not; but not because God stooped down from heaven to effect the first while the second was the effect of natural causes. Both were the effect of natural causes; but the conversion of sinners is part of God's plan for the world, and as far as we know the relative numbers of tea- and coffee-drinkers are not.

But if this is so, then the Incarnation, or rather the life of Jesus, must itself be a series of events within the 'continuous web', the product of previous states of affairs within the world, and not the irruption into the world that the traditional view would make it out to be. (The traditional view did of course hold that it was in *part* the product of previous states of affairs, notably in the history of the Hebrew people, but it also held that it was more than just

[18] Schoonenberg (1972), p. 21.   [19] Wiles (1974), p. 38.

their product, and, we might add, that many of the 'previous states of affairs' were themselves the result of divine intervention.) God is the Creator and Sustainer of all things, and gives purpose to the universe and to the lives of men and women within it; He does not work by bursting in on the world at irregular intervals, let alone by dropping in and living in it for thirty years or thereabouts and then ceasing to do so.

Of course, it may well be replied that this 'deistic' idea of God is not the only one, nor necessarily the true one either. But if we turn to more traditional views, we come across a problem that is in many ways similar. God has always been supposed to be immutable, unchanging. Can this possibly be reconciled with the idea that at a definite point in time He became a man?

We must be clear what is meant by this 'immutability'. There are of course wholly trivial senses in which God may be said to change. For instance, ten years ago He knew that I *should write* these words; at the time of writing He knew that I *was writing* them, and a few moments later He knew that I *had written* them. Obviously this sort of 'change' can be accepted, and equally obviously it does not allow for Incarnation. More seriously, acts of God in history may be allowed, even if in a sense these too seem to involve change in God. Thus in the time of Abraham God had not yet called Moses to liberate the children of Israel; in the time of Joshua He had; God had therefore changed. But this, it could be said, is not a real change in God. His will and purpose remain unaltered; it is the world that changes as it encounters different aspects of that will and purpose. Until the burning bush, Moses had not met with the calling and liberating purpose of the Lord, but that purpose was there already. It is like feeling one's way about a room in the dark: one comes across different aspects of the walls and furniture, and there is a recognizable series of events taking place as one does so; one might even say that the desk has changed, in that five minutes ago no one had ever bumped into it; but the *real* change is all in the person feeling his or her way round, there is no real change in the room itself. So we experience different phases of the divine plan without that plan's changing—let alone the Planner.

But the Incarnation is a different matter. If the traditional doctrine is true, there took place somewhere about 4 BC a permanent change in Deity; since then human nature has been taken into God. It is interesting to read the attempts of Mascall[20] to avoid the plain implication that God the Word has really changed, 'acquired a new mode of existing (as man)'.[21] The argument he advances may be summarized as follows: Some relationships are purely logical, involving no real change in either term; some are real, involving both; and some are mixed, in which one term is changed by the relationship and the other is not. Creation is a relation of the third type. 'The relationship is real in [the lesser] term precisely in that the term comes to be and exists. It is logical in the other term because the second term is totally dependent for its existence on being related to the first term *as the first is in itself*, and not by any other act.'[22] The same applies to the Incarnation, though the relationship involved is of course different, in that the human nature of Christ has no existence of its own, even as something created, except in so far as it is united to the divine Person of the Son.

This is not an easy idea to grasp, but even if we assume the validity of the distinction it seems to lead to a startling conclusion. If the created world is related to God solely by what He is in Himself ('to create demands that God acts by no other act than by the act that he is as *ipsum esse*'[23]), it surely follows that He could not have chosen *not* to create. Such an idea is not of course new,[24] but to most people it is rather puzzling. (How to combine it with God's freedom was a serious problem for Aquinas.) But even if we accept it as far as creation is concerned, can we also accept that in the Incarnation as well the lesser term is related to the greater 'as it is in itself, and not by any other act', with the apparent implication that God became incarnate by inner necessity? We saw earlier that the Incarnation seemed to eliminate the freedom of the human Jesus; it now seems that it is going to eliminate that of God Himself. On the other hand, if we say that God did become man by an act other than 'the act that He is', a new aspect really has accrued to the divine Word, and it is impossible to say that God has not changed. Certainly that change is purely one of addition. He has not lost any old characteristics, nor has He changed any of them

---

[20] Mascall (1980) quoting and developing a thesis of Dr T. G. Weinandy.

[21] p. 67. This phrase is in fact Aquinas', as reported by Weinandy, but evidently Mascall accepts it too.

[22] Weinandy, cited by Mascall (1980), p. 70.

[23] p. 69.

[24] It goes back to Neoplatonism. A few moderns have accepted it: cf. Caird (1899), pp. 154ff.; Macquarrie (1973), p. 151.

into new forms; He has merely acquired the characteristics of the man Jesus of Nazareth. To use patristic terminology, it is not a change in the divine nature (as if God were to become less wise or more just than before) but in the hypostasis of God the Son, which became 'more composite' as Leontius of Jerusalem put it.[25] But this is still a change, and a real one. The Incarnation is therefore as incompatible with, say, Aquinas' views of what God is like as it is with Wiles's.

And what of the relationship between the incarnate Word and *us*? The doctrine of the Incarnation was intended to display a special relationship between Him and the rest of the human race (other than that which is borne to us by every other man or woman). But the moment we try to say what this relationship is, we are landed with something quite incredible. It is no better than it was with Christ's relationship to Himself or to God. Traditionally, Christ has been seen as what used to be called a 'common person', one whose humanity is somehow *inclusive*. This has been put in several ways. St Paul described Him as a second Adam, who, so to speak, put the rebellion of the first Adam into reverse.[26] Others have spoken of Him as 'man, but not *a* man',[27] or said that believers are incorporated into His human nature;[28] there are various formulations. But the general notion is clear: Christ's Incarnation (and Atonement) affect us not as individuals, or not *only* as individuals, but as a single unit, humanity. We have already quoted Lowry's lines:

> Son of Man, whose birth incarnate
> Hallows all our human race;

they sum up the whole idea neatly and untechnically.

But technically or untechnically put, the idea is quite simply unworkable. H. M. Relton, a determinedly orthodox theologian, remarked on this more than seventy years ago: 'The problem is ultimately unsolvable by any finite mind. It postulates a logical

---

[25] *Adversus Nestorianos*, I. 20 (PG 86, 1485d).
[26] Rom. 5: 12–21; I Cor. 15: 21–2, 45–9.
[27] This expression is Newman's; it has been ascribed to Cyril of Alexandria, though I have seen no convincing reference, and it would be very difficult to express it in Greek.
[28] Mascall (1956b), p. 156.

impossibility—the particular cannot embody its own universal.'[29]
That Christ shared our common humanity is certainly true, but
this 'common humanity' is not a *thing* that can somehow be changed
in character by the fact that one of those sharing it was the Son
of God. It is not a particular, an individual object; it is a universal,
a characteristic or quality that particular objects can have (or, more
likely, a combination of such qualities, but that does not make any
difference). Now it is true that on one theory of the nature of universals, that of Plato, universals, or some of them, exist in their own
right independently of particulars and are indeed more real than
they. But that very fact entails that they cannot be affected by particulars. Indeed, a Platonic universal cannot be affected at all by
anything; 'becoming' belongs to this world, the world of particulars,
and not to the world of universal Forms.

Reject Platonism, then? By all means; most philosophers have
done so. But at least Platonism did allow universals to be a (very
queer) kind of individual entity; other theories of universals do not
even allow that much. And if the 'humanity' that Christ shares
with all other human beings is *not* an individual entity, then how
can the Incarnation change or affect it? The only sort of change
it can undergo is the sort of purely notional or logical change that
we dismissed as trivial when we were looking at the immutability
of God. (Thus humanity 'changed', no doubt, when I was born,
in that not until then had it ever had the property of 'being exempli-
fied in somebody called Richard Lyman Sturch'; but this is a purely
notional change, not a real one like that which is said to have come
over 'humanity' when it was assumed by the Word.) Hastings Rashdall once summed up the whole approach as 'bastard Platonism',[30]
and the description seems fair enough.

This does not apply to the converse idea which speaks of us as
incorporated into Christ's human nature. For here 'human nature'
is not a universal; it is an exemplification of a universal, the particular
example of human-ness which is there in Jesus Christ. If I say of
someone blushing that the colour of their face changed, I am clearly
not referring to the universal (some shade of pale pink, it may be)
which characterized their face before the blush; that did not change
at all except in that it was no longer characterizing this particular

---

[29] Relton (1917), p. 265. He goes on: 'But the Person of Christ is the bankruptcy
of human logic' (an attitude we have already seen must be rejected).
[30] Rashdall (1919), p. 353.

face. I am talking about an individual quality, an *instance* of a universal, and the description 'bastard Platonism' does not apply.

Yet we are no better off. For by being a particular instance of a quality (*Christ*'s humanity and not that of Herod or Pilate or William Shakespeare), it is precisely what no one else can be incorporated into. We can be incorporated into a group—the Christian Church, for example; we can perhaps be incorporated (in a rather strained use of the word) into a universal, such as 'Christianity', though I am not quite sure of this. But I cannot be incorporated into *your* Christianity, nor you into mine; nor can either of us be incorporated into any quality specified as being Christ's personal one. In so far as it is a particular quality, it is *His* and can be no one else's.

It is of course possible to say that neither of these mishandlings of the concept 'humanity' is actually required by the doctrine of the Incarnation. St. Paul, in describing our Lord as the second Adam, made no mention of universals, nor indeed of 'humanity'. Nevertheless, the importance of the Incarnation has so often been seen as lying in part at least in the difference made to 'humanity', and not just to women and men, that the impossibility of this notion is a serious objection to incarnational theologies.

4

The 'Impossibility' of Fitting Traditional Views into a True Vision of God and His World

WE are now turning, one might say, from questions about the internal content of the idea of incarnation to questions about its external relationships. No idea exists in a vacuum, isolated from other ideas and beliefs. We have already seen something of the problems involved in relating the Incarnation to the self-awareness of Jesus, to the nature of God, and to the rest of the human race, problems which suggested that the historic idea of the Incarnation was in the end untenable. We now move on to problems which suggest that even if it is tenable, it is highly objectionable. There are reasons, based on our vision of God and His world, which seem to make an Incarnation, as traditionally thought of, very improbable.

More than once people have found the traditional views ethically or spiritually wanting. There was the kind raised by a number of theologians earlier in this century, that traditional views ignored the basically ethical nature of God (and indeed of ourselves); and there are the more recent objections of Professor Driver and Mr Cupitt that they have been morally and spiritually disastrous.

The older type may be represented by H. R. Mackintosh and P. T. Forsyth. Mackintosh put it as follows (a propos of the Chalcedonian definition):

Christological relations which, in essence, are ethical and personal, have been too much expressed in terms imbued with a certain mechanical and even material flavour. This is particularly true of the term 'nature' ($\phi\acute{v}\sigma\iota\varsigma$), which is not an ethical word at all. Now non-ethical realities admit of no true unity; hence we are not surprised to find that Godhead and manhood are contemplated here as being in essence so disparate ... that a miracle of sheer omnipotence is needed to unite them, Love, it is true, is behind the incarnation ... but the methods by which this love accomplishes its purpose are not sufficiently conceived as spiritual, with the result that from the first Christ's true humanity is overshadowed, if not indeed seriously curtailed ... It becomes impossible to think of this Christ as the Head of a new redeemed race of men and Himself the pattern Man.'[1]

Hence Mackintosh sought to describe the union of divine and human in Christ not in terms of nature but of will.

If we are inspired by Christian faith to affirm that Jesus Christ is identical with God in will—a Will manifested in His achievement—we have reached a point beyond which no advance is possible; for in ethical terms, the highest terms available, we have affirmed His ontological unity with God ... Intelligent will is the organic centre of personality; and the will of Jesus fixes His absolute status in the world of being.[2]

Forsyth had taken a very similar line (and indeed Mackintosh more than once acknowledges his debt to him). It is not sufficient that the reason for the Incarnation should be moral; 'there can be no unity of spirits like God and man except in a moral way, by personal action which is moral in its *method* as well as in its aim.'[3] For Mackintosh, as we have just seen, the effect of a 'two-natures' Christology is the overshadowing or curtailment of Christ's humanity, so that He cannot be thought of as 'the Head of a new redeemed race of men'. Forsyth would have agreed; but the ill effects that he saw were more extensive. The whole 'Chalcedonian' approach (using that word to mean the method used by the Fathers of Chalcedon rather than their specific conclusions) is 'a scientific theology divorced from experience', which the vast majority of lay Christians obviously will not be able to follow. But it is presented to them as *the* key to the understanding of Christ. Hence they have to depend on the word and authority of the Church, which *does* understand this 'scientific theology'. From this beginning the 'ordinary Christian has to 'descend' to 'such personal experience as may thereupon be open to him. That is a false foundation and an inverted movement.'[4] A little later he puts it more strongly still: 'Begin everything with Christ's relation to human nature and not to human will or conscience ... begin with metaphysic more or less diluted, or you will not arrive at religion ... Is not this a ὑστερὸν πρότερόν? ...

---

[1] Mackintosh (1913), pp. 214–15.   [2] p. 304.
[3] Forsyth (1909), p. 223. My italics.   [4] Forsyth (1916), p. 86.

[The proper] metaphysic is one of ethic, of action, not of being; it is of will rather than thought.'[5]

The accusation is, then, that traditional patterns of Christological thought, by thinking in terms of being rather than of moral will, (*a*) remove the Incarnation from the understanding of the ordinary Christian, (*b*) overshadow the humanity of the Lord, and (*c*) distort the actual religion of the Church by making it depend on mere authority.

Cupitt's attack may be briefly summarized in his own words:

For Jesus's emphasis upon the divine transcendence, on the disjunction of things divine and human and the need for choice, [the doctrine of the incarnation] substituted a world-view which stressed continuity, authority and obedience. It weakened appreciation of his human work. It tended to create a cult of the divine Christ which let Deity itself fade into the background, and when God the Father was reaffirmed, he was envisaged as an old man.[6]

(Cupitt has of course particularly in mind Western iconography of the Renaissance onwards.) The similarities between Cupitt's objection and those of Forsyth and Mackintosh are clear. The absence of stress on the need for choice (including moral choice); the growth of subservience to authority; the lessened emphasis on the human side of Jesus; these are seen as defects of the tradition in both criticisms. Yet the differences too are very great. Cupitt saw Christendom as having failed to take a proper view of Deity itself—God the Father is largely ignored or seen far too anthropomorphically. More important, he sees all these defects as the results, not just of one particular approach to the Incarnation, but of the very idea of incarnation itself. Jesus' message, that there was *no* continuity between heaven and earth, human and divine, has been completely inverted, and he himself made into the Mediator who provides the continuity which he actually denied. Clearly an 'ethical' Incarnation of the kind that Forsyth and Mackintosh favoured would be just as objectionable to Cupitt as the older 'metaphysical' Incarnation favoured by the Fathers and their followers.

But perhaps the most sustained attack on traditional Christology (and most 'revisionist' versions as well) from the point of view of ethics has come from Professor T. F. Driver in his *Christ for a*

---

[5] Forsyth (1916), p. 89.   [6] In Hick (1977), p. 145.

Changing World.[7] Christology, he holds, ought to be subjected to ethical judgement. 'The procedure is not to develop a Christology first and inquire into its consequences later';[8] rather, 'the christological task is to define the role of Christ in the fulfilment of individual and social conscience.'[9] And the Churches' traditional Christologies have been seriously defective ethically. Jesus was rejected by the Jews; he was (or so European Christians supposed) white; he was male. Therefore Jews, non-males, and non-whites are liable to be regarded as 'nonpersons'. Although Christianity did not create racism or sexism, 'it was easily invaded by them and added powerful rationalizations to them because of the way it had chosen to regard Christ'.[10]

It is a mistake, according to Driver, to maintain that Jesus is or should be at the centre of the temporal world or of life generally. Such an idea renders 'weak, invisible, or ashamed' those who are unlike Christ, the centre of all things, in not being male; or in not being either white or Semitic; or in being born without inheritance; or in feeling strongly their sexuality; or in neither knowing nor wishing to know Abraham as their father; or in having no community to surround them; or in having never learned language; or in being Jews and not consenting to believe Jesus is the Christ. 'The Christ who has *already* come provides little hope for "outsiders".'[11] Christ past must be replaced by Christ future. (And this, he notes, is to a great extent true already. There have been huge shifts in the understanding of Jesus, away from the 'Christ past'—most notably in the shift which took place in Christian thought when he failed to return as soon as expected.)

To take a specific example:

[the] 'myth of the all-male male—that is, the male beholden to nothing that is not male—saturates the figure of Christ past ... It was not a feminine Logos who was in Jesus made flesh. That is why Christian feminism must necessarily have a quarrel with Christ past and with all theological doctrine bound to that figure and his Father ... I have reached the conclusion that [a christological affirmation of female autonomy] is not possible as long as the biblical Christ is regarded as final, decisive, eternal or central.[12]

[7] Driver (1981).   [8] p. 21.   [9] p. 24.   [10] p. 20.
[11] p. 45.   [12] p. 143.

Hence, although Driver is willing to applaud Chalcedon for its testimony to 'God's infinite commitment to finitude', and to agree that 'in Jesus we discern a convergence to the point of identity between what is human and what is divine', the conclusions he draws from this are, as he says, 'far different from those commonly reached.'[13]

Another criticism is related to what we have just been looking at, and also to what was said earlier about the free will of Jesus. Jesus Christ has long been held up to us as the great Example, a pattern on which the Christian life should be modelled. 'Be imitators of me, as I am of Christ', wrote St Paul;[14] 'Christ suffered for us, leaving us an example, so that you should follow in his steps', wrote St Peter;[15] and the theme has been taken up by many writers on Christian living ever since. But can He be an example if He is in fact God incarnate? It is useless to tell a sinful human being to follow the example of one who was incapable of sin. Was He really 'in all respects tempted as we are'[16] if His temptations were so drastically *un*like ours as to be doomed all along to failure? Is not even the agony of the Cross lessened in the mind of the contemplator, once it is realized who the one crucified actually was? 'If I were the Son of God', writes Mr Sydney Carter in one of his disturbing ballads,

> And if they crucified me,
> I'd think that I was luckier
> Than those who hung beside me.
> I'd know that I should rise again
> And all things would be well;
> But when you are a son of man
> However can you tell?[17]

Quite right. Both the courage displayed and the pain endured are diminished if the Jesus who was crucified was in reality the Son of God all the time. It was all very well for Him, when He was reviled, to revile not again, or, when He suffered, to threaten not;[18] as God, He was not really tempted to revile or threaten when that would have been sinful; nor was He confronted with the same terror of death as St Peter's readers were evidently likely

---

[13] pp. 59–60.   [14] I Cor. II: I.   [15] I Pet. 2: 21.
[16] Heb. 4: 15.   [17] Carter (1969), p. 15.   [18] I Pet. 2: 23.

to be, since He not merely believed He would rise again (doubt-less they believed that too) but actually *knew* it. As Dr Young puts it, 'Cross and resurrection are inseparable motifs, but if resur-rection becomes the proof that Jesus was divine or that God was incarnate in him, it immediately reduces the reality of crucifixion and death.'[19] Resurrection may still pass, perhaps, as a symbol that 'God's power to transform may be discerned within the tragic situ-ation', but as a consequence of Jesus' divinity it is positively harmful. Whether or not the King James Version's rendering of Philippians 2: 5 is correct as a rendering, it will not do as instruction to the Christian. 'Let this mind be in you which was also in Christ Jesus' demands an impossibility if in Christ Jesus God is incarnate, but not in us. Moreover, as Driver points out, though moral theologians have professed to take Jesus as their model and norm—and surely this is entailed by orthodox Christology—in actual fact they have drawn the main bases of their teaching, whether liberal or conserva-tive, from other sources. And Driver is willing to criticize here, among others, his own earlier self, having tried to discuss homosex-uality in the light of the fact that Jesus said nothing whatever about it.[20] Even if we had records of the whole of his life, instead of only tiny fragments, the gulf of time and social change that separates us from him makes him useless as a moral pattern. And is not this a serious drawback to traditional Christologies?

And what about religions other than Christianity? There have for a long time been two problems for Christians thinking about the non-Christian world. What is the ultimate fate of those who through no fault of their own—nay, often through the fault of Christians who have failed in their duty to preach the Gospel and to embody it in their lives—have not believed in Christ? And what are we to say about the great non-Christian religions, with their manifest grasp of important truths, the holiness of some of their great saints, and their frequent success in maintaining standards of righteousness among their adherents that put the Christian Church to shame?

The answer which was made to the first question in, say, the medieval West was quite straightforward and simple. 'No one', declared the Council of Florence in the fifteenth century, 'remaining

---

[19] In Goulder (1979), p. 103.   [20] Driver (1981), p. 53.

outside the Catholic Church, not just pagans, but also Jews or heretics or schismatics, can become partakers of eternal life; but they will go to the "everlasting fire which was prepared for the devil and his angels" unless before the end of life they are joined to the Church.'[21] It has however proved exceedingly difficult for Christians to maintain this position and at the same time believe in the love and compassion of God. Various expedients have therefore been devised to maintain it in form while taking away the offence in practice. Dr Hick mentions two which are characteristic of Roman Catholic thinking and one of Protestant. The first is to bring in the concept of 'invincible ignorance', familiar from moral theology. No blame can be ascribed for an action, however bad in itself, if whoever did it did not know what they were doing, provided they were not to blame for the ignorance itself. (The classic example is that of the hunter who shoots at what he takes to be a deer, but turns out to be another man; his action has the same results as a murder, but he is not a murderer!) Now applied to the present problem, this means that a Hindu, for example, who has never heard the gospel, cannot be blamed for failing to respond to it. Nor can he or she be blamed even if they *have* heard it, if they honestly find that they cannot *believe* it; for clearly they do not *know* it to be true (they do not even believe it to be true, let alone know it), and this is not an ignorance that they could have overcome by extra effort. They cannot be blamed for their failure to respond, and *a fortiori* they cannot be damned for it.

The second is an extension of the concept of 'baptism of desire'. Imagine a new convert to the Church who is being prepared for baptism, but dies suddenly before actually receiving it. Such a person clearly desires to enter Christ's Church; and it was recognized that God would take this desire as equivalent to the Sacrament itself. The idea is to extend this to anyone who desires the true religion, even if they do not know which that religion is, on the grounds that if they *did* know which it was (viz., Christianity) they would obviously profess it and seek baptism. Like the prematurely dying convert, they are prevented from formal initiation into Christ's Church by something in no way their fault, and God therefore regards them as having entered her even if they themselves never knew it.

[21] Quoted from Denziger by Hick (1977a), p. 120.

The Protestant expedient is to suggest that, although someone may have rejected, or been unaware of, the gospel in this life, they may come to accept it in the next, when the truth is displayed more fully and clearly than it was here. There is a 'second chance' available; the 'descent into hell' of the Apostles' Creed, during which Christ 'preached to the spirits in prison',[22] is taken as Scriptural evidence for this idea.

These expedients Hick calls 'epicycles', finding them reminiscent of the mathematical devices used by Ptolemy and other astronomers who believed the stars and planets to travel round the earth, and by which they explained the peculiar way in which the planets' speed, and even direction, varied from time to time. Such explanations were no longer needed once it was realized that the earth was not the centre of the universe, but that it and the planets travelled round the sun (and in ellipses at that, not in circles as had previously been assumed). The older astronomy had been hampered by its basic assumption that the earth was the unique and central point of the universe: similarly, Christian theology has been hampered by the basic mistake of assuming that its salvation is the unique centre of all true religion, and, like Ptolemy, has had to have recourse to complicated expedients which do not really convince and which are seen to have been unnecessary once we realize that we and people of other religions are none of us at the centre, but inhabit religious 'planets' on a par with one another.

Similarly with our second question. Earlier ages were content to repudiate all other religions as devices of Satan to distract his victims from the true faith. (Judaism was not of course false in the way the others were; in its case Satan did not invent it, he only blinded people's eyes to its fulfilment in Christ.) More recently, this has changed. Theologians interested in 'other religions' are willing in many cases to accept that Muhammad really was a prophet of God, that the love of God inculcated by the Bhagavad-Gītā really is a good and holy state of mind, that the compassion taught by the Buddha is something Christians could often do with a lot more of. Christ is frequently seen as the fulfiller of these religions as He was of the Jewish.[23] Even among those who repudiate this approach the attitude is often much milder than it would once have been: other religions are great achievements of the human spirit, though

---

[22] 1 Pet. 3: 19.   [23] See e.g. Farquhar (1915), or Zaehner (1958).

they are of human origin, and, precisely, *religions*, whereas Christianity is a God-given *faith*, or ought to be. (It is alas all too likely to degenerate into a 'religion' that is no nobler than any of the others.) Here too, then, we find the 'epicycle' mentality at work: Christians, with the best of intentions and the utmost good faith, are complicating their theology with new devices when the simple thing would be to recognize that Christianity is as much and as little a faith, as much and as little a religion, as the others are, and is no more easily seen as fulfilling them as fulfilled *by* them.

Now the reason for this 'epicycle mentality' is, very largely, the traditional doctrine of the Incarnation, especially as linked with the idea of the Atonement. (I will not say 'the traditional doctrine of the Atonement', as there have been many such, and there is no widely accepted formulation of it as there is, in Chalcedon, of the Incarnation.) If you believe that God has come into the world 'in these last days' to save our race, it is hard not to believe that this was the one unique and decisive act of God and that 'there is no other name given under heaven by which we may receive salvation'.[24] The rest of Christian teaching—the love and Fatherhood of God, the work of the Holy Spirit within us, the Christian life portrayed in the Sermon on the Mount, the summons to repentance, the fellowship of the Church, the gift of the Sacraments—all these could be incorporated into a 'Copernican' theology which made no arrogant claims about the inadequacy of other religions, let alone the damnation of the greater part of mankind. It is the Incarnation and Atonement that get in the way of a wider vision and prevent a closer growth together of the world's religions into what Hick calls 'a global religious life', wherein Christianity, Islam, Buddhism, and the rest would be in a relationship not unlike that of different Christian denominations today. Let it not be forgotten that the decree of the Council of Florence quoted earlier pronounced sentence of hell not only on pagans and Jews but on Christian heretics and schismatics—such as those Eastern Orthodox who refused to accept the reunion proclaimed at the Council, or even such as those Roman Catholics who were at that very time holding a rival Council at Basle and electing an alternative Pope. Hardly anyone would take that line today; we are more conscious of the things that unite us to our fellow-Christians and less insistent on the damning effect

---

[24] Acts 4: 12.

of the remaining things that divide us (or, better, separate us). Why not go further and play down this doctrine of Incarnation that separates us from other believers?

While our thoughts are in the realm of astronomy, it might be worth raising a point which is often completely overlooked, and yet, despite an almost comical appearance at first glance, is a genuine and serious one, which has bothered some Christians and made others reject Christianity. As scientific theory stands at present, it is likely that the solar system came into existence by a process that is quite common, and that there are, among the vast numbers of stars in our galaxy—let alone among the vast numbers of galaxies in the universe—thousands upon thousands of other, similar systems of planets. Even supposing that the great majority of these bear no life, and that on the great majority of those that do it has stayed comparatively primitive, still there must be a large number on which life has evolved to a level of intelligence equal to or higher than our own. Yet the gospel cannot be carried to these planets, and, given the awkward fact that acceleration beyond the speed of light is (as scientific theory stands at present) a theoretical impossibility, it is morally certain that to most of them it never will be. They are cut off from the Saviour. Now, as a Buddhist spokesman says in Professor Ninian Smart's *A Dialogue of Religions*,[25] this is no great trouble to a Buddhist, for there are many Buddhas—'the' Buddha being only the most recent—and there is no reason why someone on a distant planet should not achieve Enlightenment. (Indeed, something very like this was held by some Buddhist thinkers to have actually happened, except that they spoke in terms of 'world-systems' rather than planets.) But it is otherwise with a supposedly unique Incarnation. The traditional view is 'geocentric' to an absurd degree; it elevates our obscure planet to a dignity denied to all others.

Nor can we escape this by supposing that God has become incarnate in other worlds too—unless perhaps we abandon the doctrine of the Trinity. 'We would have to think in terms of a Quaternity or more, wouldn't we?' says another of Smart's characters.[26] A similar point has been made in more detail by Professor Roland Puccetti.[27] No single organic person, he argues (that is, no bodily

---

[25] Smart (1960), pp. 95 f.   [26] p. 96.   [27] Puccetti (1968), pp. 136 ff.

one), can be more than *one* organic person, even if he or she can be an *incorporeal* person (such as God the Son) as well. Identical twins, for instance, even if they cannot be told apart, are in different places and therefore are different people. Incorporeal persons can perhaps be everywhere at once, but corporeal ones cannot. If the Son of God has become incarnate on every planet with personal life (of which there may be 10^{18}!) 'there were or are or will be multiple organic persons in the universe who are "divine persons" in the Christian sense at the same time'.[28] Suppose, then, we are sent a picture of the non-human 'Christ' of Planet X.

We can hardly radio back 'Yes, this is the Christ' unless we mean by that no more than 'this is how the Son of God *appeared* to you'; sheer docetism again. But on the other hand we could not deny His divine status ... since He would have the same claims to this as Jesus of Nazareth ... We have Jesus Christ and they have 'X-Christ', both natures having been assumed by God ... Yet in each case the assumption of those natures is, in Mascall's words,[29] 'individualized in his person and that Person is numerically one'.

We are bound, then, to say that the Son of God is numerically one with two distinct corporeal persons who *cannot* be one with each other. 'What is more, we should have just as much reason to worship the 'X-Christ' as to worship Jesus Christ, and Christianity would embrace no longer a Trinity but a Quaternity'.[30] Either Christianity must stake everything on denying the existence of extraterrestrial 'rational persons', or it must renounce all claims to be a truly universal religion.

To turn to another complaint about traditional views: 'Not only is [a two substances Christology] open to the charge of meaninglessness,' writes Hick, 'but any imaginative meaning that it may have is of a static kind which, in the light of the modern rediscovery of the Bible, seems peculiarly inappropriate for the expansion of the biblical revelation.'[31] The God of the Bible is a living, active, dynamic God, who is seen above all in His acts, calling people and nations to Him, rescuing the oppressed, sending the prophets, judging the wrongdoer. The Jesus of the Bible is a living, active, dynamic personality, calling disciples to Him, healing the sick,

---

[28] Puccetti (1968), p. 139.
[29] Puccetti's reference is to Mascall (1956a), p. 41.
[30] Puccetti (1968), p. 140.   [31] Hick (1977a), p. 150.

sending out apostles, condemning the self-righteous, pardoning the repentant.

But move on a few centuries, and what a different picture we are being given! Listen to St Thomas Aquinas writing about God:

> The divine essence exists through itself as a singular existent and indivi-
> duated through itself; for, as we have shown, it is not in any matter. The
> divine essence is predicated of God, therefore, so that we may say 'God
> is his own essence.'[32]

> Not only is God his own essence ... but he is also his own existence
> ... That which has existence but is not existence is a being by participation.
> But, as we have shown, God is his own essence; and so, if he is not his
> own existence, he will not be essential being but participated being. He
> will not then be the first being; which is absurd. God is therefore his own
> existence.[33]

The living and acting God is being reduced to abstractions like 'essence' and 'existence'. Nor was this a process confined to medieval scholasticism. We find Boethius declaring that 'the substance of God is without either matter or motion ... In Divinity we should consider that Form which really is a Form and not an image, which is itself existence and from which existence exists ... The Divine Substance is form without matter and is therefore One and is that which it is'[34] (this last, as is shown by what follows, being equivalent to what Aquinas meant by 'being its own essence'). Or we might quote Pseudo-Dionysius to the effect that 'all essence is transcended by the super-essential Indefinite',[35] or, in the splendid but quite unbiblical ending of the *Mystical Theology*:

> He is neither soul nor intellect; nor has He imagination, opinion, reason
> or understanding; ... neither has He power, nor is power, nor is He light;
> neither has He life, nor is He life; ... nor can any affirmation or denial
> be applied to Him, for, though we may affirm or deny things below Him,
> Him we can neither affirm nor deny, since the all-perfect and unique Cause
> of all transcends all affirmation, and the simple pre-eminence of His absolute
> nature is outside all negation—free from every limitation and beyond them
> all.'[36]

---

[32] *Summa Contra Gentiles*, 1. 21. 4.   [33] *Summa Theologiae*, 1. 3. 4.
[34] *De Trinitate*, 2 (PL 64, 1250b).   [35] *De Divinis Nominibus*, 1. 1.
[36] *De Mystica Theologia*, ch. 5 (PG 3, 1045d).

This is magnificent stuff, but is this remote Indescribability the God of Abraham, Isaac, and Jacob, or the Father of Jesus?

It may be answered that Aquinas, Boethius, and even Pseudo-Dionysius, whatever the language they used in such passages as I have been quoting, did in fact believe in the God of the Bible and the Christ of the Bible, who 'obediently submitted to the designs of God His Father'.[37] Certainly this is so. But the fact that there was an unresolved conflict in their minds (even if they did not realize that it was a conflict) does not somehow mean that the 'static' side of their thought was *not* static. It was; the fact that there was a dynamic, biblical side to them as well makes them more Christian but less consistent.

And it was this 'static' way of thinking that guided the Fathers in their Christology. In the Formula of Chalcedon the only hint of anything else is in the phrase 'born from the Virgin Mary' and in the postscript 'as our Lord Jesus Christ taught us'. Otherwise it is abstract nouns and adjectives all the way: 'Godhead', 'humanity', 'of one substance with the Father', 'of one substance with us', 'the characteristic property of each nature being preserved and coinciding in one *prosōpon* and one *hypostasis*'. 'Substance', 'nature', and *'hypostasis'* all suggest fixity, immutability, stasis: and *'prosōpon'*, which in some of its meanings might not, was for Chalcedon a metaphysical term like the rest, and as static as they. It is no wonder that Dr Pittenger, who regards the charge of staticness, if applied to all forms of the 'perennial philosophy', as rather exaggerated, still feels he has to conclude that 'terms like substance, essence, being, nature (in its theological usage) and the like do appear to have an inert quality which can be devastating in its effect upon the biblical picture of the living God and his vital relationship with the world'.[38] 'Any interpretation of the meaning of Christ', he says elsewhere, 'which is to be true to the New Testament material and true also to the living experience of the risen Lord ... must be an interpretation which is in dynamic terms.'[39]

It was the belief of a number of nineteenth-century Hegelians that Christology was not really about a figure from the past at all; and this has recently been revived by such writers as Driver (p. 40,

[37] Ps.-Dionysius, *De Caelesti Hierarchia*, 4. 4 (PG 3, 181c).
[38] Pittenger (1970), p. 17.   [39] Pittenger (1959), p. 179.

above), and most notably perhaps in Ogden's Sarum Lectures. As mentioned earlier,[40] he criticizes both traditional and revisionist theories for answering their (mistaken) question 'Who is Jesus?' in terms of the historical, or, as he prefers to put it, the 'empirical-historical' Jesus; 'the actual Jesus of the past in so far as he is knowable to us today by way of empirical-historical inquiry'.[41] This position is so problematic as to be untenable. In the first place, despite the 'New Quest' for the historical Jesus by scholars like Käsemann and Ebeling, the actual Jesus of the past is virtually inaccessible to our enquiries. Even the 'criterion of dissimilarity' 'cannot be made to yield authentic Jesus-material without begging the question. Since all we know of the Jesus of the past is what we are told by the earliest available witness, there can never be any operational distinction between Jesus as he actually was and Jesus as he is reported in the earliest stratum of witness.'[42] But in any case a quest of the historical Jesus is unnecessary theologically. The real subject of the 'christological assertion' is not the empirical-historical Jesus but the *existential*-historical; and for him the 'earliest stratum of witness' is not a historical source but a theological norm. The referent of the name 'Jesus' in a formula like 'Jesus is the Christ' is not a figure of the past, to be reached, if at all, by scholarly enquiry behind the witness of the apostles, but 'the one whom we already know most certainly through the same apostolic witness, as well as all other witnesses of faith in so far as they are conformed to the witness of the apostles.'[43] It could be argued from this that even though for Ogden the christological question 'is and must be historical as well as existential',[44] we must eliminate any reference to the past Jesus from our Christology, and *a fortiori* need not look for any evidence about his alleged divinity. What we are confronted with is 'Jesus as he truly is—which is to say, as he is *believed to be* by those who ... intend to bear witness to him as the decisive re-presentation of God'.[45] We can doubtless develop a Christology on this basis, our only historical interest being in the finding of the earliest Christian witness, 'the normative witness of faith by which the appropriateness of all christological formulations must

---

[40] See Ch. 2, above.   [41] Ogden (1982), p. 43.   [42] Ogden (1982), p. 55.
[43] p. 57.   [44] p. 84.   [45] p. 58.

be justified'.[46] Indeed, Ogden proceeds to do so. But clearly it will be unlike any traditional one.

The charges of 'pre-Copernican' arrogance and of geocentricity which we looked at earlier are really only special cases of a more general defect in traditional Christology: it is simply unaware of what is going on outside itself. 'For an increasingly large portion of the world's population', writes Professor A. O. Dyson, 'it is not really a matter of moment that Christians, and Christian theologians in particular, argue ceaselessly as to what may legitimately be said about Jesus Christ ... The question about Jesus Christ is so limited, so peripheral, so small, so odd.'[47] Jesus is no doubt central to many Christian lives; he is of great importance, perhaps even central importance, to our history (though less so than used to be the case); but not to the history of the greater part of the world. And with the greater awareness that has come in modern times of the variety of cultures and societies that exist today and have existed in the past (let alone may come to exist in the future) the Christian will naturally find it harder 'to place so much weight upon one person and one point in history ... It is not necessarily replaced by any one new centre, but assumes a position as one local centre competing with many others.'[48]

We are not concerned so much with the effects this will have on our attitude towards other possible 'centres' as with the reassessment it will entail of our attitude towards the centre that is Christ. The 'faith once delivered to the saints'[49] is, if we look at things objectively, one item in an immensely complicated web of historical and social developments—and, caught up among them, must itself have changed and developed. Christian tradition is not the unchanging flow that it seems from within; it is a thoroughly mixed and heterogeneous collection of different ideas. Even in the New Testament itself the variety of ideas is enormous—and that includes Christological ideas. From the apparent idea that only at the Ascension was Jesus made Lord and Messiah,[50] by way of the idea that his virgin birth entitled him to be called 'Son of God',[51] or that

[46] p. 62.   [47] Dyson (1969), p. 13.   [48] pp. 14–15.
[49] Jude 3.   [50] Acts 2: 36.   [51] Luke 1: 35.

his Sonship was 'declared' in the Resurrection,[52] to the hints of pre-existence in the idea of one who was rich yet for our sakes became poor,[53] the 'cosmic Christ' who aided in creation[54] or is its goal,[55] and finally to the tentative applying to him of the actual name 'God',[56] the variety even there is extraordinary. It is beginning to look less certain that there *is* a 'traditional view', at least if we include the New Testament in our tradition. 'Put it thus,' says Houlden; 'if a sensitive enough instrument could be devised, every reciter of the Creed could be shown to be meaning something different by it, however strenuously he affirmed his solidarity with the Christian past and present.'[57]

The obvious conclusion is that the whole enterprise of Christology as undertaken by earlier generations of theologians was an exercise in unwarranted self-confidence. They treated the Bible and Christian tradition as a kind of monolith on which one could build (well or badly) without a qualm; whereas in fact they were building, let us not say on sand, but at best on shingle—on lots of different stones, which afford no adequate foundation, at least not for the elaborate Christological structures which they sought to erect. To quote Dyson again, 'the most significant feature of our answer to the question about Jesus Christ is precisely its fragmentary, inconclusive and paradoxical character.'[58]

Whether we are still confident enough to try and build an ambitious Christology, or whether our answers are indeed going to be 'fragmentary, inconclusive and paradoxical', we have to recognize the obvious fact that the 'definitive' Christological debates of the fourth and fifth centuries took place in a Western, and more specifically a Hellenistic milieu, and the results that were arrived at were inevitably affected by this. Even criticisms of and reactions to Chalcedon and the rest have been made within the same culture, or cultures deriving from it. We have already looked at one unhappy result of this—the obsolescence of the vocabulary used in the past and

---

[52] Romans 1: 4.   [53] 2 Cor. 8: 9.   [54] Hebrews 1: 2.
[55] Col. 1: 16.   [56] John 20: 28; 2 Pet. 1: 1.
[57] Houlden (1977), p. 16. I should add that on the next page he adds that the 'instrument' 'would also reveal how close they were'.
[58] Dyson (1969), p. 27.

of the concepts that vocabulary embodied. But there are others as well. First, even if we supposed that vocabulary and concepts were not obsolete, still there is no use in pretending that they covered all the ground that would ever be needed for discussions of the person of our Lord. 'It was the limitation of Greek philosophy', wrote Bishop F. R. Barry, 'that it had no true place for personality nor any understanding of it';[59] and Forsyth made a similar point when he said that 'psychology, and especially religious psychology, had not then come into existence; and, while the strongest assertions were made about the existence of the two natures as a postulate of faith, it was beyond the powers of the metaphysics which then prevailed to show how they could cohere in a personal unity.'[60] Questions are raised which simply cannot be answered in the old framework of thought and language—indeed, cannot be *asked* in it—but which are inevitable if we are to think and speak about Christ.

Secondly, if we tie our Christology too closely to these Hellenistic concepts, the *risk* involved is enormous. 'The whole doctrine of the two natures is an interpretation in Hellenistic terms of what Jesus Christ really means'[61]—so; but if this is declared to be the only lawful interpretation, and if those Hellenistic terms cease to be meaningful (whether they have already done so or not does not matter), then no one will know what Jesus Christ really means. It must surely be possible to express what He means in other terms as well; if not, Christology—and, it would seem, Christianity itself—will turn out in the end to have been a passing, temporary thing.

Thirdly, it is not just a matter of passing with time; it will also 'pass' as we move in *space*. Are we going to have to teach Middle Platonism and Neoplatonism to potential converts in Thailand or Zambia in order to proclaim to them the gospel of Christ? Is this what Peter and Paul did? All right, this is not quite fair: conversion to Christ has never called for a grasp of Christology as a prerequisite. But are we going to have to teach it to potential preachers and thinkers? It is interesting to note here the work of the great seventeenth-century Jesuit missionary to India, Roberto de Nobili, who set out deliberately to live like an Indian, adopting the life of a *sannyāsin* and even wearing a Christianized version of the Hindu

---

[59] *The Recovery of Man*, p. 83, quoted by Matthews (1950), p. 26.
[60] Forsyth (1909), p. 217.   [61] Küng (1976), p. 131.

sacred thread—and not only this, but to adapt Christian teaching to Indian forms and languages. Dr Robin Boyd, in his study of Indian theology,[62] has to conclude: 'De Nobili's Sanskrit and Tamil works, interesting as they are as experiments in coining new words and phrases to replace the Latin theological vocabulary, in effect simply reproduce the current Tridentine theology and make no real attempt to use Hindu terminology and thought-forms to express the Christian faith.' As a result, de Nobili's magnificent pioneering work never led to much; he had many converts but few successors. It seems that with the best will in the world Christians cling instinctively to the European forms they are familiar with—and that the evangelistic and pastoral effects are very bad. To insist on the traditional formulae is to cut off from Christ the intellects of most of the human race.

Fourthly, is not such insistence theologically unsound as well as pastorally? 'Nobody has claimed (so far as I know)', writes Pittenger, 'that any single philosophy—certainly not that of the Platonic or Aristotelian type which prevailed in earlier Christian thinking—is revealed to men as the philosophy which must necessarily be used when we are talking about the basic affirmations of the Christian faith.'[63] But this is what insistence on traditional formulae does in effect claim, even if it is formally denied. It is like the Mayor who said the town council should be chosen on a non-political basis, and so no Socialists should be elected to it! Our faith is not a matter of philosophical schemes, so no one who criticizes patristic philosophy is capable of faith! If the faith is not a matter of philosophical schemes, we must not treat it as if it were.

[62] Boyd (1969), pp. 13–14.   [63] Pittenger (1970), p. 17.

5

The 'Lack of Evidence'

WE move on at this point from direct criticism of traditional views
to indirect ones: even if the traditional views might conceivably
be true, there would be no way of telling that they were. But there
are various kinds of 'indirect criticism' along these lines, of which
we may distinguish four in particular.

First, it is claimed that the alleged evidence is historically vulnerable. Christianity, it has often been said, is a historical religion in
a way no other religion is. Not just in that it began with certain
events in the past. That is true of other religions too, such as Islam
and Buddhism. But it ascribes *cosmic importance* to these events.
Muslims and Buddhists do, of course, regard the life of Muhammad
or Buddha as important, but this is only because it was in these
lives that their teaching was given. That teaching could have been
given by someone else; indeed, Muhammad was, according to himself, only the last of a series of prophets whose message was basically
the same, and Siddhartha was only (it is held) the most recent of
a series of Buddhas, each of whom achieved and taught the same
Enlightenment. In so far as Jesus Christ was a teacher, much the
same might be said of Him: much of what He taught was also taught
by others before and after Him. But the claim was and is made
that 'God was in Christ reconciling the world to Himself';[1] that
His life and death and resurrection were in themselves instruments
of that reconciliation; that He 'died for our sins and rose again
for our justification'.[2] For the Christian, historical events are still
living and powerful for our salvation.

But this makes Christianity in a peculiar way *vulnerable*, in a
way that other religions for the most part are not. Historical criticism
may tell us that the events we ascribe cosmic importance to never
happened, or were strikingly different from the way they have been

---

[1] 2 Cor. 5: 19.   [2] Rom. 4: 25.

reported. The Fall was for long supppposed to have been *the* most
important event in history before the coming of Christ; but few
now suppose that the opening chapters of Genesis are literal historical narrative. Jesus Himself no doubt existed, but can we say more?
'Passages', writes Professor Dennis Nineham, 'in which all competent scholars would agree in recognising [that we are offered the
authentic deeds and words of Jesus] are rare, and it is important
not to claim too much ... Seldom, if ever, can we distinguish with
certainty and say "This is pure history" and "that is pure invention
or interpretation".'[3] The exact extent to which the Evangelists are
accurate suppliers of information is not at the moment our concern:
the point is simply that there is and must be doubt and dispute
over what they say—even over so apparently central an event as
the Resurrection.

Can we, then, try and build into Christianity defences against
this vulnerability? There have been attempts to do just this. Bultmann
notoriously rejected using 1 Corinthians 15: 1ff. as evidence for
the Resurrection precisely because it made the *kerygma* something
that could be verified (or disproved);[4] and Dr Van A. Harvey
sums up this position (with which he does not himself agree) as
follows:

It is a falsification of both faith and historical inquiry if the former is
based on the latter; a·falsification of faith because faith cannot change
with every new consensus of New Testament criticism or hold its breath
lest some new discovery in the Dead Sea area cast a shadow of doubt
over this particular belief; falsification of history because it is intolerable
to honest inquiry if the New Testament critic or believer decides in favour
of one historical judgment rather than another because it is more compatible
with his religious beliefs.'[5]

This will not do. The more you make a belief invulnerable against
any sort of criticism based on facts, the more you empty it of content.
This was of course at the heart of the 'Theology and Falsification'
debate of the 1950s, sparked off by Antony Flew's article with that
title.[6] There are certain kinds of proposition which really are invulnerable to this sort of criticism—truths of logic and mathematics,
for example. But any statement which makes a claim about facts

---

[3] Nineham (1963), p. 51.   [4] In Bartsch (1953), p. 112.
[5] Harvey (1967), p. 17.   [6] In Flew and Macintyre (1955).

in the real world is at once vulnerable to criticism or evidence based on facts in the real world. ('Falsifiable' is the shorthand term for this vulnerability; a little misleading, maybe, to the newcomer, for a *true* statement is in this sense just as 'falsifiable' as a lie; the word means 'theoretically capable of being disproved by some possible evidence', not 'actually fated to be disproved by real evidence'.) If (say) a Marxist makes predictions, on the basis of Marx's economic theories, about what will happen in capitalist societies, these are falsifiable, because maybe they will not come true. If the theories are correct, the predictions will come true; but at least they *might* not. But if our Marxist builds safeguards into these 'predictions' so that *whatever* happens they will always 'come true'—whether capitalism collapses, or communism does, or neither, or both, or anything you like—then nothing has been predicted at all, and the theories assert nothing.

So it is with Christian believers in (say) the Resurrection. If they believe that Christ rose physically from the tomb, they may be right or they may be wrong, but they do believe something. Much the same applies if they believe that the disciples really did have visions sent to them from a Lord who was 'risen' in a non-physical sense— alive and active though His body was still in the tomb. But if they so safeguard themselves that no imaginable evidence about the tomb or the experiences of the disciples could, even in theory, disprove their 'belief', then they believe nothing. Perhaps by 'believing in the Resurrection' they mean that their lives have been deeply affected by the preaching of Easter? But even this is vulnerable to some extent. For might it not turn out that their lives had not really been affected in the way they supposed? Not that such a 'belief in the Resurrection' is a *Christian* one anyway; it might be accepted by someone who did not believe that there had ever been such a person as Jesus of Nazareth and who regarded the teaching ascribed to him as a load of nonsense. There is simply no way Christians can escape all possibility of being mistaken except by refusing to commit themselves to anything at all. It is the *flight* from history that distorts—or attenuates—faith.

We might add, though it is perhaps something of a side-issue, that basing faith on history is surely no more a distortion of history than it is of faith. If a New Testament critic believes on other grounds that, say, God never works miracles, then he or she is quite justified in using this as a reason for disbelieving the story of the raising of Lazarus; provided, that is, that this reason is made clear, and also that he or she is honourably willing to change beliefs if it becomes beyond reasonable doubt that Lazarus really was raised.

Traditional Christianity, including its doctrines of Christ, is inextricably tied up with belief in certain historical facts (or alleged facts). And these are precarious. We do have to hold our breath lest some new discovery near the Dead Sea cast a shadow of doubt on our beliefs. But this means that Christian belief is on far shakier ground than scientific theories are, for which more evidence piles up each time a proposed law is verified, let alone mathematical disciplines which require only inner consistency. Orthodox believers have not sufficiently realized the sheer weakness of their position: they have tended too often to treat their own psychological or subjective certainty as if it could somehow be translated into objective and factual certainty of the truth of the gospel. This is not so. Traditional Christology is vulnerable; attenuated Christology is lacking in content; better abandon both, and with them the effort to keep Christianity as a historical religion.

Traditionalists may at this point feel inclined to protest that all this talk of 'vulnerability' or 'falsifiability' is very theoretical and out of touch with reality. There is nothing in what was said in the last section that is not equally applicable to someone who believes that Queen Anne is dead. The latter belief is equally 'vulnerable' and 'falsifiable'; but that does not bother people who are writing Lives of the Queens or histories of eighteenth-century Britain.

This is correct. But this is where our second objection, or group of objections, comes in. The evidence for the doctrine of the Incarnation is far too slender to bear the weight of dogma, liturgy, and homiletics that has been laid on it. This is one thing that has emerged with vast clarity from the enormous development of biblical criticism over the past two hundred years or so.

In the first place, a very large number of scholars would hold that *it is not possible to know much about Jesus at all*. That there existed such a man only a few eccentrics would deny, except perhaps in the Soviet Union, where it is or was official teaching that he never existed. But we can say very little more than that. He was a Palestinian Jew who spoke, largely in parables, about the 'kingdom of God', and was crucified about AD 30 in Jerusalem; and that is very nearly all.

Of course, to give the detailed reasoning behind this contention would be wholly impossible in this space—or indeed for this author. It is the result of increasing work on the Gospels. Source-criticism showed that often where it seemed we had two or three witnesses to a story about Jesus we had in reality only one, the seeming corroboration being the result of copying or use of a common source. Form-criticism showed that the stories had developed in the telling, and fitted uncannily well into the life of the early Church, where in all probability a great many had actually come into being. Redaction-criticism showed how the Evangelists themselves had shaped and adapted the material that came to them. At the end of it all, little was left to be ascribed to the original Jesus. The most that can be suggested is the 'criterion of dissimilarity': if a saying ascribed to Jesus is quite unparalleled in contemporary Judaism (and so is unlikely to have been taken over from some first-century rabbi) and quite unparalleled in the early Church (and so is unlikely to have arisen there) it is quite likely to be authentic. Yet even this may be going too far. To take an instructive example: Old-fashioned writers on the Gospels have often pointed out[7] that the title 'Son of Man' is never found on the lips of any speaker, or the pen of any writer, in the whole of the New Testament, apart from Jesus (with one exception, Acts 7:6[8]), and have claimed that surely here we have the *ipsissima verba* of the Lord and His own preferred self-designation. But able and distinguished scholars have maintained, not merely that some of the 'Son of Man' sayings are not genuinely dominical, being rather inventions of the early Church, but that this is true of every single one of them![9] Whether they are right or wrong is not the question here; the point is not that the 'Son of Man' sayings are certainly inauthentic, but that they are of doubtful authenticity. And if so apparently solid and rock-like a foundation can be so thoroughly unreliable, what are we to make of material that looks less convincing? 'Not a single line from the gospels can be taken as certainly reliable', is how Cupitt sums it up.[10]

But even if we assume that Jesus really did do and say much of what he is reported to have done and said, *Jesus never claimed divinity for himself.* This may seem a startling statement to make.

[7] See e.g. Barclay (1962), p. 68.
[8] John 12: 34 is no true exception; the title is merely quoted, not used.
[9] So e.g. Conzelmann (1969), pp. 131–7; Perrin (1967), pp. 164ff.
[10] Cupitt (1979), p.70.

'I and the Father are one' (John 10: 30)? 'Before Abraham was, I am' (John 8: 58)? 'He who has seen me, has seen the Father' (John 14: 9)? Yes, but all these come from the Fourth Gospel. That is a profound work, in fact the chief source (though not the only one) for the doctrine of the Incarnation, and it does include historical details which may well be as reliable as most of those in the other Gospels. But it cannot be claimed any longer as a record of the words of Jesus. The style of Jesus' speeches in John differs far too widely from his style in the other Gospels; if Jesus really did talk the way he talks in Matthew, Mark, and Luke, he simply cannot have talked the way he does in John. (The obvious analogy is with Socrates. If Socrates really did talk the way he does in Xenophon or the shorter dialogues of Plato, then he simply cannot have said the things he is portrayed as saying in, for example, the main body of the *Republic*; and though at one time some scholars did try to maintain that Plato's later dialogues did reproduce Socrates' teaching, no one would do so today.) And it will not do to suggest that John reports 'discourses and meditations of Jesus such as certainly took place in the circle of his disciples side by side with his instruction of the disciples proper, with its more rigid forms'.[11] For many of the most typically 'Johannine' discourses and debates are depicted as delivered publicly (this includes the first two of the sayings quoted above); and, what is surely decisive, they have a strong resemblance in style to John's first epistle, which is certainly not the work of Jesus!

It is no use therefore to assert that Jesus claimed divinity on the strength of His alleged words in the Fourth Gospel. We must rely on the Synoptists. Now the Synoptists themselves certainly believed that Jesus was the Son of God (cf. e.g. Matt. 2: 15, Mark 1: 1, Luke 1: 32) and represent Him as accepting this title (Matt. 16: 17, Mark 3: 12, Luke 4: 41). But these last probably represent and reflect the Synoptists' own views about Jesus, just as John 10: 30 represents and reflects John's. It is likely that the idea of Jesus' Sonship grew up out of one or both of two roots: a 'servant' Christology which shifted to 'son' through the ambiguity of the Greek word 'παῖς',[12] and Jesus' habit of addressing God as 'Abba', 'Father', in an intimate manner which suggested to his hearers that he was in some way uniquely *entitled* to use this form of address,

---

[11] H. Riesenfeld in *Studia Evangelica*, I. 59, quoted by Morris (1972), p. 47.

[12] So Jeremias (1971), pp. 53ff.

being in a special sense the Son of God.[13] Other factors may have entered in too.[14] But it may be taken as certain that Jesus did not claim to be 'Son of God' any more than he claimed to be 'God'.

If, then, Jesus did not make any claim to divinity, it is absurd for us to make the claim for him. What has happened is not unlike what happened with Siddhartha the Buddha, who certainly professed to be a human being who, once he had passed into *parinirvāna*, could influence people only through the Way that he had taught, but who somehow ended up as in effect a deity, even if that word would not be used; the visible manifestation ('*nirmānakāya*', 'body of humility') of the ultimate reality ('*dharmakāya*', 'body of the right Way', very occasionally, even, personified as 'Adi-buddha', 'the supreme enlightened one'). With the best will in the world, we may well suppose, Christians made their great Teacher first a supernatural being ('Word' or 'Son of God'), then divine, and finally one of the eternal Trinity; but he himself said nothing to justify this.

It might be argued that even if the words of Jesus about His own person do not require belief in His divinity, still that divinity is entailed by other beliefs about Him, and more particularly about His work. He is Saviour, Redeemer, Lord, Mediator, the one who 'gave his life a ransom for many' (Mark 10: 45), whose blood was shed 'for the remission of sins' (Matt. 26: 28). 'Christological expositions', says Young with absolute correctness, 'are parasitic upon definitions and concepts of salvation.'[15] The same point is made by Macquarrie: 'Christian doctrines are so closely interrelated that if you take away one, several others tend to collapse. After incarnation is thrown out, is the doctrine of the Trinity bound to go? What kind of doctrine of atonement remains possible? Would the Eucharist be reduced simply to a memorial service?'[16] Now it is indeed certain that if the doctrine of the Incarnation were to be officially abandoned, much else would go too; but the 'rewriting of creeds and liturgies, prayer-books and hymn-books' which Macquarrie goes on to mention, however daunting a task, must not

[13] See e.g. Hengel (1976), p. 63.
[14] Hengel (1976), p. 63, suggests passages from the OT like 2 Sam. 7: 14, and the self-designation of Jesus as 'Son of Man'. He doubts, however, that the ambiguity of παῖς played a significant role.
[15] In Hick (1977*b*), p. 13.
[16] In Green (1977), p. 144.

deter us from truth. And of the interrelated doctrines he cites, two, those of the Trinity and the Eucharist, are *dependent* on that of the Incarnation; the abandonment of the latter would simply remove unnecessary and embarrassing complexities. But the Atonement is another matter. Is it not the heart of Christian faith that we have been saved by Christ, and does not this salvation in the end imply His divinity?

To this a number of replies can be made. Young, in the passage just quoted, points out that although 'an exclusive claim that the only way of understanding the nature of Jesus is in terms of a unique divine incarnation has been enshrined in authoritative statements', this is not so with the Atonement. 'Exclusive claims that there can only be one way of understanding salvation in Christ have never been "canonized" in creed or definition.' It may be that some under-standings of salvation do require an Incarnation and others do not; in that case, we are perfectly free to adopt one of the latter, if it commends itself to us on other grounds, and abandon the unneces-sary and embarrassing complexity of believing in an incarnate God. This could even apply to some traditional understandings of the Atonement. The Word, said St Athanasius, 'assumed humanity that we might become God',[17] and this has been a constant theme in soteriology, especially in the East, ever since. But, as Young points out, 'a real son is not needed in order to produce adopted sons. Since we only receive an adopted sonship and a derivative divinity, the *essential* Godhead and Sonship of the one who passes it on to us is not logically required.'[18]

The same sort of point is made for other soteriological positions by Wiles.[19] He suggests that, historically, 'four pictures were of particular importance to the early church in its thought about the Atonement' (and not only in the early church, either): victory over Satan, meeting the demands of divine law, the offering of a sacrifice, and the reversal of the sin of Adam. Each must be considered in turn. If (as would be common today) the personification of evil forces is abandoned, the first one seems to be a picture assuring us that evil, 'even in its most potent and inexplicable manifestations [cannot] destroy the personal being of man in God's world'. But such assurance need not depend on any once-for-all act of God

[17] *De Incarnatione*, 54 (PG 25, 192b).   [18] In Hick (1977*b*), p. 22.
[19] Wiles (1974), pp. 61–9.

in the past. Similarly, there may be—indeed, there is—value in the ideas associated with the picture of the Cross as a meeting of the law's just demands; but precisely in so far as we try to attach this value to a literal once-for-all bearing of a fixed penalty, to just that extent the whole idea seems to lose cogency and acceptability.

Sacrifice (Wiles goes on) was the way in which Jews of our Lord's time 'gave expression to the seriousness of sin and the costliness of the way to overcome it'. That truth still needs expression; but it does not force us to believe that there must have been 'one oblation ... once offered' to embody—to incarnate—that truth. And since the story of Adam, while it may still be valuable as myth, has lost all plausibility as history—has ceased, in other words, to be regarded as a once-for-all event with cosmic implications—it cannot provide the backing it once did for the concept of the Atonement as a similar once-for-all event with reverse cosmic implications.It is significant, Wiles points out, that the difficulties which have long been seen in each of these pictures of the Atonement are all of them difficulties which crop up at the points where the pictures might seem at first to show the necessity of some once-for-all act of atonement. Of course, there may still have been such an act. We can continue to use such pictures (as pictures—but then that was always the way they were used) if there was such an act; we can also do so if there wasn't.

Conceivably it might be objected that they were more than pictures. They gave content to the vague assertion that we are saved. Can content really be given to that assertion without objective Incarnation and objective Atonement? And here we might profitably bring in some of the work of Bultmann. If 'salvation' is to be given any real meaning for present-day man, is not the best candidate what he and other existentialists call 'authenticity'?

Man has no status apart from the exclusive modes of being of authenticity and inauthenticity ... In his Being, man is concerned with himself. He loses himself, his authenticity, his ownness, when he falls victim to the 'they', the world, and thus surrenders himself as *possibility* ... Liberation consists in the fact that man accepts his whole existence as a *finite* one, for which he is responsible at every minute ... It is an existence in which he is momentarily for his time. For being in the moment is man's authentic being.[20]

[20] Schmithals (1968), pp. 97–8.

And it is God who is revealed as

the One who limits man and who brings him to his authenticity in his limitation—namely, whenever this limitation is understood as God's limitation ... He cannot set to work to carry through such a self-understanding as his own undertaking; he can only hear that and where his limit is set, for this limit is God: 'No one has ever seen God; the only Son who is in the bosom of the Father, he has made him known'.[21]

Bultmann notoriously rejected the 'mythology' of the Incarnation. The concept of Jesus as conceived by the Holy Ghost and born of the Virgin Mary, let alone the concept of Him as the Son of God in a metaphysical sense, are mythological, and 'for modern man the mythological concept of the world, the conceptions of eschatology, of redeemer and redemption, are over and done with'.[22] Nevertheless, it is still possible to speak of God as acting; He acts with us here and now, meeting us 'in His word, in a concrete word, the preaching instituted in Jesus Christ'.[23] What God has done in Jesus Christ is not a historical fact, capable of historical proof; that is the point of the mythological description of Christ and His work in the New Testament. They force us to understand Christ and His work in categories other than those of the historian. God's grace has already acted for me, but that grace is present to me now; the word I hear now is one and the same with that which was preached by the apostles.

In Bultmann, therefore, we have a clear understanding of what we may continue to call (in a non-mythological sense) 'salvation' as the act of God, yet one which is not bound up with the idea of incarnation. It is still bound up with the act of God in Jesus Christ. But should it be? Radical critics of Bultmann, such as Schubert Ogden[24] and Fritz Buri,[25] have argued that authentic existence as Bultmann describes it need not, and indeed should not, be tied to a particular event in the past, even if that is the way we ourselves came to it. 'The proclamation of the message of Christ can be the occasion for men becoming aware of their unconditional responsibi-

---

[21] Bultmann (1964), pp. 103–4.   [22] Bultmann (1960), pp. 16–17.
[23] Bultmann (1960), p. 78.   [24] Ogden (1962), p. 30.
[25] Little of Buri's work is available in English; a summary of relevant work is given in Dyson (1969), pp. 63ff. and 94ff. For his positive views see Buri (1966), pp. 77ff.

lity. All this is perfectly acceptable as long as we avoid the danger of making the one cipher absolute for all.'[26] Yet even without this further step we do have an atonement without any need for incarnation.

Obviously it is not being claimed that this existentialist view of salvation must be the only possible one and will remain the only possible one for all time. The point is simply that *a* plausible view of salvation exists which does not call for the traditional Christology. And that is all we needed. The claim had been that the traditional view was necessary in order to make sense of our salvation. But it can only be *necessary* if it is entailed by *all* views of salvation. One possible view which does not entail it is enough; the traditional Christology, true or false, is not necessary.

It may not even be sufficient! The disputes which culminated in the Council of Nicaea suggest that. 'Where Arius severed the mediator from God,' writes Young, 'Athanasius severed him from the world.'[27] If the Logos is fully divine, he is transcendent God and beyond our sufferings; if he is not divine, how can he mediate between the infinite and the finite, being thoroughly finite himself? But we need not pursue this line of thought, for all that we wanted was to show that traditional Christology was not needed. To show that it was insufficient even for the task it was supposed to perform might be gratifying as a piece of *ad hominem* polemic, but would not be a vital part of the revisionist case.

Fourthly, it seems that evidence *cannot* be available. 'The action of God', says Bultmann, 'is hidden from every eye except the eye of faith. Only the so-called natural, secular (worldly) events are visible to every man and capable of proof.'[28] He had of course his own special reasons for wanting to say this. But the odd thing is, traditional theology had equally good reasons for saying the same thing, even if it never actually got round to saying it. Again it is Young who has made this point most forcibly. 'If', she writes,' Jesus was an entirely normal human being, no evidence can be produced for the incarnation. If no evidence can be produced, there can be no basis on which to claim that an incarnation took place.'[29] At the risk of spoiling the epigrammatic brevity of this, one might expand her point a little. Suppose it is claimed that as man, Jesus

---

[26] Dyson (1969), p. 106.
[28] Bultmann (1960), pp. 61–2.
[27] Hick (1977*b*), p. 27.
[29] In Goulder (1979), p. 62.

wept at Lazarus' tomb, and as God, raised him from it. Was the raising something no one could have done without being God? We may note that consideration of similar miracles ascribed to prophets in the Old Testament or apostles in the New suggests that to the biblical writers it was not. But that is not the point just now. The point is this: If the traditionalists answer 'Yes, it was something no one could have done without being God', they are ascribing to Jesus an act that was not a human one, and are therefore falling into a mild form of Docetism. Jesus was not fully human, for He did things no human being could or would do. If, on the other hand, the answer is 'No, this was something a human being could do, at least if God gave him or her the power to do it', perhaps citing the stories of the Shunammite's son[30] or of Dorcas[31] in evidence, then the raising of Lazarus is no evidence of divinity—only of God-given power. Cupitt is, I think, making a similar point when he argues[32] in reply to the famous *aut deus aut homo non probus* argument (if Jesus talked and acted as He did, He was either evil, insane, or divine, but clearly He was neither evil nor insane) that this implies that Jesus' language was incompatible with normal human goodness and sanity; it must therefore be non-human language, and we are back with Docetism again.

And this sort of point can be made with *anything* ascribed to Jesus—supernatural insight (John 1: 47–8), power to forgive sins (Mark 2: 5–12), authority to overrule the Law (Matt. 5: 21, 38, etc.)—anything that is alleged to be evidence of his divinity. Either it is *not* evidence of his divinity (which is in fact probably the correct conclusion), or it is evidence that he was not 'consubstantial with us' in the way that the Council of Chalcedon declared he was. It follows that there can in the very nature of things be no evidence for divinity in what Jesus said, did, or underwent; and therefore on the traditionalists' own premises there can be no reason to believe in the Incarnation.

[30] 2 Kings 4: 18–37.   [31] Acts 9: 36–41.   [32] Cupitt (1979), p. 113.

6

The Basis of an Analytic Christology

I HOPE that the above summary of the case against traditional Christology will be felt to have been a fair one, and not a caricature designed to be rejected out of hand. Although later in this book I shall be arguing that none of the objections raised are in the end valid, nevertheless, there is the appearance at least of a very strong cumulative case for abandoning any attempt at an analytic Christology and confining ourselves to the revisionist kind. Not that 'confining' would be regarded by all as the appropriate word here. 'Liberating' might be thought nearer the mark; is it not theologians who feel obliged to stay within the bounds set by Chalcedon or some other confessional document who are really 'confined'? Of course, they in turn would deny that 'liberation' from this was desirable.

What they have to do—and this is why the idea of 'analytic' Christology has been stressed in the present work—is to try and think out a Christology that is capable of withstanding the criticisms that have been summarized in the previous pages. The fact that they wish to remain orthodox means that they must take into consideration not only the need to meet these criticisms but also certain basic requirements which have nothing to do with criticism but are simply demanded by the nature of the enterprise, namely, the construction of an analytic Christology that is not revisionist. Working out approximately what those requirements may be will, then, be our next task.

It may well turn out that operating under these constraints will produce something fairly complicated. That will no doubt be a pity if it does turn out to be the case, but it will not be a fatal objection to the analysis; the presented aspect of a thing may be simple and yet the true analysis be complex, as anyone will realize who reflects on what chemistry and physics have to tell us about a grain of sugar. The knowledge of Christ that is required for faith in Him to be possible may be a simple thing—indeed, it *is*—and yet the theological facts on which it rests can be quite complex.

Complexity, then, is no objection. Contradiction, however, as we saw earlier, most definitely *is*. We must at no point allow ourselves the luxury of saying 'Paradox' or 'Mystery' where what we ought to say is 'Self-contradiction!', scrap what we have just written, and look for something else. Paradox and Mystery can be pleaded; only, however, when we see that something can be true but not the method by which it has come to be true. For instance, it is legitimate for a Trinitarian to say that there is some sense in which God is Threefold and some other sense in which He is One, and to add that this is a mystery or a paradox; for as long as the senses are *different* senses there is no contradiction. There is indeed a mystery, but this is because we have no adequate insight into the Divine Nature, nor any adequate vocabulary with which to describe it, and we cannot specify precisely what these senses are. This move may or may not be justified, but clearly it is not a self-contradiction. We may have to admit that we have come up against paradox or mystery as we proceed: but let us keep a sharp look-out for logical incoherence, and avoid it.

With this warning in mind, then, let us proceed to discuss our 'basic material'. It will be taken for granted in the following pages that what we are looking for is a *Christian* Christology. This is not as absurdly tautologous as it sounds. Other religions could have Christologies. In fact, Islam does have one, in a way. Jesus was a prophet, and one of the greatest of all prophets at that;[1] he was born of the Virgin Mary, ascended into heaven, and will return at the last day, but was *not* crucified (and, consequently, did not rise from the dead either). There are even what one might call Christological heresies: the Ahmadiyyas claim that Jesus did in fact die, though not on the Cross but in Kashmir! It would be perfectly possible, similarly, for a Hindu to conceive of a Christology in which Jesus was regarded as an avatar (or partial avatar) of Vishnu; or of a Buddhist Christology which saw Him as a Bodhisattva, one well on the way to complete Buddhahood. These possibilities will not be our concern. They are mentioned only because it is important to distinguish the idea of (say) a Hindu Christology, which is of

---

[1] Al-Hallaj styled Him 'the seal of the saints' as Muhammad was the 'seal of the prophets'. For Muslim Christology, see e.g. F. P. Cotterell in Rowdon (1982), pp. 282ff.

no interest to us just now, from that of a Christology expressed in terms normally used in Hinduism. The Fathers used Greek and Latin vocabularies without adopting the pagan religions which also used them; it may be (and we shall have occasion to notice one or two attempts later on) that a Christology could be expressed in other vocabularies, still without adopting the religions in which those vocabularies developed. But to proceed.

In his book *The Shape of Christology*,[2] John McIntyre devoted a section to discussing what could be regarded as 'given' in Christology—what material the Christologist has to work on. 'Work on' is rather a vague expression. It could mean that the theologian must base his or her work on all the 'given' and on nothing else; or, at the other extreme, it might mean only that he or she ought to try and think consistently with the 'given' as far as possible. But this is not peculiar to theology: the historian and the natural scientist have similar problems. (It is perhaps to be desired that 'fundamental theology' should be expanded to tackle this sort of question in detail.) It could be that the 'given' serves chiefly a negative task—it is what we must try not to contradict, rather as natural scientists may develop theories freely, but must not contradict the experimental evidence. I shall, however, leave the idea undefined and hope that I am more or less comprehensible.

McIntyre's 'given' is obviously an idea closely related to what I called 'basic requirements', and we may well take his discussion as a starting-point. He suggests four possible candidates for the title of 'the given': the Bible; a minimal historical core to the Bible; God's self-revelation in Jesus Christ; and the 'here-and-now' Christ of Christian life and experience. But to each of these taken alone and supposed to be adequate by itself there are serious objections, and McIntyre eventually concludes that all four have to be used together. Let us consider the objections he raises (and perhaps ask ourselves whether there are others as well, or indeed other possible sources of 'the given').

The 'here-and-now' Christ McIntyre sees as being the Christ we encounter 'in the reality of the existential situation', enabling us to pass from inauthentic to authentic existence.[3] (We have already met this sort of language in the last chapter.) His difficulty with this emphasis, which he is sure must be retained as part of any

---

[2] McIntyre (1966), pp. 19ff.   [3] p. 25.

Christology we develop, is that it tends to be irresponsible, or at best equivocal, in disparaging or assessing the historical elements in the Christian faith. This is just, I think; yet might not an advocate of this approach refuse to regard it as a difficulty at all, maintaining that it is precisely the 'historical elements' which have been over-emphasized in the past and need to be cut down to size—or indeed abandoned? I should myself feel that an even more serious difficulty is the extreme subjectivism involved. It is appallingly difficult to convey in language an experience of the sort that the 'here-and-now Christ' approach usually bases itself on; and the range of Christian experience is so vast that there is a danger of confusing quite different types of experience and giving them all the same label in error. By no means all those who have 'encountered Christ' would feel that they wanted to describe this encounter in the existentialist terms which McIntyre mentions. Would someone who has been through a typical Evangelical conversion experience (if there is such a thing as a 'typical' one) wish to describe it as a passage out of inauthentic existence? Yet such a conversion surely has rather a good claim to be regarded as an encounter with Christ. And there are of course many other forms of 'encounter' as well; God (the orthodox might say) has as many ways of meeting and changing us as He chooses to have. Now nearly everyone who has been through any of these tends to regard it as, in effect, definitive, and the difficulties that arise if one tries either to base a Christology on kinds of encounter that one has never had oneself or to base it entirely on one's own pattern are obviously going to be enormous. What actually happens in many cases, perhaps most, is that the 'encounter' is interpreted in terms of a theology or philosophy that is accepted from others, whether it be Heideggerian existentialism, or rigorous Calvinism, or whatever. Nevertheless, it is certainly true that Christology will have to allow for these 'encounters'; a Christology that severs the believer from Christ alive and active (as radical revisionism is apt to do) is grossly defective.

It was perhaps to avoid such subjectivism that Dietrich Bon-hoeffer, who began his Christology with the 'present Christ', not the 'historical', spoke not of encounters or existentialism but of the Christ we meet in Word, Sacrament, and Church.[4] The diffi-culty with this approach is of course that one's theology of Word,

----

[4] Bonhoeffer (1978), pp. 43–55.

Sacrament, and Church is likely to be determined by one's Christ-ology; I doubt whether anyone, even Bonhoeffer, really could begin with these (and no presuppositions or begging of the question) and only move on to the understanding of the person of Christ after-wards.

'God's self-revelation in Christ' is suggested in McIntyre as a kind of replacement for a Bible that is no longer regarded as infallible or self-sufficient. 'The Bible points beyond itself to the self-revelation of God [which] requires no authority outside itself to establish its credentials.'[5] The trouble with this (apart from a certain exagger-ation in the way that it is put—after all, there are millions to whom this self-revelation has not yet succeeded in establishing its creden-tials) is that, as McIntyre puts it, this 'may be a perfectly good answer to a question, but not to *this* question'. Revelation 'is an account of how we come by this given, or more correctly, of how this given comes to us'.[6] It is not the given itself; it consists, not of facts or states of affairs, but of a process whereby we may learn about facts or states of affairs; or, as some would prefer to put it, it is not God but a process whereby we may learn about God. It is no more the 'given' for Christology than the experimental method is the 'given' for chemistry; when we have been told (truly) that God has revealed Himself in Christ, we still want to know *what* has been revealed.

Can the answer be then that the 'given' is, not indeed Scripture as a whole, but some minimal historical core of Scripture? McIntyre's reply is 'No' again, because any description of Jesus Christ involves interpretation as well as facts; there is no 'uninterpreted given'. This is no doubt to a great extent correct, though surely the amount of interpretation can be reduced to a tiny minimum: a list of the successive Presidents of the United States with their dates of office is very nearly pure 'given', the only element of 'interpretation' being, I imagine, the idea that it is worth compiling such a list in the first place. However, there is undeniably more interpretation in the Bible than that. Indeed, many would feel that this interpretation is itself authoritative and should be taken as part of the 'given'. And a further snag is that few could be got to agree on what the minimal historical core actually was. I mentioned earlier the disputes that have taken place over the expression 'Son of Man'. In point

---

[5] McIntyre (1966), p. 22.   [6] p. 24.

of fact the situation is far more complicated than I indicated in those passages. It is customary to divide the 'Son of Man' sayings into three groups: those referring to the then present ministry of Jesus,[7] those referring to His coming death and resurrection,[8] and those referring to His Second Coming.[9] As noted earlier, some hold that none of these sayings is truly authentic: but of those who accept that Jesus did speak of the 'Son of Man', some hold that some or all of the sayings from all three groups are authentic, others that this only holds good for the third group, yet others that it only holds for the first, and others yet again that authentic sayings are to be found in the first two groups but not in the third.[10] Where, then, is our 'minimum historical core' to be found? Besides, even if we did isolate such a core, one which all scholars agreed contained only authentic deeds and sayings of our Lord, it could still be a most misleading basis for Christology, for it might be quite *untypical* of Him. We have already mentioned the 'criterion of dissimilarity'— if a passage reflects the faith of the post-Easter Church, the presumption must be that it arose in that Church, and if it can be paralleled in the Jewish tradition, rabbinic or apocalyptic, the presumption must be that it was of Jewish origin and misattributed to Jesus, but material that is unlike either of these may be presumed to be authentic. Now it is obvious that this criterion, while it might leave us with nothing but genuine deeds and sayings of Jesus, offers no guarantee whatever that it has not in the process eliminated much that was just as genuine and perhaps more significant. Jesus was after all a Jew, and might reasonably be expected to use ideas that other Jews used; the early Church venerated Him, and might reasonably be expected to apply His sayings to its own situation. Clearly the 'criterion of dissimilarity' will only give us a 'minimum core' consisting of the more *peculiar* sayings of Jesus, ones that were both strikingly original and useless in the concerns of the early Church (though preserved by it). Of course, a lot of scholars who use this criterion do in fact supplement it with others, 'allowing in' other sayings that cohere reasonably well with the 'core' or are stylistically convincing (e.g. seem to represent Aramaic poetry); but

---

[7] e.g. Mark 2: 10.   [8] e.g. Mark 8: 31.   [9] e.g. Mark 13: 26.
[10] Cf., respectively, Hooker (1967), Bornkamm (1973), Schweizer (1971), and Vermes (1976).

even so I trust that the point has been made clear. Whatever criterion we choose, there is the risk that some quite genuine saying or action may fail to meet its demands, and in that case we shall be building our Christology on an inadequate basis. This is not so if our criterion is simply that a passage should not be demonstrably *in*authentic; but in that case we should probably be well advised to take the whole of the Gospels as our 'core', as to *prove* a passage to be inauthentic is not at all an easy task.

There is also a further problem. The events described in the Gospels, even if every one should turn out to be authentic, are only a tiny fraction of the things Jesus said and did.[11] Selection has taken place even before we begin. This is no bother, of course, to the conservative-minded theologian who takes the Bible to be in some sense the inspired Word of God. If God has providentially ordained the Gospels, He has presumably ensured that nothing necessary to us was omitted. Some of the agrapha ascribed to Jesus outside the Gospels may well be genuine, but hardly any with serious claims to our attention add anything valuable, except perhaps the saying quoted by St Paul in Acts 20: 35 ('It is more blessed to give than to receive'), which is part of the canonical scriptures. But can we then take the Scriptures as our 'given'?

McIntyre answers 'No' once more. In the first place, no one uses all the Bible as 'given' in Christology. In the second, the Bible needs interpretation; we understand it in the light of the inward witness of the Holy Spirit, in the light of creeds and confessions (though nowadays this is in 'an extremely confused mixture'). Scripture itself is interpretation, and therefore witnesses to the 'given'. 'It cannot be the given in the sense that it is ultimate or self-authenticating', for 'it derives its authority from beyond itself'.[12] Nevertheless, it may still be the 'given' of Christology 'in that it constitutes both its starting-point and its finishing-point'; it 'prescribes the problems and defines the issues'.

These comments are of rather varied weight. I do not think even the most bigoted of fundamentalists would be disturbed very much by the first. Not all Scripture is relevant for every subject, such as Christology, where we have to learn from Scripture. All the fundamentalist needs to say is that we cannot rule out any part of the Bible in advance as irrelevant; we must look and see whether it

[11] John 21: 25.   [12] McIntyre (1966), p. 21.

is or not. (Also, of course, that we cannot rule out any part of the Bible on the grounds that it is not authoritative.) We may be able to set aside, say, the Book of Nehemiah, because on investigation it turns out not to have anything to say about Christology; we cannot rule out, say, the Epistle of James on the grounds that it is strawy and of no theological value.

The second point is certainly true. We do interpret Scripture in the light of many other things: of creeds and confessions, of what we have learned of science and history, of our own preconceptions, our likes and dislikes, of biblical criticism, of philosophy and logic, and indeed, we may hope and pray, of the assistance of God the Holy Spirit. We do inevitably acquire a host of beliefs, from the Church and from the world, as well as from the Bible; but we can to some extent check them in the light of the Bible. The formula of Chalcedon is not in the Bible, nor can it be rigorously deduced from what is in the Bible, as it uses words like 'consubstantial' and 'hypostasis' which are not in it, or not in the sense in which Chalcedon uses them. The question is whether the formula is or is not legitimate, given what the Bible tells us—whether, if you like, we can reasonably interpret the Bible in the light of the formula, or whether any attempt to do so forces us into intolerable distortions of the Bible's meaning. (It is of course part of the case for biblically based revisionism that we *cannot* do this without these 'intolerable distortions'.)

The third point, that Scripture is a witness to the given rather than the given itself, is slightly confused. Certainly Scripture is not 'self-authenticating'. Nothing is, except possibly logical formulae and uninterpreted awareness of what the senses give us, which contrive to be 'self-authenticating' only because they point to nothing beyond themselves. Certainly, again, Scripture derives its authority from beyond itself. But all this does not prevent Scripture from being the 'given' in the sense that it is our basic evidence for Christology and the criterion by which our Christology is to be judged: and if this is what McIntyre meant by calling it the starting- and finishing-point of Christology, we can have no quarrel with him over that. But in that case Scripture is the given and not just a witness to it. Assuredly it is a witness: but it is a witness to *Christ*, and Christ is not 'the given' about Himself. Rather, He is the One whom we are endeavouring to understand, as far as may be possible and lawful, in the light of what is 'given' to us about Him; and, although other sources like Christian experience must be kept in mind, this means primarily in the light of the Bible.

There is of course one more very serious objection to the idea of using the Bible as our 'given'. Does it not imply a doctrine of biblical inerrancy to which few Christians would be willing to subscribe nowadays? The answer is surely 'No, it does not.' It is true, of course, that anyone who does maintain the inerrancy of the Bible must take it as (part or all of) the 'given'. But the converse does not follow. Provided that the Bible is regarded as in some sense authoritative, inspired, or God's Word to us, it can be our 'given'. Undoubtedly, if we regard it as no more than a collection of old Greek, Hebrew, and Aramaic texts whose only interest is that it includes descriptions of the events which started Christianity off and were written closer to those events than any other relevant documents we now possess—if we suppose that, things will be very different. Taken to its conclusion, this would mean that a modern book on Christology, whether historical or doctrinal, could be more authoritative than the New Testament, its distance in time from Jesus being compensated for by the greater learning and acumen of its author, rather as a modern book on the early Roman Empire may be more authoritative than Suetonius. The theology of Paul, or Matthew, or John, on such a view, has only the value of the human skill they put into their work, just like the theology of a contemporary. (Which modern book on Christology we choose might be a nasty problem to decide; the need to choose might even send us back to the Bible.) This is not the place to argue this point; it will be assumed that such a view is wrong, but not that any one particular view of the nature of biblical authority is definitive.

It may be felt that one very important possibility for the 'given' has been omitted. Should we not have singled out from the Bible, not a 'minimum historical core', but quite simply the words of Jesus Christ Himself? (Indeed, is not the 'minimum historical core' likely to be thought of in terms of Jesus' words rather than, say, Paul's or Peter's?) In effect, the argument in the last chapter, that Jesus himself never claimed to be God, was based on something very like this. Now obviously the words of Jesus have on any view of Scripture a special authority of their own—*in so far as we accept a 'high' Christology*. If Jesus was indeed God incarnate; or even, as the Arians supposed, some lesser but still superhuman being; or, for that matter, if He was, as Muslims suppose, a prophet (and a high view of prophecy is taken): then indeed we should treat His words with immense respect. (It does not follow that we should treat His apostles' words with no respect, or insist that anything Jesus did not say Himself in so many words can be ignored.) But if He was simply a first-century Jew, of, admittedly, great wisdom and spiritual intelligence, but conditioned in every way by the circumstances in which He lived, ignorant and mistaken about much that we have known from childhood, and with no greater access to the truth than any human mind might have, then it is not easy to see why His words should carry any more weight than those of Paul or John (who, after all, were also wise and spiritually intelligent). If Paul and John were right about Him, then we do right to treat Him as greater than they; if they were wrong, then, paradoxically, we should listen to them just as much as to Him. Cupitt, remarking that modern Christian 'personalist' values cannot be traced back to Jesus Himself, adds that 'it does matter, because I want the form of our relation to God to be what Jesus showed in his words. Paradoxically, I give the historical Jesus a higher religious value than do many of the incarnationalists.'[13] 'Paradoxically' is right, for there is no obvious reason (except his psychological background) why Cupitt should want the form of our relation to God to be what Jesus showed in His words rather than what Paul showed in his—or what Aquinas, or Calvin, or Muhammad, or Śankara showed in theirs; except, perhaps, that Cupitt finds that he happens to agree with what Jesus said and not with the others.

In the particular case of Cupitt there is a further paradox, which naturally is not necessarily there in others who take a similar line: he accepts 'the well-established Schweitzer-and-Bultmann view of Jesus ... that we do not know anything for certain about his life and teaching'.[14] Our knowledge, it seems, is for practical purposes that he used certain linguistic devices, notably parables; it is these devices themselves, not the content of what he allegedly said with them, which give us the clue to his teaching. (This turns out to be a rather Pauline or Johannine theme of death and rebirth.) It is perhaps worth keeping in mind, not only in this particular instance but in all cases where, explicitly or otherwise, the attempt is made to concentrate *only* on the teaching of Jesus, some wise words of P. T. Forsyth: 'We should be clear and frank that in adopting the

[13] Cupitt (1979), p. 145.   [14] p. 137.

most modern view we repudiate the New Testament as Christ's expositor, in favour of an exposition totally different, offered by modern criticism working entirely on the Synoptics, or on what is left of them by a certain philosophy of religion'.[15] 'Most modern' to Forsyth meant the views of the radicals of 1909; but things do not seem to have changed much, except in the assured results of the criticism, the nature of the philosophy, and the views ascribed to Jesus after the criticism and the philosophy have done their hatchet-work. The confidence of the radicals, and the lack of resemblance to a recognizable Jesus, are much the same.

One more point remains to be discussed. On both revisionist and analytic sides reference is frequently made to the Councils of Nicaea and Chalcedon and to general Christian tradition. Ought we to take the decisions of the Councils, or the tradition, as part of the 'given'? There is of course a long history in the Roman Catholic and Eastern Orthodox Churches of saying 'Yes'; but I shall try not to do so in what follows. (No one can wholly escape the influence of the tradition to which they belong, though some are influenced chiefly by reaction to it.) If I am trying to analyse and defend a traditional Christology, it is clearly bad procedure to treat tradition as authoritative; if I am trying to show that Chalcedon was right, I must not beg the question by assuming that it must have been. So even if the Roman Catholics and Eastern Orthodox are right, for the purposes of the present argument we may not assume that they are. And in point of fact I do not myself agree with them. I believe Chalcedon deserves respect because I believe it was right; I do not believe it was right because I believe it deserves respect. The two Councils at Ephesus, in 431 and 449, were in many ways similar. Both intended to be authoritative; both were dominated by the bishop of Alexandria; both were conducted in a deplorable manner. Yet the one is Ecumenical, the other a 'robber council'—because the first came to basically correct conclusions and the second did not.

There is perhaps one aspect of 'tradition', however, which does deserve more than a passing glance. Since the time of St Stephen at least[16] there has been a strong tradition of prayer to and worship of Christ. Most prayer is of course directed to God the Father *through* Christ; there is no question of that; but not all. There are,

---

[15] Forsyth (1909), p. 103.   [16] Acts 7: 59.

for instance, a number of prayers to God the Son in the Anglican Book of Common Prayer, as well as in the old liturgies of West and East, and of course an enormous number of hymns in all Christian traditions. Here we have a very old and very widespread practice whose significance for Christology is obvious. Nevertheless, I shall endeavour not to rely on it in the following pages, except to say this: In one of the earlier papers of the current anti-incarnationist movement,[17] Wiles wondered whether saying that Christology 'rested on a mistake' might be taken as condemning all the great incarnationist theologians of the past as incurably boneheaded. He concluded that it ought not to be so taken, 'any more than to deny the inerrancy of Scripture involves passing an unfavourable judgment on the intelligence of those earlier generations who assumed it without question'. They took the Bible to be inerrant, which few Christians do today; that does not make them fools. They also took Christ to be literally divine, which we shall not do if we are convinced by Wiles; that does not mean they were fools either. He is right. But if his rejection of the Incarnation is correct, the theologians of the past (and not only the theologians) really were something much worse than fools: they were idolaters. They worshipped as God one who was *not* God, and their condemnation by a disgusted Islam was entirely justified. We must be honest; it is possible (though I do not for a moment believe it) that the Church fell into idolatry within a few years of Jesus' death, and has remained in it (with rare exceptions, whom it repudiated) to this day. In that case our attitude towards the radical revisionists should be one, not of condemnation, but of gratitude at being saved from so outrageous a blasphemy. Even here, therefore, tradition had better not be treated as authority—though the existence of prayer to Christ within the New Testament itself is rather a different matter if the Bible is taken as 'given' material.[18]

Besides this 'given' or 'basic material', there are some theological constraints (themselves arising out of other aspects of the 'given') which will affect our analysis. Two major themes of Christian theology are normally associated with the person of Jesus Christ: Revelation and Atonement. This is not confined to the orthodox. Cupitt,

[17] Wiles (1970), pp. 75–6.
[18] For an interesting discussion of this aspect of New Testament Christology, see R. T. France, 'The Worship of Jesus; A Neglected Factor in Christological Debate?' in Rowdon (1982), pp. 17–36.

for example, felt able to write: 'If I have found salvation through Jesus' voice and person, I can quite intelligibly speak of him as the human ultimate and the crown of creation; the man who, by mirroring God, shows what the world is meant to be'.[19] Hick, again, having declared that 'Jesus was the Son of God' has no literal meaning, goes on to say that the statement 'gives definitive expression to his efficacy as saviour from sin and ignorance and as giver of new life'.[20] This is all well said, and not even the most rigidly orthodox would wish to quarrel with it, except perhaps that they might want to add 'work' to 'voice and person'. The question is how the 'salvation' and the 'mirroring' of God are to be understood, and what implications this has for Christology.

Bonhoeffer, indeed, is critical of the idea of 'referring back' the Christological question to the soteriological.[21] It is no good, he thinks, trying to move back from work to person. 'The work may appear to be good, but it can still be the work of the devil ... The work may appear to be evil, but it can still be God's work.' We must know the person first; 'only if I know who does the work can I have access to the work of Christ.' (Would not those Pharisees agree, one is tempted to ask, who said of Christ that he cast out demons by Beelzebul?) And it is possible, though wrong, Bonhoeffer continues, to interpret Christ's life as that of a religious teacher and His death as that of a hero true to his convictions; His work is done incognito. Bonhoeffer sums it up thus: 'Jesus is man and the argument back from works to person is ambiguous; Jesus is God and the argument back from history to God is impossible.' Access to Christ is, he suggests, primarily through prayer.

As a criticism of Christology 'from below', this argument, or at least the latter part of it, has some weight. But I am not happy with the insistence on Christology before soteriology. Can I come to Christ in prayer unless I believe that in so doing I am coming to my Saviour? Theoretically, perhaps; in practice, surely not. And though I agree that if we know Christ only 'after the flesh' there is no compelling reason to go on and know Him after the Spirit as well, this is not at all the same as saying that if we know Him as Saviour there is no compelling reason to go on and know Him as Lord. This latter question does need to be investigated.

---

[19] Goulder (1979), p. 169.   [20] Hick (1977*b*) p. 178.
[21] Bonhoeffer (1978), pp. 37ff.

7

The Theological Constraints

OUR next question can be raised in half a dozen words, 'Universal or individual atonement and revelation?' I am not referring to the question of 'universal or particular redemption' that was disputed between Calvinists and Arminians, nor to that of 'general' and 'special' revelation. The problem I am concerned with here is this: According to one understanding of atonement, it is an act of God whereby salvation is made available to all people, or to all the elect, who must then respond by accepting it in faith and being reconciled to God. This I call 'universal atonement'. An alternative view is that each person, or each of those who are in the end saved, is reconciled to God separately by whatever method is most suitable. Even if every human soul is in the end saved, each salvation has been brought about quite separately from all the others (though of course several may be saved in the same way or at the same time); there are as many at-one-ing acts of God as there are people reconciled. This I call 'individual atonement'.

Similarly with revelation. According to one understanding of this, God makes available a certain body of knowledge which may be learned, ignored, or rejected by those to whom it is sent. (Whether this 'body of knowledge' comes in the form of propositions, or of a Person, or by some other means, does not concern us now.) This would be 'universal revelation'. According to the other, each individual may come to know God in some sense, or may have a chance to do so but ignore or reject it; but each acquisition of knowledge is separate and distinct from all others, and so is the communication of that knowledge. The contrast is not total, of course. Obviously the 'universal' schemes have a place for the individual, in that salvation must be appropriated and revelation received by each person separately; and equally obviously the 'individual' schemes allow for the possibility that two or more people may come to salvation by similar routes, or learn the same knowledge by similar means. But in general I hope the distinction is clear.

On the whole one can say that the 'universal' schemes are what might be called 'objectivist', and begin from a starting-point that is somewhere *between* God and ourselves. There is an objective fact of atonement, and an objective fact of revelation; both come from God, both are available in the world, and both are to be received by us. By contrast, the 'individual' schemes begin more from a human starting-point, the sense of being saved or of realizing the truth, and work outwards from that; thus they may be called 'subjectivist', though not in the sense of that word which excludes the idea of *truth*. We have seen something of the same sort of contrast when we were looking at the thought of Bultmann on the one hand and of Buri and Ogden on the other (pp. 63–5, above). Bultmann, in stressing the act of God in Christ, however demythologized, is in the 'universalist' tradition, albeit on the 'left wing' of it; Buri and Ogden, in stressing individual authenticity as the starting-point, are in the 'individualist'. Clearly the latter allows for a far greater theological liberty. X may be saved by Jesus and Y by Mithras; A's revelation may be the Bible and B's the Book of Mormon: 'individualist' schemes allow for them all, and an 'individualist' theology need not confine itself to one fixed tradition. On the other hand, it does have to try and make coherent sense out of a much greater mass of material, so that, though less restricted, it has no less formidable an intellectual task ahead of it.

Traditional Christianity has of course been firmly on the 'universalist' side. There is admittedly one quite important qualification that has to be made to that statement. Individual revelations have often been recognized as real side by side with the universal one. There were many true prophets in Israel apart from those whose words have come down to us, and they too presumably had messages from God which were true revelations; but these were not of a kind to be preserved for future generations, and therefore cannot be called part of the universal revelation. The same no doubt applies to prophets of the New Testament like the daughters of St Philip.[1] Nor has the stream necessarily dried up since then. Visionaries have not been uncommon in the later Church. Perhaps some of them would be regarded (in some quarters) as part of universal revelation;

[1] Acts 21: 9.

this might be true of some of the African 'prophetist' churches. It might even be said of some Roman Catholic teachings; it has often been suggested that the doctrine of Purgatory owed its origin largely to visions of the next world (or, as Salmon mischievously put it, 'in plain English, ghost stories'[2]). But 'individual revelations' of a less authoritative kind are by no means unknown even in the twentieth century. The great Indian saint Sadhu Sundar Singh would be an obvious example,[3] and a contemporary example from America came to my notice a few days before writing this.[4] Normally, however, such revelations are seen as distinct from and subordinate to *the* revelation of God in Jesus Christ and in Scripture. And of course visions and revelations of this kind are not what 'individualists' usually have in mind. Their picture is more often of someone's acquiring an insight into valuable truth through natural, or apparently natural, means—a book, a sermon, a passing thought, an acquaintance, though more spectacular means would not necessarily be excluded.

The question is, then, whether we need the universal atonement and revelation that Christianity has traditionally asserted, and if so whether these require the traditional Christology. First of all, now, is universal or individual atonement the form Christian faith and hope should take?

In the Bultmann/Buri/Ogden debate already mentioned, it would certainly seem that the 'individualists' had the best of it. If liberation, authenticity, consists of an acceptance of responsibility, openness, a resolve to become one's own true self, or the like, then, while this may very possibly have come to Bultmann and to many others as a result of the preaching of Christ crucified, there is no obvious reason why it should *have* to come this way; indeed, the analysis of authentic and inauthentic existence which Bultmann used derives from Heidegger, who was not a Christian at all, and very similar notions can of course be found in the earlier writings of Sartre, who was an avowed atheist. 'Individualism' does seem to be called for here.

The difficulty is to see why salvation or atonement should be seen in terms of authenticity at all (and I hasten to add that most British revisionists, including the anti-incarnationists, do not in fact

---

[2] Salmon (1952), p. 85.   [3] See Streeter and Appasamy (1921).
[4] Hagin (1972).

see it so). Undoubtedly this kind of existentialism derives largely from Kierkegaard, and he in turn derived it largely from the New Testament, especially St Paul. But in the course of transmission it lost much of its original Christian content. 'This analysis of human authenticity', writes Schmithals,[5] 'is hardly conceivable without the New Testament, but ... it is *possible* without reference to the New Testament. It is not developed as the understanding of a revelation, but as the understanding which is given with existence itself, which shows itself to the man who, with death, brings the totality of human existence to mind.' I am reminded of Kant's picture of 'faith' in the *Critique of Judgment*:[6] the word, he said, 'was first introduced with Christianity, and its acceptance might perhaps seem only a flattering imitation of the language of the latter', but actually the concept, once recognized, can be seen by reason to be one which it (reason) ought to have reached by itself, though it never in fact did. But just as with Kant 'faith' has lost its direct link with God, so it has here—and it has even lost its name, as a very honest way of marking out the change. 'Faith' and 'sin' have become 'authenticity' and 'inauthenticity'; they have ceased to be relationships to God and have become qualities of people. And the change is a momentous one: there is considerable justice in Dr Donald Guthrie's remark that John's portrait of Jesus (and indeed, one might add, the Synoptists') 'shows *par excellence* what Sartre would call an unauthentic man'.[7] There is, admittedly, a certain amount of resemblance between inauthenticity (in some of its aspects) and the Pauline picture of humankind 'after the flesh'; in both, people are uneasy, anxious, and guilty. But there is far less resemblance between authenticity and the Christian life; it seems to be the *un*authentic who feel out of place in the world, whereas for the New Testament it is the faithful who—for quite different reasons—feel out of place and seek a better country.[8] And even with inauthenticity, one has one's moments of doubt. There is a celebrated passage in Sartre where it seems that the 'unauthentic mode' includes such things as the use of 'ready-made clothes, common means of transport, parks, gardens, public places, shelters made for *anyone*' in

---

[5] Schmithals (1968), p. 98.

[6] II, sect. 30 (91), p. 472 (p. 146 of Meredith's translation).

[7] Guthrie (1981), p.159. (Sartre himself does not use the 'authentic' terminology much, though his thought was for a time on similar lines.)

[8] Heb. 11: 13–16; cf. 1 Pet. 2: 11, John 17: 14.

'total interchangeability'.[9] Is this really what Christianity is about deliverance from?

Pascal and Kierkegaard, who are usually regarded as the founding fathers of existentialism (whether or not they would either of them have felt complimented by this), rendered the Christian faith great service, and, unlike their more conventional contemporaries, can still be read to the profit of the too complacent Christian—especially, perhaps, to that of the too complacent theologian. But later developments are another matter. I suspect that what McTaggart once said of Hegel applies here too: 'If orthodox Christianity, while incompatible with Hegelianism, is nevertheless closer to it than any other religion, it is natural that Hegelianism should support Christianity against all attacks but its own, and should then reveal itself as an antagonist.'[10]

If, then, this particular kind of approach is not altogether satisfactory, are there ways of deciding between universal and individual redemption in non-existentialist terms? We might note one preliminary point of considerable weight. Not only is it the case that the religions of the world offer different methods of salvation; they offer different salvations altogether. The Buddhist ideal of *nirvāna* is strikingly different from the Christian ideal of the Beatific Vision, and both from the ancient Norse ideal of Valhalla. They have little in common except being an improvement (in the eyes of their adherents) on what we have at present. Which may leave us wondering whether the routes to salvation can all be equally valid if the goals to be reached are so unlike (unless indeed we suppose that all the different heavens, or the like, exist, for different people to go to).

It is instructive, I think, to look at a major religion in which the idea of individual redemption is taken quite seriously. I refer to Hinduism. There is no one method of salvation laid down by orthodoxy; indeed, the word 'āstika', often translated 'orthodox', does not mean 'holding certain theological beliefs' but simply 'acknowledging the authority of the Vedas'. Consequently all sorts of different ideas about what salvation consists of, and what the way to it is, exist side by side in Hinduism, and it is perfectly legitimate to say that X is saved by Rāma and Y by Śiva, that A's revelation is the *Bhagavat-Purāna* and B's the *Tiruvāchaka*. This does not necessarily make Hinduism 'Copernican' in Hick's sense,

---

[9] Sartre (1969), p. 246, here expounding Heidegger's views rather than his own.
[10] McTaggart (1918), pp. 250 f.

discussed above in pp. 42ff.; indeed, Hick declares that Hinduism in some forms has developed its own Ptolemaic 'epicycles'.[11] Nevertheless, individual salvation is implied by a great deal of Hindu teaching, and the reasons for this are, I think, twofold. First, Hinduism is polytheistic in outward form, even where, as often, a strong monism or monotheism is believed to be the basic truth behind the outward form. The result is that even if there is only one true God, or one impersonal Brahman beyond God Himself, a place can and should be accorded to the lesser deities. The way to Release may quite easily lie, at least for a time, through one of these. Still more is this the case if the great recipients of theistic devotion, Vishnu and Śiva, are thought of either as aspects of one God (seen it may be respectively as Preserver and Destroyer), or if God Himself (whether Vishnu, Śiva, both, or neither) is only an appearance of Brahman, the one ultimate Reality. Devotion to Vishnu or Śiva would then be devotion, in the long run, to the ultimate God, or the penultimate, beyond whom is Brahman.

Secondly, salvation is frequently (not always) seen in terms of human works (using that word in a very broad sense). The two main routes to Release are traditionally thought of as *jñāna*, (contemplative) knowledge, and *bhakti*, devotion. But of these *jñāna* is clearly something we do ourselves, and very often *bhakti* is thought of in much the same way. It is a practice that is pleasing to God and rewarded by Him. 'But that highest Person is to be won by love-and-worship' (*bhakti*) 'directed to none other'[12]—*won*, or *attained*, be it noted. The idea of prevenient grace, of the divine love reaching out to sinners before they reach out to God, only came in later; and it is interesting that Bishop Kulandran, in his detailed comparison of Christian and Hindu concepts of grace, concluded that in spite of everything the two could not be identified: 'The need for reconciliation does not exist in Hinduism, because the soul is possessed of a worth in its own right.'[13]

Obviously, if salvation is by works (including contemplation and devotion under that heading) individual salvation will be the normal thing. This was recognized long ago in the last stages of the struggle between Christianity and Roman paganism. 'We see the same stars', said Symmachus; 'we share the same sky; one world enfolds us

[11] Hick (1977a), p. 131.
[12] *Bhagavad-Gītā*, 8. 22 (tr. Zaehner, Oxford, 1969, p. 269).
[13] Kulandran (1964), p. 239.

all: what does it matter, the manner in which each of us seeks for the truth? It cannot be that there is only one way to so great a mystery.'[14] And the reply of Prudentius was, in effect, 'What you say could well be right if we were searching for God (except that we should all fail!); but God has in mercy provided the way Himself.'[15] Yet is that an adequate answer? May not God save by grace and yet do so individually, without any need for an objective act in Christ?

Christian soteriology has tended to answer 'No. "You have not yet realized the sheer weight of sin." Something more was needed than the turning of our hearts by grace—vital though that is.' But Christian soteriology may have been mistaken. Hindu pictures of the grace of God may be inadequate, as Kulandran argued, but they do illustrate the fact that salvation by grace need not be tied to an objective historical figure.

This is certainly true. But it can be taken further. Salvation need not be tied to an objective historical figure; but if it is not, can it even be *associated* with an objective historical figure? Again let us look at the evidence from Hinduism. In the Śaivite tradition there is quite definitely *no* historical element. Śiva is never incarnate; at the most, he has occasionally vouchsafed appearances or visions of himself. The same applies to his consort Kālī. In the Vaishnavite tradition God does indeed become incarnate—not for atonement, but 'for the protection of the good, for the destruction of evil doers, for the setting up of the law of righteousness'.[16] In actual fact only one of the usual list of nine Avatars is certainly historical, and that is a late and rather awkward addition to the list, Buddha. The two previous ones, Rāma and Krishna, *may* have been real people, but if so their stories have changed greatly in the course of the centuries—far more than the critics suppose that of Christ did! Their function is really as focuses of devotion and, in the case of Rāma at least, as moral examples. They can be called Saviours, but only because (*a*) they are avatars of God, who is the true saviour, and (*b*) devotion to them is the means by which we may attain salvation (thanks, it may be, to His grace). The latter point depends, of course, on the first.

Now this simply cannot be applied to Jesus of Nazareth, *except*

---

[14] Relatio, 3. 9.   [15] Contra orationem Symmachi, 2. 91ff.
[16] *Bhagavad-Gītā*, 4. 8 (tr. Zaehner, p. 58).

by something on the lines of an incarnationist Christology. It is not hard to see why this is so. A human figure can represent Deity—inadequately, perhaps, but still representing it—provided that it is *fictitious*. In Camara Laye's novel *The Radiance of the King*, the remote figure of the African king for whom the central character is searching represents God, and there is no problem in this. Some Hindus, I think, would not be bothered too much if it turned out that Krishna never existed. It is possible to build up a 'fictitious portrait' of God, whatever is believed to be true about Him in reality (within limits, naturally). But it is quite another matter where a genuine historical figure is concerned. If Laye had written his book with a real African king as the object of the search—the King of Morocco, say, or of Lesotho—the effect would have been seriously jarring. And in actual religion the danger of idolatry mentioned on p. 78 above is far too great. A fictitious character does not exist, and so cannot receive worship; it is at most a symbol of the real God who does receive worship. (This is not to say there are no dangers here; all human ideas of God are less than the truth, and dangerous if we lose sight of this.) But a real human being gets in the way of our worship, and blocks its path from us to God. (Could it be that the historical scepticism of some anti-incarnationists is the *effect*, not the cause, of their denial of Christ's divinity—that they were unconsciously recognizing that a real Christ could not be treated the way they wished, while a figure of fiction could?) Nor does treating the historical Jesus as a helpful symbol seem satisfactory from the point of view of soteriology. 'What an extraordinary process', exclaims Moore, 'in the one being liberated: to elevate the Jesus of history to the divine level, and so to experience liberation at his hands! That makes us the saviour of Jesus, not Jesus of us.'[17]

There is of course a way by which this can be avoided, and a real human being can represent Deity without the danger of idolatry. If the human being is not *merely* a human being but is God incarnate too, then he or she can represent Deity to us as well as any fictitious portrait, indeed probably better, and yet devotion to him or her is perfectly justified, for it is directed to one who really is God. Such is of course the belief of Hindus who do not think Rāma or Krishna to be fictitious, and such is the belief of ordinary

[17] Moore (1980), p. 130.

Christians. They are all in a position to answer our question 'Can salvation be associated with an objective historical figure?' in the affirmative—but only by dint of accepting Incarnation.

It might still be possible to maintain a modified theory of individual salvation in a Christian framework by treating Jesus as one, but only one, of a number of Incarnations, like Rāma and Krishna. I mentioned earlier visiting a Hindu shrine where presumably some such line was taken, the crucified Christ being represented among the gods and avatars of Hinduism. But this would be to abandon the Jesus of real life altogether; if Jesus thought of Himself as a divine saviour at all, He thought of Himself as *the* divine saviour (as His followers indisputably did). More important still it would entail not merely retaining the concept of incarnation (which 'individual salvation' would, it was hoped, enable us to avoid) but actually extending it. We need not pursue that line of thought any further. And does it make any difference if we forget some of the traditional Christian ideas about Atonement and think of Jesus principally as an Intercessor (which of course He was and is)? Others have pleaded with God, like Abraham for Sodom and Moses for the Israelites.[18] Hardly; because surely Jesus is thought of as Intercessor for *all*. 'If *anyone* sins, we have an Advocate with the Father'.[19] We may not need a divine Saviour—Moses and Abraham were not divine— but we are no nearer *individual* atonement.

If we are going to devise a 'Christian' theology of individual salvation, it has got to be one of salvation by works—and not the 'work' of *bhakti*-type devotion, either—and the Christ it retains will be at best the old-style Great Moral Teacher, to whose work the 'mythological' side of the gospel is so irrelevant as to be highly misleading. The difficulties of such a position, and of fitting it into the New Testament picture of our Lord (even after the critics have been at work on it) are notorious; we should be better advised to abandon Christianity altogether—or admit that Christ really did come to save the lost.

The question of individual revelation can be dealt with more briefly. As we have seen, traditional theology does not in any way conflict with a belief in individual revelation, provided that the 'other' revelations are consistent with the revelation in Christ. Such revelations

---

[18] Gen. 18: 23–32; Exod. 32: 30–2.   [19] 1 John 2: 1.

might even take place outside the main Judaeo-Christian stream. (One thinks of Old Testament figures like Balaam and Melchizedek.) But this requirement of consistency with a central, normative revelation is an important one. If we could dispense with it, we might well be able to dispense with the 'revealing' side of Incarnation altogether—though, as we have seen, this would not allow us to drop Incarnation completely. Can it be done?

In theory, maybe. Not—let this be made clear—by the device of saying 'What is true for me need not be true for you', whereby those with broad minds and muddled heads have from time to time sought to cover up flat disagreements. If a statement is true at all, it is true for everybody, though not of course necessarily helpful to everybody. (Trivial 'exceptions' such as 'My name is Richard Sturch', which obviously is true if I assert it but not if you do, need not concern us.) That approach is no good at all. But there is another way in which 'individual revelations' might be retained without a definitive one to which they all had to conform. That would be by perpetually checking each alleged revelation against all the others (and of course against all known facts from sources other than revelation). Such checking is naturally done by many apologists for particular religions: a Christian, for example, may need to compare Christianity with other religions in order to claim (if he or she wishes to claim) that ideally it incorporates all that is best in them. No doubt adherents of other religions might do the same. But the aim in such cases is to show that there *is* such a thing as a central, normative revelation, even if the apologist begins by assuming for the sake of argument that there is not known to be one. In the case we are imagining the aim would be more syncretistic; one would have to treat each religion as composed of discrete units of individual revelation, real or alleged, to be kept or discarded according to how easily they fitted into some kind of composite system. While this is no doubt possible in theory, the practical difficulties would surely be insurmountable. It would be like trying to do a massive jigsaw-puzzle in which one knew that half the pieces didn't belong, but had no idea which these were, nor what the finished jigsaw would look like, and in which, to confuse things still further, many of the 'wrong' pieces fitted well with one another and even with many of the 'right' ones. One would be inclined to say 'If this is God's idea of revelation, what would His idea of concealment be like?' And note that we cannot avoid the task of checking revelations; we do not want to admit every claim of those who have 'blown their minds' on LSD—and even if we did, not all 'revelations' are consistent with one another!

If, however, there is a universal and definitive revelation, things are much simpler. It becomes a question of seeing which items of 'individual revelation' fit in with it, and, naturally, of seeing which supposed universal revelation is the true one. To revert to our jigsaw-puzzle, we should have several clear pictures already established, and the problems would be to see which of them could have pieces of the others incorporated into it, and which was the most convincing-looking final result. The task would be—is—a difficult one and a serious one, but not the bewildering chaos of the first task. Apologists have hard work ahead of them, but not necessarily *impossible* work.

Now maybe God has not made things easy for us. Maybe He does set us hard tasks. We cannot dictate what He shall do. But if He chooses to reveal Himself at all, it is unlikely He does so in a way which makes it virtually impossible to receive this revelation. Failing clear evidence that He has done this, we may assume that there is such a thing as a definitive revelation: and since we are trying to do Christology, not comparative religion or apologetics, I shall assume that this revelation is the Christian one.

8

The Implications of Universal Revelation and Atonement

THE requirements of universal revelation and atonement were summed up by William Temple as follows: 'For the former, what is necessary is that Jesus Christ should be truly God and truly Man; for the latter what seems to be necessary is that human experience as conditioned by the sin of men should become the personal experience of God the Son—not an object of external observation but of internal feeling (to use the language of human consciousness)'.[1] This seems to me to put it very well. Let us examine it in more detail.

'Revelation requires that Jesus be God and Man.' Here we run up at once against a serious difficulty. Surely God has revealed much, and still does reveal, outside the person of Jesus Christ. Did He not reveal His truth through the prophets and sages of old, and not just His truth but His very self?[2] Is He not revealed in His work in nature?[3] and have not many Christians felt the inner witness of the Holy Spirit? Yet all this, clearly, did not require that anyone should be God and Man. Why then should Jesus not be a Revealer, a 'mirror of God' in Cupitt's phrase or a 'saviour from ignorance' in Hick's, without having to be 'truly God and truly Man' either?

I feel there is considerable weight in this; but I am not sure that it is decisive. The main reason for thinking that Temple may have been right is that Scripture does seem to speak of Jesus as being in a special way the Revealer of God. 'No one has ever seen God at any time; but God's only Son' (or 'the only one, himself God'), 'the nearest to the Father's heart, he has made him known'.[4] It

---

[1] Temple (1924), p. 140.   [2] See e.g. 1 Sam. 3: 21.
[3] e.g. Rom. 1: 19–20.   [4] John 1: 18.

is interesting that Bultmann regarded this as so central to the message of the Fourth Gospel that of the thirteen main headings and sub-headings he gave to sections of the Gospel, seven included 'revelation' or 'the Revealer'.[5] The Epistle to the Hebrews, again, contrasts the varied ways in which God spoke in times past through the prophets with His speaking to us in these last days through His Son, a speaking which is no longer 'fragmentary' (NEB). Might this not be because God's revelation through the prophets was in commandments and propositions, whereas His revelation in Jesus was in a *Person*, who must therefore be true God and true Man?

And there is another—not *reason* exactly, but cause, which inclines many to stress this idea of revelation in a Person. The rise of Darwinism and of biblical criticism in the nineteenth century forced on the Church a serious reappraisal of the idea of revelation, and many theologians found it hard to continue with older notions of revelation through an inspired Scripture. One way to avoid the problem of the nature of biblical inspiration, or rather perhaps to mitigate it, was to regard God's revelation as being primarily in the *incarnate* Word rather than the *written*. And, naturally, the more stress was laid on revelation in the person of Jesus in contrast to the written Scriptures, the more important a part of His work revelation seemed to be. Now if Jesus revealed God not so much in the words that He spoke (which would have sent us back to propositional revelation, though with fewer propositions to worry about) as in His actual life, death, and resurrection, it began to look as if His character as the Revealer did require that He be both God and Man. We might *possibly* dispense with the humanity, but not with the divinity.

There is perhaps a third way to see the revelation in Christ: not so much in His words, nor even in His Person, but in the fact of the Incarnation and Atonement. 'God is love, and his love was disclosed to us in this, that he sent his only Son into the world to bring us life'.[6] The love of God, on this view, is revealed not by anyone (even Jesus) saying that God is love, nor by the fact, true though it is, that His Son displayed the divine love to the fullest extent that a human being can, but by the fact that it was the Son Himself who became incarnate and died for us.

This last does seem to require that Jesus be both God and Man.

---

[5] Bultmann (1971). Cf. Bultmann (1955), ii. 49ff.   [6] 1 John 4: 10.

But it is not (I think) the main way in which the New Testament
sees the revelation of God, and *perhaps* those passages which express
it could at a pinch be understood simply as another way of putting
across the truth of a revelation in a Person, or even in words.

What of the revelation in a Person? If we insist that this requires
that Jesus be God, would it not be best to drop the requirement
that He be fully human as well? Surely Apollinarianism makes Him
a *better* revelation of God than any view which allows His full
humanity. And if we reject Apollinarianism, and say that all that
is needed is that God direct Jesus' words and deeds so that He
reveal the true nature of the Father, then we do not need anything
as strong as the Chalcedonian position: Nestorianism is the most
that is required. And this will also, of course, allow us any revelation
in words that is necessary.

So I think, with some hesitation, that Temple may have been
wrong in saying that revelation required that Jesus be true God
and true Man. What it does require is that God be dominantly
active in Jesus.

It is the self-expressive *action* of God in Christ which is important [says
Pittenger (in a slightly different context)]; ... our purpose must be to show
that here [in the Incarnation] is no union of 'terms', but rather the bringing
into a living unity of two basic realities: the reality of God at work in
his world and above all at work in his human creation, and the reality
of manhood, itself living, dynamic, and moving, whose essential nature
is its thrust towards God and towards fulfilment in God.[7]

We might compare Hick's suggestion[8] that 'the assertion that God
is *Agapé* ... is a direct transcript of the faith that the agapé which
we see in Jesus in some sense is the eternal *Agapé* of God. If, then,
we say with Gregory of Nyssa, that the name "God" refers not
to a nature but an operation,[9] we mean that operation of *Agapé*
which was revealed in the life and death of Jesus.'

Now this appears to open the door to the idea of a 'degree Christology', which many find extremely hard to swallow. (I should add
that Pittenger dislikes the name, while accepting the idea conveyed
by it; and that Hick too seems to dislike it, or did at the time of

---

[7] Pittenger (1959), p. 179.   [8] Hick (1977a), p. 152.
[9] The reference is to *On Not Three Gods* (PG 45, 128b): all Gregory says is that
words describing God describe not His ineffable nature but His operations; θεότης,
'deity', he derives from His seeing (θεᾶιν) all things. As all operations of God are
of the whole Trinity, there is only one θεότης, not three.

the essay just quoted.[10]) God is active in many people, perhaps in all to some extent. Does a Christology based on God's activity in Christ lead to the idea that God was present in Christ in the same way that He may be present in many others, only more so; and if it does, is this a reason to reject it? Do we want to say that God was present in Christ in a different way from the way He is present in the prophets and saints?

We are not in fact committed to a 'degree Christology' by thinking in terms of God's activity in Christ, for the simple reason that this activity might be different from any activity with which He was at work in others. If, for example, the activity is described as salvation, and if God was saving us in Christ and in no other (as traditional orthodoxy would undoubtedly hold), then there is clearly no question of Christ's differing from us only in degree, or of God's relationship to Him differing only in degree from God's relationship to us. But if we are thinking of that activity as *revelation*, then 'degree' does make sense. For God has revealed truth through others besides Jesus, and perhaps something of His nature too; it might even be truth through the prophets and nature through the saints (the two classes not being mutually exclusive!). Nor is this true only of revelation. Donald Baillie suggested that we should see the Incarnation in the light of the 'paradox of grace', in which Christians ascribe every good thing in them to God, and yet feel more perfectly free than ever.[11] Certainly this allows for 'degrees'; so do most of the list which Pittenger felt should be added to 'grace': 'creation, providence, cooperation of will, attention (prayer), mystical union'— 'the whole range of divine–human relations experienced and known'.[12]

A serious criticism of this whole approach was made, apropos of Baillie and the nineteenth-century Hegelian Biedermann, by Karl Barth.[13] In Biedermann, he asked, do we not have

an exchanging of ultimate things for the penultimate to which even our little portion of Christian self-consciousness also belongs, of the act of God for its reflexion in the existence of man as determined by it? ... Even Donald Baillie ought to have considered this before—quite innocently, of course, and without being guilty of the flagrant excesses of Biedermann—he

---

[10] Pittenger (1959), pp. 188–9; Hick (1977a), p. 157.   [11] Baillie (1961), p. 114.

[12] Pittenger (1959), p. 198. Baillie does in fact suggest providence (pp. 111–13), but thinks it does not take us far enough.

[13] Barth (1956–8), iv/2, p. 57.

made it his business to try to interpret Christ in the light of the Christian rather than the Christian in the light of Christ.

I think this may not be quite fair to Baillie (Biedermann is another matter). He might have replied that he was only 'interpreting Christ in the light of the Christian' in the sense of analysing the presence of God in Christ in the light of the one way in which we directly know the presence of God, that is, in His people. He was not trying to interpret the *work* of Christ in the light of the Christian; he was not trying to begin with our lives, assume that that is 'salvation' or 'eternal life', and then go on to say that the work of Christ was to bring that to us. That really would be 'exchanging ultimate things for penultimate'. I do not think Baillie was right in the end; I think his is a diminished Christ compared with Barth's; but I am not sure that this particular criticism is well founded. So far, we may proceed on the assumption that a 'degree Christology' is legitimate.

We might go a step further. I imagined Baillie just now as claiming to interpret the presence of God in Jesus in the light of the one way in which we directly know the presence of God. But there are other such ways besides grace, as Pittenger pointed out. And consider one of his list—creation. Is not God immanent in His creation? If so, does this give us a clue to a 'degree Christology'? Something like this appeared in a number of Idealist writers at the end of the nineteenth century and the beginning of the twentieth. In the more extreme representatives of this school, like Edward Caird, Henry Jones, and (for a time) R. J. Campbell, God is immanent in all people, and it is not clear that there can be any greater degree of immanence in Jesus—does creation (or its Idealist equivalent) admit of degrees? (Hence the celebrated reply Jones is said to have made when accused of denying the divinity of Christ: 'I do not deny the divinity of any man!') In less radical hands something like a genuine 'degree Christology' appears, but the steps from one degree to another are discrete, not continuous. This is so, for instance, in Illingworth.[14] God is immanent in nature in a way analogous to the way human personality is immanent in the body and beyond it. (And, he also holds, transcendent of nature in a way analogous to that in which human personality transcends matter.) But God is also immanent in man in conscience and in inspiration.

[14] Illingworth (1900), chs. 3 and 4.

And the culmination of all this is the Incarnation, 'the climax of His immanence in the world'.[15] Illingworth himself describes this as 'progressive manifestation', which is a notion similar to that of 'degrees'. But there does seem to be a difference in *kind* involved, at least in the shift from nature to human life: conscience and inspiration are not things found in rivers, rose-bushes, or even rabbits. Even if the immanence is the same, the vehicle of the immanence is very different; but the immanence surely is not the same. The part played by God differs as well as the part played by the vehicle.

Illingworth also drew a distinction between the immanence of the human personality in the *body* and in its *work*; the spirit of great artists 'is immanent in the painted canvas and the printed page'.[16] But here an ambiguity creeps in. The Father is completely immanent in the Son, and through Him in creation, His work. But the 'Son' here is the eternal Second Person of the Holy Trinity; it is not clear what kind of immanence there is in Jesus of Nazareth. (To confuse things still further, Illingworth here quotes Colossians 2: 9, 'in whom dwelleth the fulness of the Godhead bodily', which does refer to the *incarnate* Christ.) It would seem natural, however, to take it that for Illingworth the relationship between God the Son and Jesus of Nazareth is more nearly analogous to that between us and our bodies than to that between us and our works. (It is not of course identical—that would be too close to Apollinarianism.)

Here, then, we have a Christology in which the difference between God's relationship to Jesus and His relationship to other people could be described *either* as a difference in degree *or* as a difference in kind. God is 'more' immanent in Jesus than in you or me, but this is because He is immanent in Jesus in an extra way in which He is not immanent in us, over and above the ways in which He is immanent in us all. If this is a 'degree Christology', that too is orthodox (whether or not it is correct).

Several other theologians during the same period urged a 'degree Christology' (again not their term) of a different kind. Must we not speak of 'degrees of incarnation' in *Christ himself*, what Forsyth was willing ('speaking carefully', agreed) to call 'a progressive incarnation'?[17]

God and man met ... in action rather than in being; and the unity of

---

[15] Illingworth (1900), p. 77.   [16] p. 68.   [17] Forsyth (1909), p. 330.

being is just such as is required for mutual action and communion ... We have on the one hand the perfect God who cannot grow; and yet, as the *living* God, He has in His changeless nature an eternal movement which He implanted as growth in the creature He made in His image. And on the other hand we have this waxing man, who only grows into the personality that communes with God.[18]

The baby in the manger, and even the boy in the Temple asking the scribes questions, were not yet complete or adequate vehicles for the action of God in humanity. 'He is not at birth perfect in the sense of complete attainment; but only in the popular sense of being free from sin and from the lack of anything necessary to Him at the stage of life in which he was', wrote Frank Weston.[19] And Mackintosh sets it out in detail:

Real growth is predicable also of Christ's person [as well as of his work]; the union of God and man in him was more completely actualised at death than at birth, when he rose than when he died ... There is the ever-increasing degree in which his body became ministrant to the spirit; there is the growing moral stability which comes from duty done, from new responsibilities accepted. There is advance in his reasoning thought, in his mental fitness to be the vehicle of truth, his adjustment of personal relationships, his holy aversion to sin mingled with the knowledge that he is identified with the sinful, his awareness of supremacy over man and of oneness with the Father.[20]

Fr. Jon Sobrino has recently taken a similar line:[21] 'Jesus gradually fashioned himself into the Son of God, became the Son of God.' But Sobrino's reason for saying this is that

the relationship of Jesus of Nazareth to the Father has a history, and hence I would maintain that Jesus is not only the Son of the Father but also the Way to the Father ... The Son does not simply reveal the potential filiation of all human beings with God. He also reveals the very process of filiation, the concrete way in which human beings can and do become children of God.[22]

(I should add that Sobrino is also clear that we have to end with the statement that the Son became man.)

A 'degree Christology' seems, then, to be implied within the life

---

[18] Forsyth (1909), p. 336. [19] Weston (1907), p. 291.
[20] Mackintosh (1913), p. 495. [21] Sobrino (1978), p. 338. [22] pp. 339–40.

of our Lord Himself, and why should the idea not be illuminated by the experience of grace or the sending of revelation? Revelation in Christ, we may say, requires that God be active in Christ; and we may well go on to say, in view of the stress laid (notably by John) on the crucial importance of the revelation in Christ, that God was active in Christ to a greater degree than in anyone else. (This does not involve us in a 'pre-Copernican' outlook, as no other religions as far as I know require revelation *in* a person in the same sort of way.) Of course, those who regard John's Gospel as lacking in authority will feel this last is not needed; but if we are going to keep to the position suggested earlier, that the closer we are to the biblical witness the better, it *is*.

According to the second part of Temple's dictum, Atonement requires that 'human experience as conditioned by the sin of man should become the personal experience of the Son—not an object of external observation but of internal feeling'. Here we are coming to a critical stage of the argument. For nearly all revisionist Christ-ologies—not only those which *deny* the Incarnation altogether, but also those which assert it—deny that human experience has become the experience of God the Son, or, failing to take the alleged necessity of this into account, develop a view of the Incarnation which leaves no room for it. Incarnation, where it is asserted at all, becomes a purely one-way process: God is active in Jesus Christ (we remember the declared preference of many revisionists for 'categories of action rather than being'),[23] but there is no reciprocal process whereby He is passive through Jesus Christ as well.

In the modern era, this goes back at least to Schleiermacher. To see the Incarnation, as he did, primarily in terms of the supreme 'God-consciousness' of Jesus, is to see it as a process in which our Lord's humanity is purely receptive as far as its peculiar relationship to God is concerned. Of course Jesus was active, not merely passive, towards other people, and indeed towards God in obedience and prayer. But in the feature which set Him apart from others, His unique and unclouded awareness of God, He is, precisely, conscious of God, receptive of Him. If He is also conscious of anything else, that affects Jesus the man, but not God. And this Schleiermacher himself perceived and acknowledged.

It is fairly clear that such a view of the Incarnation will not square with any of the 'traditional' theories of the Atonement, and Schleier-

---

[23] The phrase is Hick's (1977*a*), p. 150.

macher rightly saw that he would have to abandon these and develop one of his own. The so-called 'classic' theory saw the devil as seizing on 'prey' which turned out to be too much for him; but this required that the 'prey' in question should be divine in *passivity*—that the devil's action in attacking Jesus should turn out to be an attack upon God, not simply that God should have been active in the man attacked. Substitutionary theories require that God Himself should bear the weight of human sin or vindicate the divine honour in human flesh. Even a pure 'Abelardian' theory requires that it be God who loves even to death and so wins over human hearts:

> Ours are the crimes, dear Lord, not Yours but ours,
> The crimes whose punishment You make Your own.[24]

All require, as Temple said, that human experience, especially the experience of death on the Cross, become the experience of God. 'We needed a God made flesh and put to death in order that we should live again', said Gregory of Nazianzus,[25] and so far he seems to have been right.

It has also been powerfully urged that in the Cross of Christ we see, not exactly a *solution* to the ancient 'problem of evil', how the existence of a good and all-powerful God can be compatible with the existence of evil, but at least an *answer* to it. The classic statement of this must surely be that of Charles Williams:

The distress of the creation is so vehement and prolonged, so tortuous and torturing, that even naturally it is revolting to our sense of justice, much more supernaturally. We are instructed that He contemplates, from His infinite felicity, the agonies of creation, and deliberately maintains them in it ... This then is the creation that 'needs' (let the word be permitted) justifying. The Cross justifies it to this extent at least—that just as He submitted us to His inexorable will, so He submitted Himself to our wills (and therefore to His). He made us, He maintained us in our pain. At least, however, on the Christian showing, He consented to be Himself subject to it.[26]

And again: '"O fools, and slow of heart, *ought* not the Christ to have suffered these things, and entered into His glory?" Yes; He ought. He said so: "The Son of Man *must* ..." But then also He

---

[24] *Hymnarius Paraclitensis*, XLIV:

> Nostra sunt, Domine, nostra sunt crimina:
> Quid tua criminum facis supplicia?

[25] Letter 234 (PG 32, 869b).   [26] Williams (1958), p. 132.

did.'[27] The same theme is found in another ballad by Sydney Carter, whom we quoted earlier on, the unnerving *Friday Morning*, with its accusing refrain

> It's God they ought to crucify
> instead of you and me,
> I said to the carpenter
> a-hanging on the tree.[28]

Blasphemy indeed—*unless*, as the Church has always supposed, the crucified carpenter was also the crucified God, and 'the Word of God suffered in the flesh'.[29]

Some of the Antiochene Fathers, as a matter of fact, claimed as a positive merit for their Christologies, which, like that of Schleiermacher, allowed in effect only 'one-way traffic' between the Godhead and the man Jesus, that it did *not* allow us to say that 'God suffered in the flesh'. Nestorius seems to have argued that the union of God and Man in Christ must be voluntary (i.e. 'active' on the side of the Word) because a hypostatic or natural union would 'make subject to the suffering of many sufferings Him who is consubstantial with Him who is impassible'.[30] Similarly, Theodoret held that, just as the Resurrection was that of the body and soul of Jesus, not of the Divinity, so also with the Passion: 'the divinity is not separated from the humanity, either on the Cross or in the tomb; however, being immortal and immutable, it did not undergo either death or suffering';[31] and, more specifically, 'The "form of a servant" suffered, the form of God being of course with it ... So it was not the Christ who suffered, but the man who was assumed by God from among us.'[32] It is a fairly safe bet that no modern 'Antiochenes' would claim this merit for their views; indeed, the doctrine of the divine impassibility is rather unpopular at the present time, among traditionalists and revisionists alike. For instance, Bishop J. A. Baker, whose position is fairly 'traditionalist', says that God, 'by forming his grand design as Creator ... exposed himself to the possi-

---

[27] Williams (1958), p. 139. [28] Carter (1969), ii. p. 6.

[29] Cyril of Alexandria, 12th Anathema (PG 76, 450a).

[30] Nestorius (1925), pp. 178–9; cf. p. 38. Nestorius is here criticizing Apollinarius, but clearly has Cyril in mind too.

[31] *Haereticarum fabularum compendium*, 15 (PG 83, 504cd).

[32] *In anathemata Cyrilli* (PG 76, 450b).

bility of having to suffer ... [The word "impassible"], usually construed as meaning "incapable of suffering", certainly produces insuperable difficulties if it is taken in this narrow sense. But philosophically all that it necessarily implies is that God cannot be acted upon against his will.'[33] Again, from a moderate 'Antiochene': 'It is hard to see how a rigid acceptance of the doctrine [of divine impassibility] can leave room for any belief in costly divine sin-bearing at all ... Perhaps we can conserve both sides of the truth by saying, paradoxically, that while there is suffering [for human sin] in the life of God, it is eternally swallowed up in victory and blessedness'.[34] And lastly, from a radical revisionist: 'A God who is in his essential nature impassible cannot become passible; and therefore could not become incarnate and experience human pains and emotions. But on the other hand the contrary doctrine of unceasing divine sympathy and suffering removes this particular need [for God to submit Himself to the pains of the world he has made], since God is already fully involved in all his creatures' joys and sorrows.'[35]

I should not like to subscribe to all the details of any of these statements. Neither Nestorius nor Theodoret thought impassibility only meant God could not be acted on against His will; for the Passion was not against God's will, yet they thought it could not affect Him. Again, Cyril clearly thought it quite possible that God suffered and bore our sins in the flesh while impassible in Himself; while the first part of Hick's remarks unfortunately overlooks the teaching summed up in the *Quicunque Vult* that God and Man are one in Christ 'not by conversion of the Godhead into flesh, but by taking of the manhood into God'. But the general thesis of all three, that a God of love must be passible, does seem quite a natural assumption. The biblical *locus classicus*, Isaiah 63: 9, is not now usually rendered 'In all their afflictions he was afflicted';[36] yet God is said to be grieved,[37] to repent,[38] to be angry,[39] and so on—all things the doctrine of impassibility would reject. And

[33] Baker (1975), pp. 315–16.   [34] Baillie (1961), pp. 198–9.
[35] J. Hick in Goulder (1979), p. 81.
[36] RSV and NIV retain the older rendering, but all other recent versions I have to hand follow the LXX and avoid this.
[37] See e.g. Ps. 76: 40; 95: 10; Eph. 4: 30.   [38] See Amos 7: 3.
[39] See Isa. 9: 12.

if it is mistaken, we do not it seems need that human experience become that of the Son.

The doctrine of impassibility rests on three main pillars: the idea that God cannot be caused to be anything; the idea that He is unchanging; and the idea that He is in eternal bliss and glory. Of these the first is surely wrong. God is certainly the cause of all there is, but why should He not let Himself be affected by that which He makes? (How else could He be aware of all that goes on in His creation, unless of course He is Himself the direct agent of it all?) The second is (I believe) true, but does not imply impassibility; for God is not (I believe) in time, which He created, and which is no more part of His being than space is. But this no more implies that He cannot be affected (timelessly) by the world than it implies that the world cannot be affected by Him.

The third is the most serious. We recall C. S. Lewis on 'the demand of the loveless and the self-imprisoned that they should be allowed to blackmail the universe: that till they consent to be happy (on their own terms) no one else shall taste joy: that theirs should be the final power; that Hell should be able to *veto* Heaven.'[40] If Hell cannot spoil the joy of the saints, still less can it spoil that of the Lord of the saints, at whose right hand there is pleasure for evermore. The self-inflicted misery of the damned is in a sense their own wretched concern. God will, we may be sure, do all that omnipotent love can do to save them from it; He has already done the seemingly impossible and died for sinners' sake. But neither He nor His saints are to be made eternally miserable by the evil will of others.

Yet the damned are not the only sufferers in the universe. Does God not react to the sufferings of the sick, the poor, the hungry, and the oppressed? Of course He does. Whether this involves Him in a shadowing of His joy, though, is another matter. Can one not be sorry for someone and act to help them without being unhappy (to some extent) oneself? Traditional orthodoxy is sure that the incarnate Lord felt the emotions of pity and compassion, and acted upon them. But was it similar emotions in the eternal Godhead which led to the Incarnation, or did the will to love and save come first and produce the emotions by way of the Incarnation? It seems that God has not chosen to tell us. My personal inclination is to agree with Baillie that any suffering there is must surely be 'swal-

---

[40] Lewis (1946), p. 111.

lowed up in victory and blessedness';[41] but I feel that there is no *need* to postulate suffering in the Godhead in the first place.

The point is that certain modern Christological revisionists use rejection of the divine impassibility to allow them to retain a God of compassion while denying that the Incarnation is a 'two-way' affair. Hick we have already quoted. Young insists that 'Jesus is not the only evidence for the suffering of God'; in Daniel, Jeremiah, and Isaiah 53 'what is expressed is universal insight into the suffering of God's faithful, a suffering which tells of God's suffering'.[42] It is difficult to know quite what to make of this. These passages do indeed express the sufferings of God's faithful, and *if* we believe that God shares the experiences of His faithful, then they tell of His suffering. But they do not of themselves give any reason to suppose that He does share our experiences. Would we have any reason to think He did, but for belief in the Incarnation in Jesus Christ? Wiles comes close to the same mistake in his *The Remaking of Christian Doctrine*.[43] 'It was the pain', he suggests, 'of Hosea's continuing love for his unfaithful wife which gave rise to the distinctive emphasis in his oracles on the compassionate love of Yahweh for his erring and suffering people.' Very likely—though one wants to point out *ad hominem* that on Wiles's quasi-deistic principles Hosea was merely guessing; his 'oracles' did not come from God any more than those of a false prophet, or a thriller by Edgar Wallace. Now I do myself believe that Hosea was inspired by God, and that therefore we can move from his words to truth about God. Yet, though Hosea was inspired to see in his continued love for Gomer a reflection of God's continued love for Israel, are we entitled to infer, from the unhappiness which undoubtedly accompanied Hosea's love an analogous unhappiness on the part of God? Hosea himself drew no such inference. It seems to me that even if God does suffer alongside His creation, our only indication of this is in His life on earth, as revelatory of what preceded it; but that it is more natural to suppose that the suffering He underwent then was something new and deliberate as part of His plan of salvation. To see the suffering itself as revelatory has very grave difficulties, as we shall see later on.

[41] Cf. also Caird (1899), ii. 145–6: 'Moral suffering contains or carries with it what may be called an element of compensation, in virtue of which it is transmuted into a deeper joy ... [that] masters all the anguish.'

[42] In Hick (1977*b*), pp. 36–7.   [43] pp. 71 f.

Wiles has, indeed, urged that the doctrine of the Incarnation, so far from enabling us to see God as one who shares our pains (whether because by taking our nature He enabled Himself to suffer, or because in the incarnate life He revealed something which was eternally true in His Godhead), actually does the opposite. 'If it is logically conceivable ... for God to be actually identified with a human person without in any way taking away from the full and genuine humanity of that human person, it follows that God does not, in fact, draw near to us as individual men and women or share our suffering as directly as he could'.[44] The idea is that in the Incarnation (as orthodoxy takes it) God draws as near to Jesus the man of Nazareth as it is possible to draw—namely, to the point of identity—and shares Jesus' sufferings as completely as it is possible to share them—namely, by making them His own. But apparently He does not do this with the rest of us. If, of course, His drawing so near to Jesus, and sharing his sufferings so completely, destroyed a part of Jesus' humanity, as Apollinarius taught, then naturally He could not do this with the rest of us. But orthodoxy rejects Apollinarianism. So He could—yet apparently did not.

There are, I think, two answers to this. One is simply that Wiles has misunderstood the nature of 'sharing suffering'. If I have rheumatism, it is likely to be of great help to me to know that you sympathize, that you are moved by my plight. It would be of no help at all to know that you had rheumatism too, or rather that you experienced a rheumatic twinge every time I did, which is what Wiles is demanding that God do. I think he may have confused the sharing of a *pain* with the sharing of a *condition*. It could well be—indeed, I am sure that it was—a help and comfort to the lepers among whom Father Damian worked, that he not only sought to help them (that could have been true of a doctor who treated them at arm's length in a cloud of antiseptic and left by helicopter the moment this had been done) but lived among them, sharing their condition, to the point in the end of becoming a leper himself. But this, orthodoxy believes, is just what God *has* done. He has shared our condition, and even our death. That indeed was why Damian went to live among the lepers.

I might add, incidentally, that the proper conclusion for someone who does want God to experience a rheumatic twinge, or rather my rheumatic twinge, every time that I do, is of course not deism

[44] In Goulder (1979), p. 8; cf. Wiles (1974), p. 72.

but pantheism. This was argued (in a rather different form) by Mr Richard Francks in an article[45] on 'Omniscience, Omnipotence and Pantheism'. The form is different because Francks' basis was the doctrine of omniscience. God's knowledge, he argued, must be not only complete but *perfect*, 'of the highest order'. Suppose now my knee hurts. Must not God, to have perfect knowledge, feel my pain? 'If God's knowledge of my pain is only that of the perfect physiologist, then I have an awareness, a perspective, which God lacks' and in that case His knowledge is not perfect. God therefore feels my pain, and every other sensation that I have, or you have, or any other sentient creature has, exactly and precisely as we feel them; and it seems to be impossible to draw any distinction between God's feeling of them and ours. We feel them to be peculiarly 'ours'? Yes, but God has that feeling too. The natural conclusion is pantheistic, or at least 'pantozoistic'—God is identical with all creatures that live and feel.[46] (He may of course be more than this.) Now we may decide that we do not believe that God's knowledge has to be perfect in this way; but it seems clear that this is what Wiles wants to say. (Not perhaps to believe; he is arguing *ad hominem*.)

The second answer is this: Wiles seems to be assuming that incarnation is a relationship into which God entered with an independently existing human being (so far, that is, as any created being can be called 'independently existing')—the Antiochene position, in fact. But this is not necessarily the only possible form of incarnationist Christology. Orthodoxy does hold that the humanity of Jesus was full and complete. Nevertheless, it was 'anhypostatic'. The exact meaning of this word depends on the meaning of 'hypostasis', and this is a vexed point, as we shall see.[47] But it certainly seems to imply that Jesus of Nazareth would not have existed at all but for the Incarnation; that God did not 'take over' (or even 'draw near to') a human being who would otherwise have developed normally, but started as it were from scratch. Jesus of Nazareth did not and does not exist independently of or separated from God in the way that we do. 'We offer Thee ourselves', says the Prayer Book; may it be true of us all, but it was not true of Jesus, because His self was God's human self from the very start. God can only draw near

[45] Francks (1979), pp. 395–9, esp. p. 396.
[46] Francks also argues from omnipotence for full pantheism; but that is not now our concern.
[47] See Excursus VI.

to us in the way Wiles suggests at the price of making us unable
to surrender ourselves to Him—well, that perhaps we could do without if necessary—and also maybe of making us all one person, different aspects of God incarnating Himself. There was something Jesus
lacked which the rest of us have (apart from sin, that is), to wit,
complete distinctness from God. It did not make Him any less
human. Nevertheless, if Wiles lacked it, would he be Wiles? and
would I, if I lacked it, be who I am? We might be—we should
be—better than we are; but God has not chosen to make nothing
but God-united perfection, or this world would never have been
created. He chose to make us *separate beings*; and He chose to
redeem us. God follows, it seems, the pattern He laid down, and
that includes His pattern for the human race as part of His creation;
indeed, Wiles believes He does so so completely that He never acts
in any special way towards anything or anyone within that creation.
I should not go so far myself. I believe He does act from time to
time in grace and revelation, and that once He took the greater
step still of entering the world Himself in a human person; but
I am sure that it would be inconsistent with what we seem to know
of His ways that He should relate Himself to every human life in
the strange way that He did with the life of Jesus. It seems, then,
that even if God is not impassible, a full two-way Incarnation is
required to show us His sharing of our troubles, and His bearing
of our sin. 'The work of atonement is His own work, incarnate
in the Passion of Jesus Christ because it is "eternal in the heavens"
in the very life of God—the love of God bearing the sin of the
world.' So Donald Baillie.[48] And if he is right—and if God is passible he surely *is* right—his own analysis of the way that work became
incarnate turns out to be deficient, for the Passion of Jesus Christ
is not the Passion of God, but only caused by it; it is the Passion
of the Man whom God sent to the Cross, as a revelation of God's
suffering love, to die in pain which God Himself did not bear. We
are terrifyingly near the monstrous God of the Gnostic Basilides,
who let Simon of Cyrene be crucified in his place. Of course no
Antiochene, ancient or modern, ever meant any such thing; they
would have recoiled from it in horror; but for all that, their teachings
do theoretically imply something very like it. 'We would claim to
see in the crucifixion the supreme manifestation of the divine nature',

---

[48] Baillie (1961), p. 194.

says Dr Hanson[49]—but what sort of a nature if the Incarnation is only a matter of God's action? That of a God who, as Dr Baker puts it, is declaring 'Truth can only be given to them in a personal existence ... But this life will involve the most terrible suffering. *I will therefore send someone else to do the job.*'[50]

Still more does this hold if God is indeed impassible. Then we should have a situation where, in Lady Oppenheimer's words, 'his [Christ's] sacrifice is reduced to an unhappy miscarriage of justice and the heavenly Father is left on high untouched by the evils of the world'.[51] We have seen the problems this raised for the Antiochene Fathers, and it would seem that some of their later followers had to modify their teaching a little: thus we find the Nestorian teacher Narsai (d. 503) writing:

> The soul suffers not in the body when its limbs
>   are scourged,
> And the Godhead suffered not when that body
>   suffered in which it dwelt ...
> The soul suffers with the body, in love and not
>   by nature
> And the sufferings of the body are by figure
>   attributed to the soul.[52]

In the idea of 'suffering in love' Narsai seems to be coming close to some of the modern passibilists. But his analogy of soul and body (used also by the Chalcedonian *Quicunque Vult*—and by Monophysites!) points surely in a different direction.[53] One would normally say that the soul did suffer by nature when the body was scourged, and that it did not require love to produce this. (Maybe, though, by 'suffer' Narsai meant something more like 'undergo injury'.)

We began by considering the Atonement, and noting that all the classical theories required that 'human experience should become the personal experience of God the Son'. But we seem to have moved on from that. It is beginning to look as if the only way to make sense of the Cross *at all* as part of God's deliberate plan is to allow

---

[49] Hanson (1975), p. 99.   [50] Baker (1975), p. 317. (Baker's italics.)
[51] Oppenheimer (1973), p. 214.
[52] *Mimra*, 40. 17, quoted by Wigram (1910), pp. 272ff.
[53] It is significant that Nestorius himself did not use it.

this two-way Incarnation. A purely 'Antiochene' Christology will not do. We must either introduce an 'Alexandrian' element as well or regard the Cross as an irrelevant and regrettable waste of a rather striking young life.

9

Approaches to Analysis

METHODS of approaching the task of analysis vary very widely. No doubt most or all of those who have undertaken analytic Christology have in fact approached the task quite simply by way of faith in their Lord and Saviour, seeking to draw out the implications of this faith and its basis in Scripture. But at least as they set their analyses out different procedures seem to be involved. And the differences themselves differ from one another. We may perhaps distinguish four main kinds of difference.

One well-known distinction is between '*Word/flesh*' or 'Alexandrian' Christologies and '*Word/man*' or 'Antiochene' ones.[1] The former expression, taken literally, is Apollinarian. The Word enters human flesh, but no mention is made of a mind or soul, and by Apollinarius himself it was explicitly denied that the Lord *had* a human soul. Realization of what this implied led to acknowledgement that what the Word entered or assumed was a complete human nature, body and soul together; although in writers like Cyril this is still often called 'flesh', which could be misleading, they were simply using a long-accepted expression which goes back, of course, to the prologue of St John's Gospel. Nevertheless, the human side of Christ is still apt to be considered in abstract, impersonal terms.

By contrast, a 'Word/man' Christology sets out to describe the unity between God the Word and a definite, concrete human being, Jesus the son of Mary from Nazareth. Extreme versions like that of Paul of Samosata held Jesus to be a normal man in whom the Word, a quite distinct entity, dwelt as in a prophet or a saint, only more so. Recognition of the difficulties in this led again to modifications which insisted on the unification of the two elements in a single Christ.

It is clear that most of the theologians we have been discussing

---

[1] See e.g. Kelly (1960), pp. 281ff.

belong to the second group. Even the actual opponents of incarnational theologies could perhaps be seen as an extreme wing of
this group, according to whom God and Jesus are so totally distinct
that it is not proper to speak of 'incarnation' at all. But 'Word/flesh'
thought took deep root in the Church, predominated in her until
recently, and is perhaps the natural impression the ordinary church-
goer gets from the recital of the Creeds, which, by using 'Jesus
Christ' as a name for the pre-existent Son, suggest that the Incarnation was an episode in a continuous life extending both before
it ('before all worlds') and after it ('whose kingdom shall have no
end'). The 'Athanasian Creed' or *Quicunque Vult* is far more 'Word/
man' in approach, but it is hardly ever used.[2] Hence perhaps the
impression given, one gathers, to the youthful John Wren-Lewis:

> I have heard it said again and again that the ordinary person sees Jesus
> as a good man and no more ... I am sure they are quite wrong, even today.
> Certainly up to the Second World War, the commonest vision of Jesus
> was not as a human being *at all*. He was a God in human form ... very
> much like the Olympian deities were supposed to be when they visited
> the earth in disguise.[3]

(There is of course no 'quite wrong' about it; the people whom
Wren-Lewis thinks wrong were talking about ordinary *non-Christian*
people, while he himself was thinking of ordinary *church-goers*. But
the impression he received is interesting.)

A second distinction is between Christologies that begin from two
abstract natures and those that *begin from a single concrete person*.
(To some extent these correspond to the two previous groups.) The
distinction is put very forcefully by Pannenberg:

> From the very beginning Christian theology was forced to say both that
> Jesus is truly God and, at the same time, truly man. *Vere deus, vere homo*
> is what the formula of Chalcedon says. ... The formula of the two natures
> or substances in Christ affirmed something completely different. [Why so,
> we may ask? Because] the formula of the true divinity and true humanity
> begins with the fact that one describes one and the same person, the man
> Jesus of Nazareth, from different points of view. The unity ... is given,
> and both things are to be said about this one person: he is God and he
> is man. The formula about the two natures [starts from] the difference

---

[2] I have myself heard it used just once.
[3] In the symposium *They Became Anglicans*, quoted by Robinson (1963), pp.
65–6.

between the divine and the human, creaturely being in general ... Jesus now appears as a being bearing and uniting two opposed substances in himself. From this conception all the insoluble problems of the doctrine of the Two Natures result.[4]

The catch with this is that there is a difference between the divine and the human—even Pannenberg has had to speak of 'different points of view'!—and, though it may be inadvisable to *begin* with this, it is almost impossible to avoid getting to it sooner or later. And in fact beginning with the one person has its own dangers: for one thing, since what we see of that one person is, inevitably, for the most part human, the risk is obvious that we may lose sight of the divine, the Word in heaven.

Thirdly, there are *'Christologies from above'* and *'Christologies from below'*. The first asks, in effect, 'How might God become man?', the second, 'How and in what sense might this man be called God?' Again, these are to some extent respectively 'Alexandrian' and 'Antiochene', but not always. I think it might be true to say that the original 'Antiochenes' of the patristic age were asking a mixed question—'How might God become *this* man?'—that is, stressing the particular character of the man Jesus rather more than their 'Alexandrian' contemporaries, but *not* seeking to 'build up' from this man and somehow reach divinity from there. But such 'building up' is by no means uncommon. It was finely advocated by Luther as the way the Scriptures used; 'but', he added, 'the philosophers and doctors have insisted on begining from above, and so they have become fools. We must begin from below, and after that come upwards.'[5] And this need not be done by 'Antiochenes' alone; for it is the natural approach of apologetics, which can be carried out by either school. C. S. Lewis, for example, was certainly 'Alexandrian' in his Christology; yet the figure of Christ is introduced in his *Mere Christianity* as 'from below': 'Among these Jews there suddenly turns up a man, who goes about talking as if He was God...'[6] The whole classic argument *'aut deus aut homo non probus'* which Lewis goes on to develop is a 'from below' approach. Nevertheless, in general it is clearly likely that an approach which

---

[4] Pannenberg (1968), pp. 283–4.
[5] Quoted by Mackintosh (1913), p. 232, from Luther's *Works* (Erlangen edition), xii. 412.
[6] Lewis (1955), p. 51.

is exclusively 'from below' will probably try to link Jesus and God by a 'Word/man' Christology, and one which is exclusively 'from above' will probably try to depict 'the Word made flesh'. The tendency for many centuries was to try to work 'from above', sometimes to the point of almost forgetting that our Lord really was a man—or even of denying it, as in Newman's notorious saying 'Though man, He was not, strictly speaking, in the English sense of the word, *a* man.'[7]

Lastly, there are *ontological* and *functional* Christologies. The ontological (which was characteristic of most Christology until quite recently, though elements of the other were present in the Antiochene Fathers) sees the concepts and categories in which the doctrine of the Incarnation is to be presented as metaphysical ones—concepts like substance, nature, person, and the like. The functional, to quote J. A. T. Robinson, asserts identity 'in terms of verbs rather than substantives or substances. The Christ', he continues, 'is the one who does what God does, who represents him ... The issue is whether in seeing him we see the Father, whether, in mercy and judgment, he *functions* as God, whether he *is* God to and for them.'[8] In point of fact, Robinson, and Dr C. A. van Peursen whom he is to some extent echoing, add a third type, the 'mythological'. This uses neither metaphysical nor functional concepts, but what may be called poetical ones—such as 'Son of God' or 'Lord of glory'. I shall not, however, treat this separately: in the first place, because it would land us with yet another meaning for the unfortunate and overworked word 'myth', and in the second because I think all theologians would agree that one must at least *try* to formulate Christology in more 'scientific' terms. The poetical (or mythological) terms must stand, for they are the ones given to us in Scripture, and would-be 'scientific' expressions of Christology have perpetually to be checked by them; what is more, they may well convey meaning which cannot be expressed without them.[9] But for the purposes of analytic Christology they are part of the 'given', in that they provide most of the language in which the 'given'

[7] *Parochial and Plain Sermons*, vi. 62. (I owe the reference to Strange (1981), p. 57.)

[8] Robinson (1973), pp. 183–4.

[9] See eg A. M. Farrer, 'Poetic Truth', in Farrer (1972), pp. 24ff.; R. W. Hepburn, 'Poetry and Religious Belief', in Toulmin (1957), pp. 85ff.; C. S. Lewis, 'The Language of Religion', in Lewis (1967), pp. 129ff.

is expressed; they do not belong in the analysis itself. Ontological and functional terms do, or at least may; we must see.

Which of these, then, shall we choose? Or— an obvious possibility— are we forced to choose at all? Can we not rather insist on retaining all eight insights? The most difficult to reconcile or use together is almost certainly the first pair, so let us tackle the pairs in reverse order, leaving the hardest till last.

Ontological or functional, or both? Undoubtedly many Christ-ologists of the past would protest that they had always combined the two. The Person of Christ and the Work of Christ were always indissolubly linked, and the Work obviously *had* to be described in functional terms. Mind you, ontology was seen as the basis of function, perhaps even as its preliminary. 'The Lord', wrote the Byzantine theologian Nicholas Cabasilas, 'allowed men, separated from God by the triple barrier of nature, sin and death, to be ... united to Him by the fact that He has set aside each barrier in turn: that of nature by His incarnation, of sin by His death, and of death by His resurrection.'[10] The ontological barrier, on this view, had to be set aside first by an ontological change; then the incarnate Lord could 'function' to set aside those of sin and death. I think, however, that some contemporary 'functionalists' are want-ing more than this. They want to eliminate the ontological side altogether as unhelpful. Description in terms of function is to be moved back into the Incarnation itself, and to displace all other.

But can ontology be eliminated? I very much doubt it—and I am quite sure that those who wish to eliminate it have not succeeded. Most people would say that a function must be exercised by a per-son—in this case, the person of Jesus. A being—a substance, even— lies behind the function. And most people would say that God too is a being (even if some theologians would prefer to drop the indefi-nite article and write 'being' with a capital 'B'). Can Christ then 'function as' God without being God ontologically? To quote Forsyth, 'could God's plenipotentiary' (compare Robinson's 'repre-sentative') 'for the last purposes of the soul and the last destiny of the race, be a creature?'[11] Even to answer 'Yes' is to ontologize to some extent; but in fact the answer is surely 'No'. An analogy may help. Someone may perhaps 'function as' Prime Minister without

---

[10] *On the Life in Christ*, quoted by Lossky (1957), p. 136.
[11] Forsyth (1909), p. 84.

holding that office, in the sense of deputizing for the real Prime Minister during absence or illness, because the office is itself a function. They cannot 'function as' Mrs Thatcher (though they can of course act for her), even if Mrs Thatcher is the Prime Minister, because she is a person, and there is no such thing as 'Thatchership' to be a function. If 'God' is the name of an office, like 'Saviour' or 'Messiah', Jesus might be able to function as God without ontology's coming into it. (I doubt even this; the office is too exalted. A cat cannot function as Prime Minister, even if the real Prime Minister is absent.) But if 'God' is not the name of an office—and surely it isn't—the thing is impossible. The only way out seems to be to drop ontology completely. If ontological thinking is in some way objectionable in itself, quite apart from Christology—if verbs are to be preferred to nouns—then the nouns 'Jesus' and 'God' must be translated into verbs as well, and not just the nouns that expressed the relationship between them. Something like this was proposed by the idealists of 'Orbis Tertius' in the imaginary language of Tlön, which had no nouns at all but only 'impersonal verbs qualified by monosyllabic suffixes or prefixes which have the force of adverbs, so that "the moon rose over the sea" is written as "upward behind the onstreaming it mooned"'.[12] Failing something as drastic as that, ontology will stay with us; and it is seldom that anything so drastic is proposed. Occasional talk of the 'Christ-event' (or even 'the event Jesus Christ'[13]) is usually the nearest, and even that seems mainly designed to emphasize (very properly) the fact that the whole life of Jesus has to be kept in mind.

Perhaps we should make an exception here for some of the 'process theologians',[14] who have made a serious attempt, following A. N. Whitehead, to express not just the Incarnation but everything else in terms of *becoming* rather than *being*. An entity, on this view, is not a substance to which things happen, but a process—the process of growing together into a unity of its (the entity's) relationships with other entities, its 'prehensions' in Whitehead's terminology. Hence we can express Jesus' divinity in terms of His prehensions of God and God's of Him. I suspect that in order to do so the Whiteheadian concept of God with which process theology began

[12] J. L. Borges, 'Tlön, Uqbar, Orbis Tertius', in Borges (1962), p. 22.
[13] P. Hamilton, 'Some Proposals for a Modern Christology', in Pittenger (1978), p. 154.
[14] e.g. Hamilton, or Pittenger himself.

would have to be modified, but I may be wrong, and of course no one supposes Whitehead was infallible. In any case, however, ontological, 'being'-style *language* would still be, as indeed it is, used for convenience; we should still use nouns like 'God' and 'Jesus', or for that matter 'Mount Everest', to refer to what in the last metaphysical analysis were processes, not static 'things'. And in that case we might also use adjectives to represent their prehensions of one another, and continue to say that Christ was 'consubstantial' with the Father, or that in Him the Word was 'incarnate'. 'Representing' God or 'functioning as' God would have no advantage over these simply by being, grammatically, verbs; for verbs, adjectives, and nouns would all be describing the same sort of 'proceeding' reality.

Setting aside, then, questions of the technicalities of process theology, it seems doubtful whether we can get by on function alone; ontology does seem to be needed as well. Function must certainly be kept. There is little point in Christ's being God and Man if He doesn't *do* anything with this. But I do not see how it can stand on its own, the more so as it is not easy to fit into it the reciprocity or 'two-way traffic' which we have seen to be needed if Christ is to be either the Revealer or the Reconciler. We do seem to need a both/and here, not an either/or.

What about 'from below' and 'from above'? The case for saying that the proper approach is 'from below' to the virtual exclusion of 'from above' has been made very forcibly by Pannenberg.[15] In the first place, he argues, Christology's most important task is to present the reasons for confessing the divinity of Jesus—not presupposing it, as 'from above' Christology does. Secondly, a 'from above' Christology has difficulty in recognizing the significance of 'the distinctive features of the real, historical man, Jesus of Nazareth'. And thirdly, to construct a 'from above' Christology we should have to be able to stand in the place of God Himself.

Now on the first of these points Pannenberg is certainly right, as we have already acknowledged. Apologists do have to present reasons for confessing the divinity of Jesus, and they may of course go on from this to develop a Christology 'from below' if they so choose. But they do not need to. They may, having established the Lord's divinity, proceed to ask 'But how could God have become

---

[15] Pannenberg (1968), p. 34.

a man?' and develop their Christology 'from above'.[16] If, that is,
they wish to go in for analytic Christology at all. Suppose detectives
investigating a burglary find the fingerprints of Bill Sikes on the
window-frame by which the thief entered, and conclude that Sikes
is the thief; they do not necessarily have to trace Sikes's footprints
back to his home. They may equally well go on to trace them for-
wards to wherever Sikes is now, or indeed leave the tracing to others
while they get on with other tasks. Similarly, the apologist may
establish the divinity and then hand over to the Christologist, to
work 'from below' or 'from above' as he or she thinks best. What
perhaps has misled Pannenberg into thinking that Christologists
must also be apologists is the fact that with the growth of anti-
incarnationism within the Church herself they very often do have
to be just that. Gore and Forsyth, for example, about the turn of
the century, were having to begin their writings on the person of
our Lord with a survey of the biblical evidence, not just as a 'New
Testament Christology', but as apologists against a 'liberalism'
which reduced Jesus to the Great Moral Teacher. And something
very like this may well be needed today. But once this intra-
ecclesiastical apologetics has been carried out, 'above' and 'below'
are both (as far as the present argument goes) valid options.

The second point is a very serious one indeed. It is uncommonly
easy for the Christologist 'from above' to reduce Jesus of Nazareth
to a kind of schema, an outline figure of whom nothing is needed
except that He be human. Karl Rahner has complained bitterly
of this: 'Has the abstract formalism of Christology contributed to
a decrease of interest in a theology of the mysteries of Christ's human
life? In the ordinary textbook-Christology current today, one has
to keep a pretty close lookout to find anything even about Christ's
Ascension.'[17]

This is indeed serious, as I said. But is it peculiar to Christologies
'from above'? Is it not perhaps a risk in *any* Christological work
(the present one not excepted)? As far as my own reading suggests,
Christologists 'from below' fall into the trap just as easily as their
colleagues. For Christologists are attempting to analyse the whole

---

[16] See Sobrino (1978), p. 339: 'An authentically orthodox Christology must end
up with the ontological affirmation of the Incarnation. Epistemologically, however,
it must work in the opposite direction.' (Though Sobrino is not thinking primarily
of apologetics.)

[17] Rahner (1961), p. 190.

'event of Jesus Christ'; unless the distinctive features of the historical Jesus affect that analysis, they may well feel those features are not their concern. This may change. They may move from Christology to commentary, as (for instance) William Temple did between *Christus Veritas* and the *Readings in St. John's Gospel*. But while they are doing analytic Christology (proclamatory Christology is another matter altogether) they may well pass over the details of Jesus' life and personality—though they had better keep those details somewhere in mind lest they start talking nonsense. I understand that some seventeenth-century Roman Catholic writers held that Jesus must have been *the* supreme mathematician, doctor, orator, philosopher, and so on.[18] If so, they certainly *had* neglected the 'distinctive features of the real historical man Jesus', totally. Those 'distinctive features' have got to be kept in mind as a check and control on human speculation. But need they be more important than that, in analytic Christology? A geologist need not be blind to the beauties of a landscape just because, as he is working on the rock strata that underlie it, his reports contain no reference to that beauty—though, if he is about to recommend that the whole area be turned over to open-cast coal-mining, he had better keep that beauty well in mind.

It is Pannenberg's third objection that seems to me the strongest. Can we answer the 'from above' question 'How might God become man?' without in effect imagining ourselves as God pondering how to do it? And surely this is not only impertinent but impossible. I think this is right, and if so it rules out any Christology that purports to describe the process of God's becoming human in other than Scriptural terms ('mythological' ones if you prefer), which are given to us by God. It remains possible, however, or so it seems to me, that a Christology might be devised which only purported to describe the *end product* of the 'process', and yet, because it is thinking of that result precisely as a result of God's act, might still be called a Christology 'from above'. Perhaps it would come closer the mark to call it a Christology 'from the middle'. No doubt this is only a matter of names. The point is simply that the elimination of approaches that require us to think God's thoughts for Him does not automatically mean that the only possible approach is one which tries, as it were, to wring the divinity out of the humanity.

---

[18] I owe this to Robinson (1973), p. 71, who in his turn derived it from Brown (1968), pp. 44ff.

It is not altogether fair to say of earlier theologians, as Dr Robinson does,[19] 'Christ established there [at Nicaea] as a person or *hypostasis* of the Trinity, fully God in every sense of the word, *this* was the datum that could not be questioned—not the fact of his existence as an individual, historical person'. None of the orthodox ever dreamed of questioning the latter fact. The trouble was that some of the heterodox, namely the Arians, *had* questioned the former one, and it needed to be emphasized and reiterated. In a sense, it had itself been established by a 'from below' process (of apologetics, including 'intra-ecclesiastical' apologetics); the individual, historical person had been acknowledged as Lord and Messiah by His immediate followers, and the main 'from above' element that entered into the debate from then on up to and including Nicaea was the element of *revelation* which, it was supposed (rightly, to my mind), had led to that acknowledgement in the first place[20] and to its development in the writings of the New Testament. Once, however, the divinity of the Lord had been established, it did no doubt seem legitimate to try and analyse the Incarnation 'from above'. As I have said, I am not at all sure that it was legitimate; but if it was not, this was only because we do not have enough understanding of God, and not because the inner nature of the Incarnation has got to be of a kind that only analysis 'from below' could lay bare. 'From above' approaches certainly have their dangers; but then so do 'from below' ones.

To begin with the divine pre-existent Son makes better sense of the New Testament approach, especially of Paul and John [writes Guthrie]. If we begin from 'above' we shall take account of revelation, whereas if we begin from 'below' we shall be concerned with concepts within our own experience and develop them in accordance with our existent knowledge of humanity, which leaves little room for revelation.[21]

A purely 'from below' approach runs the risk of supposing that we have not been told anything about the Son of God's coming to be among us, which is not the case. The two really have to act as checks on one another. Our *knowledge* of Christ begins chiefly from His human life (though not entirely, thanks to revelation); it does not follow that our completed theology must. The distinction

---

[19] Robinson (1973), p. 102.   [20] Matt. 16: 17.   [21] Guthrie (1981), p. 402.

between *ordo essendi* and *ordo cognoscendi* must not be forgotten; and *ordo analysandi* may follow either—preferably keeping both in mind. Rahner, whom I mentioned earlier as seeing clearly the dangers of the 'from above' approach, nevertheless wants to combine the two:

> In giving a justification for our faith in Christ, the basic and decisive point of departure, of course, lies in an encounter with the historical Jesus of Nazareth, and hence in an 'ascending Christology' ... [but] if Jesus as the Christ has ever actually encountered someone, the idea of a God-man, of God coming into our history, and hence a descending Christology, also has its own significance and power.[22]

And he concludes that the combination of the two methods 'need not be a disadvantage, but rather it can serve as a mutual clarification of both'.

Christologies 'from two abstract principles' and 'from a single person'? Here I am inclined to say that *neither* is legitimate, not if the two descriptions are to be taken literally. We begin with God and Jesus Christ. We may use the idea of 'two natures' as we go on; we may conclude that we are dealing with a single person, not two; but the starting-point cannot be either of these. We do not *begin* with the formula *vere deus, vere homo*, nor with that of the two natures, except in this sense, that we may wish to assume as done all the work that led to one or the other of these formulae. (Thus the second council of Constantinople took for granted the work of Chalcedon, and Chalcedon took for granted the work of Nicaea and Ephesus.) In such a case we should in effect be beginning in the middle; and if we are, it could well be that to begin with the two natures would land us in difficulties (though Pannenberg's description of the problem as 'insoluble' is begging the question). But then to begin with the single person might also have its drawbacks, on the lines pointed out by Guthrie. Christology, after all, is not bound to be an easy task, or one free from all risk of making serious mistakes. But I should have thought that the least risky method was to begin with neither of these, but with God and Jesus Christ, in the light naturally of what was said previously about basic requirements and constraints.

Are we now in a better position to judge between 'Word/flesh' and 'Word/man' Christologies? It seems to me that either is

[22] Rahner (1988), p. 177.

legitimate; we cannot declare in advance that either method is to be ignored. If we had been able to rule out ontology, or to insist that Christology had to begin 'from below' only, then 'Word/man' would undoubtedly have had the best of it. But it does not seem that we can do either of these. We are certainly confronted in the 'given' of Christology with God and with a Man; we are also told of the Word being made flesh, of Christ Jesus coming into the world to save sinners, in language which does suggest the 'Word/flesh' pattern. We can only decide between them (or combine them) by trying to develop a Christology without presupposing either, and then seeing which pattern it more nearly fits. But in the process we must be alert for the dangers that beset the two patterns. We must not construct a 'Word/flesh' Christology which in the slightest way implies that Jesus was not a human being like us, in the full, ordinary sense of the words; we must not construct a 'Word/man' Christology which prevents two-way traffic between heaven and earth. These are two negative criteria for any Christian understanding of Christ.

10

The Link between God and Man in Jesus

IF there is to be some kind of link between Jesus of Nazareth and God the Word (or, since we must not prejudge the 'Word/flesh' and 'Word/man' decision, between God and man in Jesus Christ), and if this link is to allow the two-way traffic of which I have spoken, we would seem to have three possibilities. First, that there are *at least* two different kinds of link joining Jesus and the Word, or God and man: one sort which allows God's purposes to affect Jesus' actions, and another sort which allows us to say truly that when Jesus suffered God was bearing our sins. Secondly, that there is a union between the two of only one kind, but one which resides in something they have in common, and which can provide what one might call a channel between them. And thirdly, that there is a union between the two of only one kind, but which resides in something *external* to both, so that both act and are acted upon together. These are not of course necessarily exclusive of one another; and since if there are two or more kinds of linkage they might include some of the second or third types, we had better leave multiple-link Christologies to the last.

Union residing in something external to the items united is common enough in ordinary life. A pack of cards held together in a box, a bundle of sticks tied together with string, a pantomime horse; all these fit the description well enough. Something like this seems to have been the view of Nestorius. Hodgson suggested[1] that for Nestorius the πρόσωπον, which was for him the uniting element in the Incarnation, might be translated 'appearance', so long as this was *not* contrasted with 'reality', but was the appearance 'considered as an objectively real element in the being'. It describes

---

[1] Nestorius (1925), appendix iv. Cf. Vine (1948), p. 100.

'the external undivided appearance of the whole'.[2] In such a union
the elements united are a single unity if compared with anything
else in the whole of existence. Jesus is more closely linked with
God the Son than He is with any other person or thing, and similarly
God the Son is more closely linked with Jesus than with any other
person or thing, with the possible exception of the other Persons
of the Blessed Trinity, and probably not even that. (It would, by
the way, be extremely difficult to use this Nestorian model if one
were also using a 'two natures' approach.)

There are two main difficulties with such a Christology. One,
as I have just suggested, is whether we might want to say that the
bond between God the Son and the other Persons of the Trinity
is as close as or closer than that between God the Son and the
human Jesus. But this is not certain (the two closenesses are of
such different kinds that to try to say which is the greater is very
likely a waste of time), and even if correct might not really spoil
Nestorius' case. The other is, of course, that it does not seem to
allow room for the 'two-way traffic' we spoke of earlier. An act
directed to the πρόσωπον as a whole is indeed directed to both
the Word and the Man; if, for example, I pray in the words of
the Prayer Book Litany 'Graciously hear us, O Christ', my prayer
is addressed not to God the Son alone to the neglect of His humanity,
nor to Jesus formerly of Nazareth to the neglect of His divinity,
but to both elements of the πρόσωπον together. But the Crucifixion
was not directed to the πρόσωπον as a whole; only the man Jesus
was crucified, dead, and buried. (Applause directed at the pantomime horse, if one may continue that ludicrous but helpful analogy,
is due to and received by both actors; but a collision with the scenery
is only undergone by one at a time.) I think, therefore, that the
Nestorian view (if it was in fact Nestorius'), while true enough as
far as it goes, does not go far enough. And it seems unlikely that
there is some other form of union residing in something external
to the items united which will do the work that πρόσωπον did
not do. (We shall see, though, that this assertion may need to be
qualified.)

[2] Perhaps the image of the pantomime horse is not wholly inept; we can conceive
of one pair of 'legs' as entirely in accord with the will of the other ... There is
a difference in that the costume of the pantomime horse is literally external to the
players involved, whereas the πρόσωπον, if Hodgson is right in his understanding
of Nestorius, is not separate from the entities that share it, but is theirs jointly,
a part, not of one nor of the other, but only of both together.

Union residing in an element common to both is less common in ordinary life, but by no means unknown. Siamese twins are an obvious example. It has certainly been prominent in Christology: Apollinarianism is clearly an attempt to explain the One Christ on this basis, and some defences of an 'enhypostatic' Christology are too. But Apollinarianism is rightly rejected as a heresy, and many theologians have felt that this is bound to be the case with any Christologizing along these lines. *Whatever* the 'element in common' is, clearly the pre-existent Christ had it (or otherwise it would not be common to Him and to the man Jesus); and clearly the man Jesus did not have His own separate one (for the same reason); but clearly all other people *do* have their own separate ones, or it would not be part of human nature, and therefore not part of Jesus. Therefore Jesus lacked some element of human nature which all the rest of us have—whether mind, soul, spirit, ego, or ὑπόστασις makes no difference—and was not consubstantial with us, which is contrary to Chalcedon and, more important still, contrary to the obvious full and normal humanity of the historical person Jesus of Nazareth.

Can some element be discovered which is not open to this criticism? It appears that the fifteenth-century theologian John Capreolus suggested that what was 'missing' in Christ was 'a properly created *act of being*'.[3] The idea is, as I understand it, that in each created thing there is to be distinguished the essence or nature of the thing— that which makes it a star, an angel, a warthog, or a human being— and the 'act of being' which makes it an actually existent star, angel, warthog, or human being as opposed to the mere idea or possibility of one. Christ's human *nature* is complete, but the 'act of being' by which He is a real man and not a fictitious or imaginary one is that of God the Word, because He already existed before He became man. There is no separate 'act of being' which belongs to the man Jesus alone. Schoonenberg objects that such a view 'makes Christ's human nature completely unreal'; it is an 'ontological Docetism' which takes away from Christ not just that which made Him a rational being (as Apollinarianism did) but that which makes

---

[3] I owe this to Schoonenberg (1972), p. 60, who also mentions that the view was revived in the twentieth century by Louis Billot; my comments are based solely on what he says.

Him a being in the world. 'Jesus Christ is no longer a man ...
he is no longer as a man.'[4]

This does not seem fair to me. Surely Capreolus' view does not
make Christ's human nature unreal, it simply says that what makes
it real, the instrument of its reality, is not something created but
something divine. Schoonenberg is right to say that on this view
Christ '*is* no longer as a man', if by this 'is' he means 'exists', and
if by this 'as' he means 'because'. Christ exists, not because He
is human (though He certainly is) but because He is God incarnate.
If, however, Schoonenberg means (and I suspect he does) that Christ
does not exist *qua* man, in His capacity as a man, then he is certainly
wrong; Capreolus was not denying this. Mr Gladstone did not exist
'as a Prime Minister', if that means 'because he was Prime Minister';
but that does not make him or his Premiership unreal!

Nevertheless, Capreolus' view does seem unsatisfactory in other
ways. In the first and most important place, I am not convinced
that the 'act of being' can be treated as an element in Christ (or
in anyone or anything else) in the way that is required. It does
not seem to be a part of anything; if it were, it would belong to
the nature, which it doesn't. It seems to be equivalent to the *fact*
of a thing's existing; and if that is so, can it provide the link between
eternal Word and first-century Jew that is needed for revelation
and atonement? Secondly, on the usual view of Thomists like
Capreolus, God has no 'act of being' distinct from His essence;
in Him essence and existence are one and the same. If so, it seems
that Christ's humanity is real, He exists as a human being, directly
in virtue of the divine nature (and the divine nature of all three
Persons of the Trinity at that, one presumes), which I cannot make
much sense of, and which, if it does make sense, entails surely that
God is a first-century Jew by His very essence. Thirdly, even if
in God essence and existence are distinct, the fact that God the
Word exists and the fact that Jesus of Nazareth exists are surely
quite separate facts; and can they be separate facts if the 'act of
being' is one and the same for Word and for human? And fourthly,
to quote Mackey, 'What it could mean for a nature which is complete
of its kind to exist but not by its own proper existence is something
of a conundrum to the shrewdest metaphysical mind.'[5] Is an act
of existence not to be picked out and defined in terms of the object

---

[4] Schoonenberg (1972), pp. 60 and 73.
[5] Mackey (1979), p. 246 (discussing Aquinas, not Capreolus).

whose act of existence it is? How then can Christ's humanity, given that Christ really exists, *not* have its own act of existence? It exists, of course, only by the creative will of God; but then that (as Mackey goes on to point out) is true of all created things. Indeed, one might add, do not the various parts of Christ's human body have their own 'acts of being'? His hands and His feet were real things, which really existed; are we to say that they too only existed by the 'act of being' of the eternal Word, whereas our hands and feet have their own 'acts of being'? It really does not look as if 'act of being' will do for our link.

Is there any other alternative? The term 'ego' has been suggested. Thus Fr. Jean Galot writes: 'if there is in Christ a unique divine person, the ego of the human consciousness of Christ can designate nothing other than this person ... There is in him no human ego [*moi*], there is human consciousness of a divine ego.'[6] This looks a little more promising. The principle 'what is not assumed is not redeemed' might just possibly not affect it, as the ego or *moi* could be so much a matter of the *individual* that to talk of its being 'assumed' is nonsense. Moreover, as the *moi* is what has the body, mind, and soul, it has what is redeemed, and to talk of *its* being redeemed (or not redeemed) as contrasted with them is also absurd (just as it would be absurd to say of someone that their body, mind, and soul were all healthy and then raise a question whether they themselves were).

Yet there are difficulties here too. Some I think are slight. Mascall, although he greatly admires Galot, feels that 'ego' ought to be replaced by 'person', 'if we wish to express it in a strictly theological form'.[7] With respect, this is surely just what ought not to be done. Christology in the English language has been complicated quite hideously by the ambiguities of the word 'person': does it represent the Greek πρόσωπον, or the Greek ὑπόστασις, or does it bear its modern meaning of 'human or (in certain contexts) other rational being', or does it have overtones of the modern word 'personality', or what? Galot was surely making a creditable effort to be more precise, and should be allowed to go on doing so.

Pittenger's treatment of similar ideas (writing before Galot) is far more critical:

---

[6] Galot (1971), p. 115, quoted by Mascall (1977), p. 164.
[7] Mascall (1977), p. 164. Galot did in fact adopt this usage to some extent in Galot (1980), pp. 283 ff.

'In the sense in which the word 'person' is commonly used today—that
is, as the psychological centre of subjective experience—the 'person' of
Jesus Christ as an historical figure, in his manhood, must necessarily be
human. To think of his 'person', in this sense, as divine would be equivalent
to saying, with Apollinarius, that the normal human centre of consciousness,
the psychological ego, was replaced by the divine Word. If that were so,
our Lord would not be truly human at all ... Interpretations of Jesus Christ
as one in whom *God* is the sole 'experiencing' centre are not only absurdly
untrue to the actual remembered historical picture of our Lord in the Gospels but also tend to be (and usually are) heretical in terms of classical
christological formulations.[8]

The objection is evidently twofold: theories like Galot's (Pittenger
probably had in mind those of Relton[9] and Davenport[10]) make
God, not a man, the sole experiencing centre of Jesus' life, and
in so doing make nonsense of the Gospel picture of Jesus; and by
denying that He had a human ego they are Apollinarian. But while
the former accusation may perhaps have been justified against
Relton and Davenport, it is not justified against Galot (as far as
Mascall's quotations from him go at least). To say that the Word
became the ego of Jesus' manhood[11] is to suggest that, say, the
tiredness felt at the well of Samaria[12] was, so to speak, a minor
adjunct to the thoughts of the eternal Logos, as closely related to
them as to the thirst Jesus felt at the same time. But Galot's words
are that 'there is human consciousness of a divine ego'. It is not
the Word but the *ego* of the Word that 'has' Jesus' experiences,
and I do not see that this in any way goes against the picture given
to us in the Gospels. The Gospels make it clear that our Lord's
earthly experiences were human ones; they do not say that they
were not in some fashion linked with those of the Logos (e.g. by
centring in the same ego).

The second part of Pittenger's criticism is more serious. Does
not the idea of an ego which is not human imply, not perhaps
Apollinarianism (for that said much more than just the ego was
superhuman), but at least the same mistake as Apollinarius made?
This really depends on what meaning we are giving to the word
'ego'. In the Freudian sense, clearly any human being will have

---

[8] Pittenger (1959), p. 114.   [9] Relton (1917).   [10] Davenport (1925).
[11] Davenport, (1925), p. 249.   [12] John 4: 6.

a human ego, and the notion of a divine one is in itself absurd, let alone that of a human being having a divine one. But of course neither Galot nor Pittenger means any such thing. Pittenger's own definition is 'the conscious subject of [subjective] experiences, a subject which is distinct from yet in close relationship with other subjects ... the organizing centre of the totality of experiences; it is the "self"'. But', he goes on, 'the emphasis seems to be placed on the awareness of the "self" and its capacity through that knowledge to direct the activities of the system.'[13] (It is not clear whether he means the awareness the 'self' has of other things, as might be supposed from the connection with 'directing the activities of the system', or the awareness it has of itself, which is suggested by a reference in the next sentence to 'self-consciousness'.)

Now if the ego, person, *moi*, or self is defined in this way, with a multiple capacity, as subject of experiences, related to other subjects, organizing centre and director of activities, Pittenger is right. The thing described is part, and a large part, of the human soul, and if it was missing from the human aspect of Christ, that aspect, and His humanity, were incomplete; not as incomplete as Apollinarius supposed, but still 'heretical in terms of classical Christological formulations'. How exactly Galot understands the term I am not sure. He begins with the use of the word 'person' or 'hypostasis' in Western Trinitarian theology, where the Persons of the Divine Trinity are distinct from one another through their relations to one another, and sees the human person as an imperfect version of the same idea; 'a person only exists as a relation to other persons ... an "ego" (*moi*) has meaning only in its relation with other "egos"'.[14] But he also regards it as that which is 'incommunicable' about me, that is, that which (unlike my height, weight, IQ, political opinions, and so on) I cannot have in common with anyone or anything else.[15] '[Jesus'] "I" remains exclusively his own.'[16] Now I find the first part of this rather hard to assess. The idea that a person only is a person in relation to others is one familiar in philosophy, especially perhaps Idealist philosophy, though the 'others', it has usually been thought, need not necessarily be other *persons*.

[13] Pittenger (1959), p. 112. Strictly speaking, he is defining 'person', but as we have seen, this is taken as equivalent to 'ego'.

[14] Galot (1969), pp. 42ff., cited by Mascall (1977), p. 155. Similarly also in Galot (1980), pp. 283ff.

[15] Mascall (1977) p. 155.   [16] Galot (1980), p. 333.

'We only realize our personality in so far as our consciousness has a content—a manifold to which the centre is formed by that I, awareness of which constitutes personality. And this content of consciousness involves for us the recognition of an Other.'[17] We may accept that an ego (whether Jesus' or anyone else's) requires relationships to something not the ego. But this is hardly enlightening to the Christologist; no picture of Christ, orthodox or unorthodox, has ever denied that He was in various ways related to things and persons other than Himself.

The other half, though (the ego as that which is 'incommunicable'), has interesting possibilities. It is an appeal, in effect, to the idea of a 'substance' distinct from its attributes. It has often been held that metaphysical analysis of anything will show that it has certain attributes which it has in common with other objects (or could in theory have in common with them even if in fact it is unique) and an 'underlying' element or 'substance' which is peculiar to it, which indeed *is* it. For instance, I am six feet two inches tall; well, many thousands of other things are too. I am a human being—millions have that attribute. I bear the name 'Richard Lyman Sturch'; it is probable that no one else has ever borne that name besides myself, but there is no reason why they shouldn't. But no one can be identical with me except myself.

Many philosophers would reject the idea of 'substance' in this sense as unnecessary. 'Retaining "things"', wrote Bertrand Russell, 'does not enable us to dispense with qualities, while bundles of qualities fulfil all the functions for which "things" are supposed to be needed.'[18] Now this may well be the case; it may well be that not all groupings of qualities must have some centre to hold them together. But a very strong case can be made out for saying that even if Russell and those who agree with him are right, such a centre is required for any consciousness, whether human or of some other kind: not indeed a centre of *attributes*, but one of *experiences* and *actions*. The case in question derives largely from Kant, and it is of interest that when Temple was trying to find some modern equivalent for the Greek ὑπόστασις, he suggested that the nearest might be Kant's 'analytic unity of apperception'.[19]

The first argument for this position may be very briefly summar-

---

[17] McTaggart (1906), p. 204.   [18] In Schilpp (1944), p. 697.
[19] Temple (1924), p. 136.

ized as follows:[20] If I, or any other conscious being, am aware
of two or more related things, then it must be the same 'I' who
am aware of both. Otherwise I could not be aware of the two as
related to one another. In a consciousness which had no unifying
centre of awareness, two sensations—let us say, seeing a clock and
hearing it strike—might indeed occur together, but there could be
no realization that they were there in the same consciousness, even
if they actually were. We might, of course, point out in reply that
a third sensation is also involved in such cases, namely, the sensation
of 'being aware that the two are together in the same consciousness'.
But this is itself part of my experiences; how can we use it to unite
the others unless it is itself united to *them*, presumably by a fourth
sensation and so on for ever? Indeed, does not the idea of 'being
in the same consciousness' already presuppose something like an
'I'? If someone else, God perhaps, is surveying all my thoughts and
sensations, He may be aware that they all form part of a single
stream distinct from those of other creatures, for His own sensations
are outside the 'stream'. Can *I* know they form a single stream
unless there is some element in my awareness which is *not* a sensation,
so that it too is no part of the stream? God sees all my thoughts
as parts of the same object; I am aware of them as the thoughts
of the same *subject*. Even, then, if we reject the substance/attribute
analysis of things in general, we need something very like it, a sub-
stance/sensation analysis, to account for the unity of experiences
in one conscious subject.

A second argument, related to this, was advanced by McTaggart.[21]
If I know that I am aware of X, I must know what the word
'I' means here. Of course in ordinary circumstances we learn
how to use the word 'I' quite properly without any metaphysical
speculation. But in a special case like this introspective one we can
only justify using the word if it refers to something which we are
directly acquainted with.

I am not too sure of this argument. The obvious reply, that 'I'
here refers to the set of thoughts and sensations associated with
the speaker's body (or, to put it more crudely, to the speaker him-
or herself), McTaggart rejected on the grounds that many people
can say 'I am aware of X' without any beliefs about the relationship

---

[20] For a fuller version, see Campbell (1957), pp. 75ff.
[21] McTaggart (1934), pp.72ff. I should add that McTaggart's view of what constituted the 'self' was not that taken here.

between mind and body. But is any explicit belief required? We know that our minds and bodies are intimately linked, even if we do not know (nor even have beliefs about) *how*. I think McTaggart was probably right, but am by no means as convinced by him as I am by the preceding argument, or by the one that follows.

This third argument pointing in the same direction can be derived from our sense of personal identity. It is common to suppose that a person X is identical with a person Y if and only if there is bodily continuity between them: for instance, Queen Elizabeth II is identical with the Princess Elizabeth of York alive in 1934 because there is a continuous history of a human body between the one and the other. Alternatively, it has been suggested that *memory* can provide an adequate link: X is identical with Y if X can remember events from Y's past (from Y's point of view, naturally). For instance, claims about reincarnation are sometimes made on the basis of alleged rememberings of events in a dead person's life. But there are times when we are aware of *neither* of these, and yet are aware of ourselves. In a dream, I may not recall anything from my waking life, and certainly I am not aware of my body at all, yet I am surely aware of being *me*, of my own being and identity; it is not some other person who has the dream. The most natural explanation of this is that there is a 'centre of consciousness', an 'ego', which can be aware of itself, though it need not be so at all times, nor need the awareness always be explicit.

Now if there was only one such ego in the Incarnate Lord, the requirement that 'human experience as conditioned by the sin of man should become the personal experience of God the Son—not an object of external observation but one of internal feeling' is clearly fulfilled. The 'self' who undergoes the joys and pains of Jesus of Nazareth, who *is* Jesus of Nazareth, is also the 'self' of God the Son.

The first and most obvious objection to this is that, once again, we are back with the error of Apollinarianism. Something is missing from Jesus' humanity. (As we saw, Pittenger raised just this objection.) But this is mistaken. If the human 'centre' is, as we have described it, that which 'has' all a human being's experiences (in the widest possible sense, and including acts of will, desires, and so on), then the expression 'A human centre' does not mean 'A centre of the particular type we call "human"', which can be distinguished in itself from centres which are centres of other kinds of conscious beings' but 'A centre with human experiences inhering in it, a centre which belongs to a human being'. (The centre of a square in no way differs from the centre of a circle as far as its own nature is concerned; it is what surrounds it that is different.) Similarly, a 'divine centre' is the centre of divine experiences (if 'experiences' is the right word to use of God—if not, of whatever is analogous in the divine life to human experiences in ours). We might illustrate the position being advocated here by a diagram of two separate squares which touch one another at a corner. The geometrical point at which they meet is a corner of both squares, yet neither square lacks any necessary feature, nor would it cease to do so if the other square vanished. We cannot say that the 'human' square is in some way incomplete, nor for that matter that the 'divine' one is. Such a view, then, is not Apollinarian, nor open to the objections to which Apollinarianism was open.

A second and more formidable objection is that we are staking everything on a metaphysical theory, and one, at that, which is by no means universally held. There may be all sorts of defects in this theory—indeed, most contemporary philosophers think that there *are*; and yet are we not coming close to saying that Christianity stands or falls by it? This is folly, and more than folly; the gospel cannot depend on any piece of human philosophizing.

This is so. And in fact a similar analysis of the Union could probably be constructed without depending on this particular metaphysical theory. Suppose for the sake of argument that the unity of an experiencing subject is not after all to be conceived of in terms of a *moi* or substantival self. Suppose that my awareness of two or more sensations, and of myself, can be explained without it: that all there is in such cases is another awareness by the side of the normal ones, and that the experiencing subject can say 'I experience both X and Y, and I am aware of my own identity as a person' although there is no 'ego' for which this word 'I' is a label, or which constitutes this personal identity.

All this applies, of course, to Jesus of Nazareth, who was an 'experiencing subject' like other men and women. It also applies, we may presume, to God the Son, although certainly His 'experiences' must be very different from ours. (If it does *not* apply to God the Son—if He, unlike us, does have a central self or *moi*—then there is no real problem; that central self has both the divine experiences and the human ones in the same way as suggested earlier, except that our smaller, human square had better be a circle now, with no corners, as humans do not have the 'central self' the corner represented.) In that case, we need only say that besides the human awareness 'I experience X and Y', which Jesus has like the rest of us, there is also a divine awareness 'I experience X and Y and also P and Q', where P and Q stand for experiences of God the Son. X and Y (the experiences of the Passion, for example) then form part both of Jesus' life and of the life of God the Son, but the human life does not include an awareness of this fact, although the divine life does. (Of course, this holds good on the 'substantival self' theory as well—on that theory God the Son is aware that X and Y are His own experiences, even though Jesus of Nazareth is not aware that P and Q are *His*. The point is that it can be held without that theory.) There is the same unifying factor in the life of the Incarnate Word as there is in yours and mine. We may therefore have a substitute for the πρόσωπον type of unity, which we wondered earlier might be found: the unity lies in the awareness on the part of the Word that the life of Jesus is His, the Word's, life (which, as I said, is the same kind of unity as your and my lives have too), and this may properly be described as a unity lying outside the two elements that are united, in that without the Incarnation no such awareness would ever have existed. At the same time, it ensures that Jesus' experiences are the Word's, as truly as mine are mine.

Why then drag in the 'central self' at all? First, because I think this theory is in fact *true*, and I should prefer to express an analytic Christology in terms of a metaphysic I believe in rather than one I don't. Secondly, because I think the 'central self' theory may have advantages for when we try to link our Christology to our understanding of the Trinity, though I am far from certain about this. (See Excursus II.) And thirdly, because I think it enables us to avoid certain difficulties which have been raised over another presentation of a 'two minds' Christology, that of Dr Thomas V. Morris.[22]

Morris holds that there is an 'asymmetric accessing relation' between the two minds. 'The divine mind had full and direct access to the earthly, human experience resulting from the Incarnation, but the earthly consciousness did not have such full and direct access to the content of the overarching omniscience of the Logos, but

---

[22] Morris (1986), pp. 102 ff.

only such access, on occasion, as the divine mind allowed it to have.'
But this sort of 'accessing' holds of us all; God is He to whom
all hearts are open. And of course He can reveal any contents of
His omniscience to anyone He chooses. What, then, does the unique
nature of the Incarnation amount to? Morris eventually decides
that it amounts to this: that Jesus did not have 'a personal set of
cognitive and causal powers distinct from [those] of God the Son.'[23]
But this is getting very close to Monothelitism (which Morris has
already very properly rejected in his discussion of the Temptation[24]).

What a 'central self' theory gives us, and Morris's, similar though
it is, does not, is an awareness on the part of the Logos (and perhaps
at times on that of the earthly Jesus: more of this later on) that
the human life 'accessed' is *His own*. We might imagine a human
telepath (to take an illustration of Morris's own) having access to
the thoughts, volitions, etc. of another person; but they would not
be his own. Nor would they *seem* his own; he would not think
'I am seeing a tray of cheeses; I am choosing a piece of Sage Derby',
but '*So-and-so* is seeing a tray of cheeses; *she* is choosing a piece
of Sage Derby.' Whereas, on the theory we have been working out,
the eternal Logos is aware that the thoughts, etc. of Jesus the Nazarene are His own. Jesus' human, bodily causal powers, however,
are not those of the Logos, except at one remove, in that they are
those of the man with whom the Logos is one.

A third objection to the kind of view advocated here has been
raised by Mr A. N. S. Lane.[25] It does not strike him as Apollinarian
so much as embarrassingly close to Nestorian (though not, he agrees,
actually *becoming* Nestorian). It separates the two natures, he
argues, in a way that Leo, for one, would not have approved, and
runs contrary to Chalcedon's 'without division, without separation'.
As far as Leo is concerned, I must admit he is right. We cannot,
if the unity of our Lord's person is to be found in the 'central self',
say that He wept over Lazarus as man but raised him as God; both
were the acts of a man, though of one who was one with God
the Son. But I am not convinced that this is to separate and divide

---

[23] pp. 161ff.
[24] pp. 150ff. For an interesting criticism of Morris's book, see Hick (1989). So
far as I can tell, the points raised by Hick do not affect the position taken in the
present work.
[25] 'Christology beyond Chalcedon', in Rowdon (1982), pp. 278–9.

the natures, any more than Leo's distinction is. The one Logos remains the subject of all that either nature does or undergoes, and in addition is in His divine life fully aware of all that is happening in the human life, and that it is *His own life*. This is distinction, if you like, but not division or separation.

Objection number four, again in terms of 'classical Christological formulations', would perhaps be this: According to Chalcedon, Christ was in two natures, the human and the divine. Now a 'nature' is a combination of attributes. But we have rejected the idea that attributes must be united in a single underlying 'substance'; the 'central self' we have been advocating unites thoughts and experiences, not attributes. The divine attributes of the Logos and the human ones of the Carpenter are not therefore united by our 'centre', so that the two natures are separated after all. This is no objection really. It is not required of Christological analysis that it should find some element that unites the two natures directly and immediately; as we saw earlier, it is an error to begin from the two natures. Provided that God and man are united in one Christ, the two natures are automatically united as well. Any being which is God partakes of the divine nature, and any being which is a man or woman partakes of human nature, by definition; that is what a 'nature' is. The natures are united because Jesus is both divine and human, not vice versa.

Bishop Montefiore, in his contribution to the symposium *Soundings*,[26] wanted to eliminate the concept of 'nature' from Christology altogether, and of course if he was right we need not have raised this last objection at all; but I think he was mistaken. He argued that we do not know what either divine or human nature truly is. 'The nature of God is beyond our human comprehension', he wrote, truly enough, adding 'If we had really known the nature of God, there would have been no need of an Incarnation to reveal Him to us.' (Significantly, Montefiore, who advocated a 'functional' Christology, overlooked here the possibility of other reasons for Incarnation besides revelation.) As for man, no absolute line can be drawn between him and the higher mammals, nor can we know his future potentialities. Even if we set these points aside (reasonably enough, seeing that the Jesus of whom we speak was neither *Australopithecus* nor some being from the remote future of science fiction)

---

[26] In Vidler (1962), pp. 153ff.

we are unable to define what constitutes human nature *now*. And of course this is true.

But the mere fact that we cannot *define* human nature, or divine, does not mean that we cannot speak of it. We cannot define 'man' or 'God', if by that is meant specifying all the qualities that are essential for a being to be man or God; yet we speak of them. (So does Montefiore.) Why not also of their 'natures'? Human nature consists of those qualities or disjunctions of qualities which are had by all men and women and are had in their entirety by nothing else; and similarly with divine nature. Whether we can specify what all these qualities are is beside the point. And orthodoxy says that the Incarnate Lord had both sets, which, if the unity of the 'central self' is the key, was in fact the case.

Here we come to yet another objection. Apollinarius agreed that Jesus Christ had a human body, but not that He had a human soul; have we not come close to the reverse position? We have not indeed denied that Jesus had a human body—of course He did—but we have treated it as irrelevant; our proposed unity is a unity of mind or spirit, described in terms of thoughts and experiences alone, and makes no mention of the 'holy and glorious flesh'.

I am bound to say that I can see no way to meet this objection except by admitting it, and holding that our Lord's body was united to the Godhead not directly but by way of His human soul or mind animating it.[27] This runs contrary to (for example) the tradition that the body of Jesus in the tomb was still united to the Godhead; on our showing it was not, but was reunited to the Godhead at the Resurrection. But I do not myself feel this objection to be fatal. It implies indeed that for a short time our Lord's humanity was incomplete, but only in the same sense that all human beings who have died so far have incomplete humanities; He was consubstantial with us in this also. We need not be seriously bothered by this argument.

Objection six: even as far as the spiritual or immaterial side of our Lord's humanity is concerned, is not the unity proposed inadequate? Even my mental life is more than a centre plus a series of experiences. Have we not overlooked the *will*? Or, if we answer that though the will does not consist of experiences alone, it includes them (I can hardly do a voluntary act without knowing it!), are

[27] So e.g. Aquinas, *Summa Theologiae*, 3, q. 6, art. 2.

we not still dealing only with the surface of the mind? Thus we find Moore writing: 'The concept of the "self" as distinct from the ego, the concept of an identity incomparably wider and deeper than the one I live with, is indispensable for a modern Christology. The union of the person with Christ cannot be adequately conceived if we ignore those hints that come . . . of an altogether larger self.'[28] Again, what of the 'unconscious'? Sanday's famous attempt to understand the Incarnation in terms of the 'subliminal conscious ness'[29] failed, no doubt, but can we eliminate the 'subliminal' altogether? If we do, are we not back—it is becoming a little monotonous—at a new form of Apollinarianism? Does not the unconscious need redeeming too?

It does, unless (as some, such as Freud, have thought) the unconscious is basically a matter of brain processes. If it is, then presumably it is redeemed along with the body. But in so far as it is not, it is surely causally connected with conscious mental events, and if these are normal and human in Jesus, so is His unconscious, which, like His body, is united to the Godhead by these. The 'wider and deeper' identity of which Moore speaks is an identity within the human nature of our Lord: body, conscious mind, 'larger self', unconscious, all are linked to one another in Him in the same way as they are in the rest of us, but there is *also* the link to the Godhead by way of that which constitutes the unity of the conscious self, which conscious self is far from being the whole person, and yet is the crucial part of the person without which the rest are a mere jumble.

So far, then, the current suggestion seems to have held its own. But the last objection is the most serious of all. If the central self of Jesus is one and the same with that of God the Son, then the requirements of Atonement are probably satisfied. But what of the requirements of Revelation? If all the acts of Jesus, bodily and mental, are purely human, does the mere fact that the central self to which they are linked is also that of God the Son make them a revelation of God? We have only half our 'two-way traffic' after all; we need some form of causal link whereby the Godhead affects the deeds of the Man, and the idea of a 'substantival self' provides no such connection. We have committed the exact reverse of the Antiochene error; in anxiety to maintain that 'the Word of God

---

[28] Moore (1980), p. 135.   [29] Sanday (1910), p. 159.

suffered in the flesh' we have provided no way by which the Word might be *active* in the flesh as well.

There must therefore be, as we knew might be possible, *two* kinds of link joining God and man in Jesus Christ; or of course more than two. That which we have been discussing, identity of central self, I believe to be one; but there must be at least one other besides that. And here some of the ideas which we have been criticizing as inadequate *total* Christologies may well come back into their own, and take a place in our understanding of the Lord's Person and Work: ideas of a functional Christology; ideas of revelation or grace as keys or models for our understanding; ideas of Jesus as inspired like prophets and saints only in greater degree; and the like. But here we run up against a problem. Such ideas have usually been designed as accounts of the union between the Word and Jesus of Nazareth. As such they were inadequate; but as accounts of God's *action* in Jesus we may wonder whether they need to be, or should be, expressed in terms of God the Word at all. Christ's ministry, the time above all when God was active in Him, began at His Baptism; and at that Baptism, while it is false to say with some early heretics that the Word came on Him then, it is true to say that the Holy Spirit did. And the first public words of Jesus that St Luke records after that Baptism are a taking to Himself of the opening of Isaiah 61, 'The Spirit of the Lord is upon me',[30] while St Peter could tell Cornelius that God 'anointed Jesus with the Holy Spirit and with power'.[31] Should we not see this side of Christology in terms of the Third Person of the Holy Trinity rather than the Second?

This point was raised after a fashion in the patristic period; oddly enough, it was the Antiochenes of those days who emphasized the Spirit's part in the work of Christ, while their modern successors do so far less.[32] Cyril's ninth anathema singled out anyone who said 'that the one Lord Jesus Christ was glorified by the Holy Spirit, so that he used through him a power not his own and from him received power against evil spirits', insisting rather that 'it was his own spirit' (or 'Spirit'?) 'through which he worked these divine

---

[30] Luke 4: 17–21.   [31] Acts 10: 38.
[32] An exception is the late Professor G. W. H. Lampe (see 'The Holy Spirit and the Work of Christ', in Sykes and Clayton (1972), pp. 111–30, and his Bampton Lectures, *God as Spirit* (Lampe (1977)). But Lampe was so to speak forced into this position by his wish to abandon the doctrine of the Trinity completely.

signs'. Nestorius' counter-anathema was against anyone who said that 'the form of a servant' (that is, our Lord as man) 'is of like nature with the Holy Spirit, and not rather that it owes its union with the Word, which has existed since the conception, to his mediation, by which it works miraculous healings among men'; and his ally Theodoret listed a whole string of references to the part played by the Holy Spirit in the life of Jesus. This was so obviously right that Cyril had to give way a little and explain that 'an anathema is called for, not against those who say that Jesus was glorified by the Holy Spirit, but rather against those who shamelessly say that he used the power of the Spirit as one might use the power of another person (ὡς ἀλλοτρίωι δυνάμει)'.[33]

I say the point was raised 'after a fashion', because the Fathers seem to have been thinking almost entirely about one aspect of our Lord's ministry, the miracles. (Theodoret himself evidently thought that as far as *knowledge* was concerned it was the Word, not the Spirit, who inspired Jesus: He 'knew as much as the indwelling Godhead revealed'[34]). But the New Testament does not so limit the Spirit's work in Christ (cf. e.g. Luke 4: 1, John 3: 34); nor need we. If the Holy Spirit spoke through the prophets, we may also suppose that He spoke through the prophet Jesus of Nazareth in Galilee, being source alike of divine power, divine knowledge, and divine revelation.

Now if this is joined with what we were saying earlier of the identity of the central self in God the Son and in Jesus, it seems to me that we do have a Christology which allows for both Revelation and Atonement; which takes into account the biblical linking of our Lord's work both with the Word and with the Spirit, and which is, I think, quite compatible (if that be desired) with Chalcedon—as indeed with such post-Chalcedonian developments as *an-* and *enhypostasia*. The 'experiencing centre' of Jesus did not have to be specially created at the time of the Incarnation, because it already existed as that of the Logos. If this centre can then be taken as corresponding to the ὑπόστασις of the Fathers,[35] then the humanity of our Lord was anhypostatic 'in itself', but not in reality; it did not lack a centre or ὑπόστασις, all it lacked was one peculiar

---

[33] See PG 76, 433a, or Wace and Schaff (1890), pp. 214–15.
[34] Quoted by Sellers (1940), p. 146.
[35] See below, Excursus VI.

to itself. This, I think, is where Pannenberg goes wrong in his criticism of 'ego' theories of the Incarnation.[36] If the Dyothelite decision of 681 is followed, he argues, 'one probably would have to speak of a divine ego and a human ego side by side, since will (and consciousness) are not conceivable apart from an ego centre'. They are not. To this extent Pannenberg is correct. But the question is whether they need to have *separate and distinct* 'ego centres'. A square (to revert to our geometrical parable) is not conceivable without corners; yet as we saw two squares may *share* a corner and still remain two: two squares, though a single geometrical figure.

The idea of two consciousnesses in Christ has seemed highly objectionable to many. 'We cannot predicate of Him two consciousnesses or two wills', wrote Mackintosh, in words already quoted: 'the New Testament indicates nothing of the kind, nor indeed is it congruous with an intelligible psychology'.[37] Forsyth had said much the same a few years earlier, denying that we could have 'two streams parallel while unmingled'; 'There could not be two wills, or two consciousnesses, in the same personality, by any psychological possibility now credible'.[38] Yet others had accepted it without much trouble, from the time of the *'extra Calvinisticum'* onwards at least. Thus (to go no further back than the nineteenth century) Liddon, in his once celebrated *Divinity of our Lord*,[39] could write that 'His Single Personality has two spheres of existence; in the one It is all-blessed, undying and omniscient; in the other It meets with pain of mind and body, with actual death, and with a correspondent liability to a limitation of knowledge'. In Denmark, Bishop Martensen (best known nowadays as the first target of Kierkegaard's *Attack upon Christendom*) wrote similarly: 'The Son of God leads in the economy of the Father a twofold existence ... He lives a double life in His world-creating and His world-completing activity'.[40] And Gore, in support of Martensen, went so far as to say that 'the personal life of the Word [was] lived as it were from more than one centre'.[41] This was the wrong way round; we need only one centre (and perhaps

[36] Pannenberg (1968), pp. 329–30.
[37] Mackintosh (1913), p. 470. Cf. Schoonenberg (1972), pp. 69–70.
[38] Forsyth (1909), p. 319.
[39] Liddon (1891), p. 472. This passage is not, I think, typical of Liddon's usual approach.
[40] Martensen (1874), p. 277.   [41] Gore (1895), p. 215.

two personal lives!); but a 'twofold existence' does seem to be implied, and in its turn to imply a twofold consciousness.

I think the difficulty some people have had over this has arisen largely, perhaps entirely, because of one of the less fortunate legacies of the patristic period. Many Fathers tended to say that Jesus acted now as man and now as God: that, to take an instance cited earlier, He wept at Lazarus' tomb as man but called him out of it as God. This certainly suggested that the human personality of Jesus was at intervals interrupted by the divine—almost that He alternated between a divine life and a human. Since the same Fathers also held that there were in Christ two natures, human and divine, and since this was later held (correctly) to imply two wills, human and divine, it was easy to suppose that these expressed the 'alternating personality' idea, which I entirely agree is in no way supported by Scripture. Jesus was not a pathological 'split personality'! But this is not what Chalcedon said; nor is it implied by what it did say, even if those who drew up its formulae might have agreed with it. The divine nature remains distinct from the human, and epithets applicable to one are only applied to the other by a special way of speaking, the *communicatio idiomatum*. The will and consciousness of God the Son were those of the same person (πρόσωπον and ὑπόστασις) as those of the first-century Jewish carpenter, but they were not, so to speak, present in His human brain. Jesus wept over Lazarus' tomb and raised him from it as a human being, though one empowered by, and in fact one with, God. There *are* two wills and two consciousnesses, but in the whole πρόσωπον, not in either of its two component parts; in each of these there is but one will and one consciousness, though the human ones were guided and enlightened by the Holy Spirit, and the divine knows all that passes in the human life as its own. Weston's objection to some kenotic theories, that 'they require two centres of activity in the lower state: a centre of His self-abandonment and a centre of His divine-human or human activities once the self-abandonment has taken place'[42] raises in effect the point I am trying to make, though in terms of 'activity' rather than 'consciousness'; if there is a double activity (or consciousness) in the *lower* state, that is, in Jesus of Nazareth, then we do indeed run into intolerable difficulties. But a double activity in the whole Person, God and Man (which is all Liddon

---

[42] Weston (1907), p. 158.

and Martensen at least were saying), has no particular difficulties. 'Incarnational Christology', as Brian Hebblethwaite rightly says, 'attributes two consciousnesses, not to Jesus, but to God incarnate'.[43]

[43] Goulder (1979), p. 90.

The Charge of Obsolescence Discussed

WE turn now to consider the objections to traditional Christology which were raised in the earlier parts of the book. Will this development of our own analysis enable us to meet them, or are they still valid? In the latter case we should have either to start looking again for a better analysis or to agree that the choice lies between a revisionist Christology and none at all.

The first objection, it may be recalled, was that the vocabulary used in traditional formulae like that of the Thirty-Nine Articles or Chalcedon was obsolete: 'nature' and 'person' were indeed still in use as words, but not in the sense in which the Fathers or even the Reformers used them.

As far as 'person' goes, this is correct. We should nowadays use this word to refer to the human Jesus considered simply as a human being, or possibly to God the Son considered simply as one Person of the Trinity (and there are quite a number of problems *there*!). It was partly because of this that I avoided using the word in propounding my own views, and tried to confine its use to places where I was reporting the views of others. For of course if an orthodox Christology can be devised which does not use the word 'person', then the fact that the word 'person' has changed its meaning is interesting but irrelevant.

I am not at all sure that the same applies to 'nature'. This is a word still used in much the same sense as Chalcedon used it. 'You can't change human nature' may be a foolish saying or a wise one, but it is perfectly intelligible, and it certainly uses 'nature' to refer to that which human beings have in common. 'Divine and human nature', as Schoonenberg says, 'quite simply indicate everything pertaining respectively to the divine and the human, by which Jesus is one in being respectively with the Father and with us.'[1]

[1] Schoonenberg (1972), p. 62.

However, this too can be avoided, and in the constructive section of this book it was avoided as far as convenient. Indeed, it is normal to avoid it; it is not often that the ordinary usage of the Church includes the word (though the Prayer Book Collect for Christmas Day is an instance to the contrary). We say that Jesus is truly God and truly Man, rather than use the more abstract way of saying exactly the same thing, namely that in Him God's nature and ours are joined. Abstractions like 'nature' do serve a useful purpose, but only from time to time; they are normally used when a contrast is needed with some other abstraction. Thus we may contrast 'nature' and 'nurture', or, as at Chalcedon, a nature with that which is *of* that nature ('person' or 'hypostasis'). The word is not, therefore, all that common; but it exists, and it is not obsolete.

It will be best to take the charges of obsolescence in ideas as a unity, since our reply will apply equally well where the ideas are embodied in an old-fashioned vocabulary and where they are not. There are various ways in which an idea or a theory may become obsolete. The first and most obvious is by *new discovery*. Concepts like 'phlogiston', 'luminiferous ether', 'animal spirits', and 'caloric', which once figured in scientific treatises, do so no longer; new discoveries have made them useless. The concept of the luminiferous ether suggested that the speed of the earth through space should be calculable by measuring the difference in the time light took to travel a distance in line with the earth's motion and across it; when it was discovered that there was no such difference, theories had to be devised which did without the ether.

Rather similar would be obsolescence because of a *shift in ethical ideas*. A famous theological instance would be Anselm's 'feudal' idea of sin and atonement, in which a central idea is the infringing of God's honour. 'Nothing is more intolerable than that a creature should deprive his Creator of due honour, and not repay that of which he deprives Him'.[2] I will not say that notions of infringed honour have totally disappeared, but they are certainly far less important than they were in Anselm's day, and to have a whole understanding of the nature of sin or of the Atonement based on them would be impossible today. And if the ethical shift is in the right direction, this is of course very similar indeed to obsolescence by new discovery.

[2] *Cur Deus Homo*, I. 13.

A third is by *literal unintelligibility*, where it is quite simply no longer possible to know what the original ideas were. This is most likely to occur where there is an actual change of language. We do not at present understand the Etruscan language (as far as I know); we therefore cannot understand any ideas expressed in it. But of course the same kind of unintelligibility arises whenever there is a specialized terminology belonging to a particular science or other discipline (I should not, for example, be able to understand a paper in topology or biophysics); and this can also happen with a religious terminology (I do not understand much of what is said in such Taoist writings as I have come across, and doubtless many Taoists would find equal difficulty with many Christian writings). Hence it may happen that a religious terminology becomes obsolete because, quite literally, no one remembers what it meant.

Now none of these apply to traditional Christology. It is clearly not true that we have forgotten the meaning of the words used, or that moral changes have affected their plausibility. It might, however, be thought that scientific progress has rendered 'nature' obsolete. It has certainly removed its function as a scientific term. A 'nature' in Aristotelian thought (which was not necessarily that of the early Church) was something from which the behaviour of an object having that nature might be inferred; it was the nature of earth to move downwards, for instance, and that of fire to move up. Undoubtedly this sort of thinking is out of date. But 'nature' as in 'human nature'—that is, the qualities or disjunctions of qualities that all normal human beings have in common—remains a perfectly useful term, almost unaffected by the passage of the years.

However, there are other methods of obsolescence which may look more relevant. An idea may become dated because we tend to ask different questions or use a different conceptual framework from that used by those among whom the idea was current. St Thomas Aquinas devotes a section of the *Summa Theologiae* to the question 'Was Christ's priesthood after the order of Melchizedek?'[3] This is a question it is hard to imagine a present-day theologian raising (though one might easily discuss the question 'What did the writer to the Hebrews mean by calling Christ a priest "after the order of Melchizedek"?'). Indeed, Aquinas also provides a good example of a great theologian who used a strikingly different concep-

---

[3] *Summa Theologiae*, 3, q. 22, 6.

tual framework from that of most people today. It needs a good deal of mental effort (not to mention study) for most of us to understand what he is getting at in some parts of his writings; and, more dangerous still, we may *think* we have understood what he is getting at when really we haven't.

But though an idea may become dated in this way, that does not of itself mean that it is valueless. The fact that we do not ask a particular question does not mean that the question cannot be, or ought not to be, asked. Suppose we have established precisely what the author of Hebrews meant by 'a high priest after the order of Melchizedek'; it still remains possible that he or she was right to call Jesus such a high priest, and possible that he or she was wrong. A question very much to the same effect as Aquinas' (though not identical) remains to be answered. Similarly, it may be that few people today would raise questions like 'Was Jesus consubstantial with the Father and with us?' (although the continuing Christological debate suggests otherwise); still, this does not mean that the question is meaningless, nor that it cannot be answered, nor that the traditional answer 'Yes' is mistaken. If, then, as was suggested in Chapter 1, no replacements have arisen for words like 'person' and 'nature', this may well be because we do not often ask quite the same questions as people did in the sixth century, or the sixteenth; but this does not mean that the words, or the answers that used them, are worthless.

Conceptual frameworks are a different matter. It could be that some conceptual frameworks are positively *mistaken*, and that an idea dependent on them is therefore useless. I think this is indeed the case. But it is not at all easy to show that a given metaphysic or other framework is mistaken, and certainly the mere fact that it is not widely believed today is not enough. So obsolescence caused by a mistaken conceptual framework is an undeniable possibility, but exceedingly hard to prove. In any case, it is hardly our concern here: for we are not dealing with ideas inextricably bound up with a given framework, except the framework of theism. The Incarnation can be, and has been, believed in by people with an immense variety of such frameworks; it is not obsolete unless all of them are—if then.

What I suspect is often meant by 'obsolete' is 'unfashionable'. This comes out very clearly in the arguments quoted from Wiles and Cupitt in Chapter 1. Wiles realizes that the fact that the idea of a divine intervention was more of a natural category of thought in the first century than it is today[4] does not disprove the idea of the Incarnation. But unless there is reason to think it is a *mistaken* category of thought, its unpopularity today does not justify *any- thing*. The most it does is make it psychologically easier to doubt the Incarnation—and this should if anything be a reason for even greater caution before venturing to doubt it, as we realize the possibi- lity of our being biased. Wiles thinks that the shift in thought makes it necessary to raise the question 'Is Christianity separable from the idea of the Incarnation?' If by this he had meant 'People believe in divine intervention less readily than they used to; in order to keep them from thinking inaccurately in spite of this unfortunate mental block, it is necessary for Christians to show them (what previous generations took for granted) that Christianity cannot be separated from the idea of the Incarnation', he would have been justified. The same might hold if what he meant was 'We must see if we can have Christianity without the Incarnation, because perhaps that way we shall be able to persuade people to be Christians who would otherwise be put off by their mental blocks'. But neither of these is what he means. What he seems to be saying is more like this: 'People believe in divine intervention less readily than they used to; it is, therefore, necessary to see whether we can separate Christianity in our own thought from the specific form of divine intervention we call the Incarnation.' And this is a *non sequitur.* The question of separating Christianity from Incarnation can be raised as soon as it is seen to be logically possible that God does not intervene in the world, or indeed sooner; for perhaps He does intervene, but not in this particular way, as Jews and Muslims would in fact believe. It can only be said to have become necessary now- adays either because we are concerned with apologetics, as suggested above, or because we ourselves disbelieve in divine intervention, and are therefore driven to wonder whether we can or cannot go on calling ourselves Christians in spite of this. The latter is, of course, the position Wiles is in; for him it genuinely is necessary to raise the question of separation, for the sake of intellectual honesty and

---

[4] If it is a fact. Not only do many people at the present time believe firmly in divine intervention; it is worth remembering that many in the first century did not. The main schools of philosophy at that time were either pantheist, like the Stoic, or quasi-deist, like the Epicurean and Aristotelian, and regarded special divine inter- vention with almost as much scepticism as Wiles does himself.

peace of mind. But it is not necessary in itself, or rather is no more necessary than it was at any other time. There may be more people in Dr Wiles's position than there were once, that is all. 'Obsolescence' does not come into it; and, to be fair to Wiles, he does not himself use the word.

Cupitt's argument looks at first glance like one based on ethical change. Kenotic theories originated in nineteenth-century bourgeois society, we are informed, which needed to validate the duty to 'condescend to men of low estate'. With the social changes since then, 'condescension' has come to be a term of disapproval, not commendation, and kenosis has become hopelessly inappropriate. (As a matter of fact, 'condescend' seems to have acquired its unpleasant overtones before kenosis became popular, but let that pass.) It is just possible that the idea of kenosis did arise because of the social factors Cupitt describes, though one had thought that the class divisions which allegedly inspired it were older than the nineteenth century. And if kenotic theories turned on the idea of the divine condescension in the way that Anselm's ideas about Atonement turned on that of injured honour, there might be some reason to query them. In fact, of course, they do not, and any connection between them and nineteenth-century bourgeois morality is irrelevant to their truth or falsity. Nor has the shift in social relationships since then, with, shall we say, a certain loss of confidence in the 'upper' classes and a certain loss of deference among the 'lower', done anything to disprove kenosis. Take a parallel. For most of the history of the Church the normal form of government was monarchical, and God was seen as the King of the universe (as Cupitt himself has pointed out with some vehemence). Today monarchies are rare; most countries have Presidents, who owe their position either to election or, frequently, to the forcible seizure of power. But I should think it very odd if this shift in social relationships were taken as evidence for thinking that God owed His supremacy either to election by the world or to seizure of power from the previous Cosmic Dictator, like Zeus and Kronos in the Greek mythologies. The fact that God is supreme by *right* and not by force or election was brought out in the image of Him as King, and will survive, I trust, even if there should not be a single king left in the world. The fact that Christ humbled Himself and took on the form of a servant was perhaps brought out most of all in kenotic Christologies, but it is a fact whether they are true or false, and whether condescension is thought of as good or bad, or not thought of at all.

It is worth thinking back to the Introduction if we want to see one possible reason why Wiles and Cupitt, who are not fools, have fallen into the old 'genetic fallacy', or at least come close to it (the fallacy of supposing that if you can see the causes which have led someone to a particular belief you have somehow shown that belief to be false).[5] We distinguished at the start between analytic Christology and proclamatory. The proclamatory Christologist asks, it may be remembered, not so much 'What must have been true to give us our Christian starting-point?' (what McIntyre called the 'given'), but 'What new truths does this starting-point lead to?' Now for proclamatory Christologists trends and fashions are important. They want to lead people onward into new realizations, and to do so they must begin where those people are; nor must they try to lead their hearers into truths which they cannot understand or accept. Hence, if 'condescension' (in a good sense) is a currently popular notion, they will do well to show how God in Jesus Christ condescended to our low estate; if it is not, they will do better to emphasize, perhaps, the idea of Christ as 'the firstborn among many brethren'. Social changes will affect their message, for they are in their theological way *preachers*, and preachers who take no account of their audience preach badly. What neither they nor anyone else must do is suppose that this affects *truth*. It does not. It may be that the truth is one which social changes make unpalatable to most people, and yet which is absolutely vital. Maybe this is the case with the idea of divine intervention. In that case, preachers of Christ have an uphill task ahead. They may be able to commend Christ to some extent without bringing in the unpalatable part, and (so to speak) soften up the opposition that way; but sooner or later the 'scandal' of particularity and discontinuity is going to be seen for what it is. Perhaps we should see Wiles as a kind of preacher, even sympathize with his predicament; eager to commend his splendid superstructure, he is trying to move it off the foundation, nearer the passers-by. That could make things easier, as they were for the

---

[5] Wiles is, as I said, aware to some extent of this danger, but not sufficiently. The alleged readiness of the first century to believe in divine intervention is not enough even to make it easier to see incarnation as a temporary 'interpretation of Jesus'. If there are good reasons to doubt the Incarnation, we do not need facts about ancient mental habits; if not, perhaps those habits were *praeparatio evangelica* for a binding truth!

man in the parable who did not wish to build his house on the rock. But the result in either case is a ruinous crash.

As far as the question of 'historical relativism' is concerned: It is true and obvious that Christian thinking has throughout its history been seriously affected by its environment, social, cultural, and intellectual, from the Jewish background against which it began to the Marxist revolutionary movements of the present century. But does this justify the relativist's claim that it is impossible to maintain any continuity of doctrine over the generations, and that this impossibility is actually desirable? Is not such a view one of those which actually undermines its own self? Cupitt has put it rather well (in a slightly different context): 'If the proposition that "every item of our knowledge is relative to an interpretative framework" is known to be true, non-relativistically, then it is itself an exception to the rule it states: but if it is itself true only relativistically, then it might be untrue in another perspective.'[6]

This might be objected to as mere logic-chopping; but in fact the logical difficulty (which even on its own is serious enough) points beyond itself to a deeper difficulty in relativism: unless I can to some extent step back from my own framework, I cannot know that I *have* such a framework. But I do know it, and so I can to some extent step back from it. Indeed, I cannot realize that there is a difference between my own natural framework and that of (say) St Paul, unless I can not only step out of mine but also to some extent imaginatively enter his. Otherwise, even if I recognize the way my own thinking is affected, I cannot see how Paul's was; for all I know, he may have been affected in exactly the same way as I am.

This does not mean that I must be able to accept Paul's framework as true, or as just as good as mine. I may think it defective, or wholly misguided; or I may think it is better than mine and try to adopt it. It does not matter. The 'stepping back and entering in' process is one of imagination rather than belief. But it is a real process. It is the work of a good historian of ideas to help us go through it. Indeed, Houlden, whom I cited in Chapter 1 as an advocate of relativism, himself does what on his own premises ought to be impossible: in a later chapter of his book he sets out to help us see how the main writers of the New Testament thought and

---

[6] Cupitt (1976), p. 112.

what they were getting at—'stepping out and entering in', in fact. We may not be able to carry out this process perfectly, but we are often able to make a shot at it. The very existence at the present time of people who call themselves (say) Calvinists, Thomists, or Marxists should give relativists pause. Perhaps it is undesirable that these people should stick to an oldfashioned framework of thinking, but it can be done. Such people exist; they differ from one another and from the rest of us; does this not suggest that they do have something in common with their founders, that there is continuity of thought across the generations?

And of course our thought is shaped *both* by the environment in which we live *and* by the past: by previous generations who were shaped in *their* turn by their past, and above all by the Bible, which is after all itself a survival from the past. Houlden is not quite right to depict us as standing in a circle side by side with St Paul, 'looking inwards at that from which both derive', because our line of sight goes through Paul himself (and of course the other biblical writers, and others after them). Even if we believe that we have direct access to some kind of personal knowledge of God and His Son, that knowledge is shaped by what we have learned from Paul and the rest. Even if we deny them 'inspiration' (which I should not myself do) we have to grant them 'authority', because there is too little else to go on. The past is not alien to us, for we are its children.

12

The Inner Coherence of the Traditional Position

IT should be made quite plain that if there really is logical incoherence in the doctrine of the Incarnation, then that doctrine must be abandoned. There can be no pleading of 'mystery' or 'paradox' to cover up what is really a self-contradiction; to that extent the objectors are right. On that understanding, we proceed to the argument that the common definition or understanding of the word 'God' contains elements which are incompatible with elements in the corresponding definition of the word 'Man'. We saw that the traditional Christologies sought to avoid contradiction by distinguishing qualities belonging to Christ's divine nature from those which belonged to His human; or, if we prefer to avoid using the word 'nature', between those qualities which are His in virtue of being God and those which are His in virtue of being human.

But will this really do? Some philosophers and theologians, such as Dr R. T. Herbert and Dr Thomas V. Morris, anxious to defend the idea of Incarnation, have made very heavy weather dealing with alleged contradictions between the 'divine' and 'human' qualities.[1] Christ as God, it has been pointed out, existed before the time of Herod; but Christ as man did not. Hence a contradiction. Christ as God knew all things; Christ as man did not. Hence another. And so on. No one and nothing can both exist before Herod and not exist before him; no one and nothing can both know all things and not know some of them. Drs Herbert and Morris are certain that these alleged contradictions can be dealt with, but they take a great deal of time and paper to do so, unnecessarily so, it seems to me.

[1] Herbert (1979), ch. 4, and Morris (1986), respectively. Morris's position, as already noted, is a 'two-minds' Christology not unlike the one defended in this present essay.

For there are two quite familiar ways in which a single person or thing can have apparently incompatible qualities. One is where each part qualifies the person or thing *in a particular capacity*. Martha has dual nationality, British and Ruritanian. As a Ruritanian citizen, she has no right whatever to assistance from the British Consul if she gets into difficulties abroad; as a British citizen, she has a very definite right to it. There is no contradiction.

But if it is replied that 'being God' and 'being human' are not capacities, so that this is irrelevant, then we can appeal to an even more familiar situation. One person or thing may have incompatible qualities if they are qualities of parts of the person or thing. There is no contradiction in my saying 'Islip church was built in the twelfth and thirteenth centuries', even if I add 'The tower is fourteenth-century in date'. For of course part of the church was built in each of those centuries. Part of Christ, the eternal Logos, existed before the days of Herod; part of Him, the Galilean carpenter, did not. Part of Him knew all things; part did not. And so on.

The only place where a real problem arises is where a divine quality seems to be of such a kind that it would have to affect the humanity, or vice versa. Thus, as we saw in Chapter 2, not only is God good, he could not conceivably be otherwise; whereas Jesus of Nazareth, good though He was in actual fact, might conceivably have been bad. 'If Jesus is able to will evil, he is not divine, and if he is not able to will evil, he is not human'.[2] Talk about capacities or parts will not help us here.

But this argument, plausible though it looks, is in fact mistaken. The apparent contradiction is between the propositions (1) 'It was possible that Jesus should will evil' and (2) 'It was not possible that Jesus should will evil'. Now statements of possibility are usually *relative*. 'I may possibly be away next week', 'It is possible that we left the electric fire switched on', or 'Is it going to rain?' 'Quite possibly' are none of them statements of abstract logical possibility; they all state a possibility relative to the speakers' knowledge (or at least that part of their knowledge that they are actually drawing on while speaking). Given the information available to me, it is possible that I shall be away next week; perhaps, if I come to know more, I shall come to see that it is not possible after all. But that does not mean that I was a liar, or even mistaken, the first time.

---

[2] K. Ward, review in *Theology*, 81 (May 1978), p. 215.

To borrow an illustration from Avicenna,[3] a man is capable of being a bird in so far as he is an animal, but not, obviously, in so far as he is human. Given as our background information only the fact that Dickie is an animal, we may assert quite truthfully that it is possible he is a bird; given the further information that he is human, we may not. Similarly, given as our information the fact that Christ was human, the assertion 'It was possible that he should will evil (even if in fact he never did)' can be made; given also that He was divine, it cannot. Again, no contradiction.

Incidentally, exactly the same 'contradiction' can arise in cases where divinity is not involved at all. 'If Jane is not able to will evil, she is not human' looks fine. But then add 'If Jane is able to will evil, she is more than a week old'. Does it follow that if Jane is human, she cannot be less than a week old? Of course not. Neither then does it follow that if Christ is human, He cannot be divine. The assertion 'If X cannot will evil, X is not human' is all right as a general rule, but not if X is less than a week old; nor if X is also God incarnate.

It is, unfortunately, not at all clear what Goulder means by the word 'mystification', which we ought to discuss next. His examples are too varied. They include the eighteenth-century 'phlogiston' theory of combustion, which got into the position of having to say that phlogiston had negative mass, and the belief apparently current among the Dorze of the Sudan that leopards are Christians, despite the fact that, unlike other Dorze Christians, they do not fast on Fridays. His point seems to be that it is unclear *what* is being asserted in such beliefs; instead of asking 'How might this belief be reconciled with assured facts?' (as with a genuine paradox) we are reduced to asking 'What, if anything, can this mean?' One might feel that as far as the Dorze are concerned, the belief may well be unintelligible even without the failure to fast on Fridays, but that if it is intelligible before that is taken into account, the addition of the failure to fast reduces the belief into self-contradiction rather than mystification. ('All Christians fast on Fridays; All leopards are Christians; Not all leopards fast on Fridays' is a model self-contradictory set of statements, an antilogism.) The 'negative mass' of phlogiston is certainly hard to imagine (though not perhaps more so than much

[3] *Sufficientia*, 2. 1. 24.

of more recent physics), but might have been 'cashable' in terms of experimental results, or capable of being fitted into the mathematics of Newtonian physics; if it was not, then it was simply false. It is not clear what the two have in common; what 'mystification' means to Goulder is, frankly, mystifying.

However, if we turn to what Goulder says about the Incarnation itself, he becomes much clearer. There is, he claims, no element of *continuity*; the differences between the pre-incarnate and the post-incarnate Logos are clear enough, but what was identical throughout? We shall have occasion to refer to this later in Excursus III, on kenosis; Goulder seems to have assumed in advance some sort of kenosis on the lines of Thomasius or Godet. For of course on most other Christological theories the ordinary attributes of the Logos continue as before during the Incarnation. Even on a kenotic theory some meaning could be attached to the assertion of continuity, as we have seen; if after the Resurrection the Logos had the memories both of His pre-incarnate life and of His incarnate one, He had at least as much continuity as we have when recalling a dream.

The same would hold if, as is possible, Goulder is really asking for an element of continuity between the pre-incarnate Logos and Jesus during His incarnate life, not between two stages of the life of the Logos. But in any case, as the main point of Chapter 10 was to show just how there could be a common element to Logos and Galilean even apart from memory, we need not pursue this matter further; it has only been raised here for the sake of tidiness.

Schleiermacher's objection, that to talk of a 'divine nature' is impermissible, needs careful handling. It is clear that in one sense he is right. God is not one among a class of beings sharing a group of common qualities, like comets, tomatoes, or human beings. The divine nature is not 'revealed in a variety of appearances'. (We might feel that a reservation ought to be made here because of the doctrine of the Trinity: does not God the Son share the divine nature with God the Father and God the Holy Ghost? But this is doubtful; certainly it is not in the way that Mary, Peter, and John share human nature.) But the fact that only one being exists in a certain class does not mean that we cannot talk about the nature of that class. Only one battleship of the *Vanguard* class was ever built; but that does not mean that we cannot compare that class with earlier ones.

There is indeed an extra complication in the case of God, in that not only is there only one God, there only *could* be one; but I do not see how this could affect the question of a divine nature.

But of course this was not Schleiermacher's only argument. He also pointed out that in one sense of 'nature' God and nature are normally contrasted with one another, so that to attribute nature to God in this sense was impossible. This is true but irrelevant (and indeed I think Schleiermacher was only raising it in passing); in *that* sense nothing and no one 'has a nature'. Either they are part of nature, like you and me and the galaxies, or they are the God who created nature. Thirdly, Schleiermacher points out that even in phrases like 'animal' and 'vegetable nature', or 'noble' and 'ignoble' ones, we are always talking of a limited existence. Now this is really very close to begging the question at issue. It is certainly true that when we talk of any nature other than God's we talk of a limited, finite nature; but that is simply because all beings other than God are limited and finite. We cannot show that *all* natures must be finite unless we already know that the one infinite being, God, does not have a nature—i.e. already know that which Schleiermacher is attempting to prove. After all, when we talk of goodness or wisdom in any case other than that of God, we are talking of a finite and limited goodness or wisdom; it does not follow that God cannot be good or wise. Nor, indeed, does the fact that all other real things are finite show that God cannot be real.

The genuinely interesting logical point that Schleiermacher makes is this: How can 'divine' and 'human' be brought together under any single conception, as if they were instances of the same universal? To develop this point (I hope in a way that is not unfair to what Schleiermacher was getting at): When we talk of the divine wisdom, we are not suggesting that God is rather like Solomon or Confucius on a grander scale. God's wisdom is something quite different from human wisdom. It is, at the most, analogous to ours, playing the same part in His life and being as human wisdom does in human life and being. At the very best, then, God's 'nature' can only be analogous to the 'nature' of a human being, a horse, or a lizard. But whereas there is great point and convenience in talking of God's wisdom, since the effects of that wisdom really are like those of human wisdom (only far greater), 'nature' plays no such useful role. It makes a great deal of difference to the world that God is wise; it makes no difference at all whether He has something analogous to a 'nature' or not. We have to speak of God's wisdom, goodness, power, and love as if they and human wisdom, goodness, power, and love were instances of the same universal, though qualifying this at once; we have no reason to do the same with 'nature'.

But this is not quite true. For 'nature', if it is a universal at all, is a second-order one. 'Human nature' is not a property or quality like 'human wisdom'; it is an expression used when we want to refer to certain human properties taken together (namely, those which are common to all normal human beings, those which no one could lack and still be a normal human being). Similarly, the 'divine nature' is not a property of God to be compared to human ones; it is an expression used when we wish to refer to certain properties of God taken together (namely, those which no being could lack and still be properly called 'God'[4]).'Nature' does not refer to a universal or quality, it is a word used to enable us to speak of such qualities in a particular way. Its use is primarily logical and not descriptive, and the vast difference there is between God and us humans does not affect the use of the word. Consequently, Schleiermacher's point, interesting though it is, is not in the end valid.

We pass, then, to Cupitt's difficulty, that if we wish to say 'Jesus is God', it seems impossible to treat the word 'is' either as one of identity or as one of predication. As a matter of fact Cupitt has himself given us a clue to the resolution of his own difficulty: 'few theologians', he remarks, 'would accept that formula without qualification'.[5] Since, however, they would accept it with qualification, the question is what qualification(s)?

The answer is, I suspect, of an almost appalling simplicity. The qualification that orthodox theologians would normally make is of course 'and Man'; and I think that, surprising as it may seem, this is the solution to Cupitt's logical problem. For it greatly reduces the difficulty in trying to make the 'is' one of predication. That difficulty, it may be remembered, was that the 'is' could only be one of predication if 'God' were a common or general term, so

---

[4] For example, God might presumably not have created me, and in that case He would have lacked the property 'creator of Richard Sturch'; yet He would still be God. It is not, then, part of His nature. But He could not be God if He were not good; goodness, then, is part of His nature.

[5] In Goulder (1979), p. 31.

that 'Jesus is God' became in effect 'Jesus is **a** God'. And to the Christian 'a God' makes no sense: there is only one God, nor could there possibly be more. The 'is' could only be predicative if Jesus' being God, or a God, were contrasted with at least a possibility of there being other gods. If one may illustrate the point with an analogy: There is at the time I write only one living emperor, the Emperor Akihito of Japan, and only one living Pope, John Paul II.[6] But it makes perfectly good sense to say 'Akihito is a living emperor', because, although there are in fact no other emperors alive, there could be; the 'is' is one of predication. On the other hand, it makes no sense to say 'John Paul II is a living Pope', because there can be only one living Pope at a time. Similarly, if there were only one God, yet others might have existed, 'Jesus is a God' might have made sense: He would be contrasted with other possible (but not actual) Gods, as Akihito is with possible (but not actual) other emperors. If there *can* only be one God, this is not possible, and 'Jesus is (a) God' makes no sense.

If, however, the correct expression is 'Jesus is both God and Man', the predicative 'is' becomes possible after all. For the contrast is not between one person to whom the predicate applies and another to whom it also applies or conceivably might have applied; it is a contrast between one predicate applying to a particular person and another predicate also applying to him. It makes no sense to say 'John Paul II is a' (as opposed to 'the') 'living Pope', because the 'a' here seems to suggest that there could be other living Popes, which is not so. But it does make sense to say 'John Paul II is a living Pope and a living Pole', because we are not interested here in the possibility of there being other Popes, but only in the possibility of John Paul II's being something else as well as Pope. 'Living Pope' here can and does function as a predicate. And similarly with 'Jesus is God and Man'.

But we can go further than this. Orthodoxy speaks of a joining of the two natures, divine and human, in the one person of Jesus Christ. And it is not difficult to see that such a joining would lead to a need for careful linguistic handling. Again an analogy may be of help. Near the city of St Louis, in the United States, two of the world's great rivers, the Missouri and the Mississippi, join together. The river below this junction is known by the name of

---

[6] I have been reminded that the Coptic Patriarch of Alexandria is also known as 'Pope'; but this, I suggest, is using the word in a slightly different sense!

one of them, Mississippi, but is of course a combination of the two. Now it is interesting to note that a lot of the linguistic problems that arise if we try to say 'Jesus is God' *also* arise if we try to say 'This' (referring to the river below the junction) 'is the Missouri'. Clearly to deny that it is the Missouri would be even more misleading than to assert it; but equally clearly to assert it without qualification would also mislead. If we are thinking in the same sort of pattern as St John in his Prologue, we might say something like 'The Missouri turns south and is joined to the Mississippi'; if in the same sort of pattern as St Thomas after the risen Lord appeared to him, we might address the combined river as 'My beloved Missouri!' Language applied to the Missouri above the confluence may also be applied to the combined river (e.g. statements about its source, its total length, or the quantity of sediment it carries). Or the combined river could be said to be one with the Missouri, or the Missouri be said to be in it. But the unqualified assertion 'This is the Missouri' ought not to be made without adding 'and the Mississippi'—just as it would not be correct to assert 'Jesus is God', without adding 'and Man'. In other words, the apparently perplexing difficulties over calling Jesus 'God' are exactly what we should expect if the orthodox doctrine of the Incarnation were true. They can hardly, then, be used as an argument to show that it is not true—unless it is also possible to prove that the Mississippi and the Missouri cannot flow into one.

Possibly it might be objected that we can surely say 'Jesus is human' without the qualification 'and God'; why not, then, the reverse? The answer is simply one of nomenclature. The name 'Jesus' or 'Jesus Christ' is used both for the man from Nazareth irrespective of His divinity and for the whole Person or πρόσωπον of the Word made flesh in that man. It is not normally used for the Word considered apart from His incarnation. We cannot therefore say 'Jesus is God' without qualification, but we can say 'Jesus is human', using the name in the first of these two ways. We can also of course say 'The Word is God' without qualification, but not 'The Word is human'. There is no real asymmetry.

Ogden, it will be recalled, argued that Christologists were for the most part asking the wrong questions. If by this he meant simply that Christology ought not to be considered in isolation, that our ideas about the person and work of Christ must inevitably affect and be affected by what we believe about God and ourselves, and that mere 'belief' without what he calls the existential element is spiritually valueless, he would be right, and no theologian would disagree. But he clearly intends to say something stronger and less universally acceptable. I think that perhaps we can best see what he means by considering the episode of Peter's confession at Caesarea Philippi, which Ogden himself adduces (Matt. 16: 13ff.).

Jesus' question 'But who do you say that I am?' does indeed call for a personal confession, as Ogden says; and according to Matthew it did indeed need a revelation from God to elicit one. Peter's reply had implications far beyond the formal identification of his friend Jesus with a figure described as 'the Christ' or 'the Son of the living God'. But Ogden does not think in terms of implications. On the next page we find him calling questions about the meaning of our existence 'logically prior' to questions about Christ. But can this really be applied to Peter's confession? Surely the thrust of the story in Matthew is against this. Peter is depicted as making his confession without full understanding. He has not worked up to it by considering his own existence or ultimate reality—on the contrary, not 'flesh and blood' but God produced his reply. And he has not understood his own terms—in a few moments he will be addressed as 'Satan' for his total misunderstanding of Jesus' Messiahship.

Although Christian assertions about God, oneself, and Jesus Christ are intimately linked, there is no *temporal* priority in any one set of assertions. Some, like Peter and his fellow-Apostles, know something of God before they meet Jesus. Some know their own need before they know either God or His Son. And some come first to feel the claims of Jesus Christ upon them, and move on from that to a better understanding both of their own existence and of the 'ultimate reality' that is God the Father. But can we properly speak of *logical* priority here?

Older-style systematic theologians usually discussed the doctrine of the person and work of Jesus Christ after that of God and man and before that of justification. For God exists independently of us and of His Incarnation, and the human race existed before Jesus of Nazareth, while justification is only a reality thanks to Christ. To this extent they acknowledged a 'logical priority', though not quite the one found in Ogden. Theirs is a priority in the *ordo essendi*, not necessarily in the *ordo cognoscendi*, which Ogden seems to be thinking of. We can be saved by Christ, and moreover can know this and acknowledge Him as Lord and Saviour, without having consciously answered, or even asked, questions about the meaning of our existence or about ultimate reality; we may indeed infer these from our knowledge of our salvation. No hard-and-fast rule can be laid down about the way our questions are asked and answered.

It is possible, very possible, that many orthodox theologians have tended to be too systematic, too fond of drawing boundaries where they should not really be drawn and pigeon-holing doctrines into separate compartments so as to obscure the interconnections between them; and it is well that we should be reminded of this 'fallacy of misplaced concreteness', as Ogden calls it in a phrase of Whitehead's. But the opposite error, that of blurring all distinctions and gliding imperceptibly from one region of thought to another, is no less dangerous. It is unlikely that many traditional Christologists really lost sight for long of the way in which other parts of Christian doctrine bore on their subject and it on them. It is very likely that Ogden, and others too, can lose sight of the fact that in gliding from one region of thought to another they have carried with them assumptions that belonged only to the first region, that in refusing to make sharp distinctions they have overlooked genuine differences. Thus Ogden, having said that the question 'Who is Jesus?' is not the only question Christology answers, goes on to say that questions about God and ourselves (or rather their answers) are presupposed in early Christological formulations. The latter is quite correct, and perhaps the former too. But his next step is to criticize other views on the grounds that 'instead of being the question about the meaning of Jesus for us, given the logically prior questions about the meaning of our own existence and about ultimate reality ... it becomes the very different question about the being of Jesus in himself'.[7] Almost imperceptibly the questions about God and ourselves have become 'logically prior'[8] and the question 'Who is Jesus?' has disappeared altogether. A change of great importance has come over the whole discussion without its being made clear what has happened, let alone any justification being given for the change. We must avoid fallacies of both kinds.

---

[7] Ogden (1982), pp. 28–9.
[8] Might not this itself be a case of misplaced concreteness?

13

Incarnation and 'Inner Life'

DOES our proposed analysis offer any help as far as the problem of describing the mental life or self-consciousness of our Lord is concerned? It probably does as far as His knowledge is concerned, yes, as we have seen. But the real difficulty comes with His will. We have seen just now that although, given only that Jesus was human, His sinning was a possibility, still, given also that He was divine, it was not. Does this not land us in Monothelitism, and, what is more, in denial of His freedom? And surely freedom of the will is part of human nature?

As regards the risk of Monothelitism, this has already been answered (in effect) when we looked at the question of 'two consciousnesses' in Christ. There can indeed be two wills in Him, one human and one divine; but the one functions in the sphere of operation of the Divine Word, the other in that of the son of Mary, the link being that it is the same subject who 'wills' in both. It is the question of freedom that is the really knotty one.

Some would hold that freedom consists of the ability to do something if one wishes or chooses to do it. A similar idea may be put in negative form: freedom is the absence of compulsion to do a thing. This is probably the view most prevalent among philosophers, at least in the English-speaking world.[1] If this is correct, then there is no problem. Jesus was as capable as anyone else of carrying out His purposes—more so, in fact, than most; and no one compelled Him to do anything. 'No one takes my life from me; I am laying it down of my own free will', He said, and even in the Agony in the Garden He *chose* to go on: 'Do you suppose I cannot call on

---

[1] e.g. Moore (1912), ch. 6; Nowell-Smith (1954), chs. 19–20; A. Flew, 'Divine Omnipotence and Human Freedom', in Flew and MacIntyre (1955), pp. 144ff. All three are atheists, but the view is also found in Christians, e.g. Edwards (1754), part I, sect. v and *passim*.

my Father, and He would at once send me more than twelve legions of angels to my aid?'[2]

However, Christian theologians and philosophers have often defended a stronger sense of 'freedom', in which one is only free if one's actions were not causally predetermined by factors outside oneself.[3] For if an action is thus predetermined, it seems that I, the agent, could have done nothing else; it may be that no one *compelled* me to do it, and that if I had chosen to do something else, I should have succeeded in doing it; but *I could not choose* anything but that which I actually did choose, and someone who had access to all the relevant facts and to the relevant scientific laws could have accurately predicted my action without any consideration of my 'free will'. And if this were always the case, human responsibility would disappear; we could neither be praised for our good deeds nor blamed for our bad ones, except in the way that one may praise or blame the weather. Rewards and punishments alike would not be *deserved*, but would be merely useful reinforcements of behaviour patterns; for the causes of our actions would lie outside ourselves, before, it may be, we were born or thought of.

Can we ascribe freedom from this sort of determinism to our Lord? It seems that we must. If we deny it, then, in Schoonenberg's words, 'incapacity for sin would always have been determined before Jesus' human insertion of will; with such a course of affairs, however, his human will is not redemptive and our human will not redeemed ... In particular, we should then be doing wrong to what the New Testament tells us about his temptations.'[4]

The second of Schoonenberg's points we may be able to meet. Temptations could be real events in our Lord's life even if there were an absolute certainty that He would overcome them. A temptation is, presumably, the thought that a certain wrong act or omission could be carried out, plus the thought that it is to some extent a desirable act or omission. Such thoughts could occur even to one who was proof against ever actually carrying out the tempting deed. 'Evil', says Milton,

> into the mind of God or man
> May come and go, so unapproved; and leave
> No spot or blame behind.[5]

---

[2] John 10: 18; Matt. 26: 53.　　　　[3] e.g. Lucas (1970); Plantinga (1975).
[4] Schoonenberg (1972), p. 142.　　　[5] *Paradise Lost*, v. 117ff.

Perhaps it is a bit more awkward for those of us who take seriously the personal part played by Satan. Would he waste time trying to tempt someone whom he knew to be incorruptible? Well, maybe: Satan is stupid, or he would not have become what he is. His desire is to lure people into evil, and there is no particular reason to suppose that he would pass anyone over, whether or not he thought himself likely to succeed. And this is the more likely in that it is not likely that Satan occupied himself much with working out an analytic Christology of his own to see whether temptation of Jesus was bound to fail or not.[6]

Schleiermacher, indeed, held that the very idea of temptation implied the idea of sin in the one tempted, if there was 'even an infinitesimal element of struggle involved'.[7] If that were so, we should indeed find ourselves in difficulties with the New Testament accounts. Schleiermacher himself suggested that while pleasure and pain were (naturally) possible in Christ, these 'never passed over into desire or repulsion'. But this is no real solution. What kind of humanity is it that feels no desires or repulsions (at least towards pleasures and pains)? And surely the Agony in the Garden, for instance, is unintelligible if there was no desire to avoid crucifixion, and no repulsion from it. 'He began to be greatly distressed and troubled'; 'Now is my soul troubled, and what shall I say? "Father, save me from this hour"?';[8] the Gospels are agreed. However, Schleiermacher's solution is unnecessary; his problem can be dealt with without it. Struggle implies only a felt desire (or rather two felt desires), not a wrong desire consented to; there is nothing evil in itself in the wish not to be crucified, and nothing wrong therefore in feeling such a wish. Knox has indeed argued: 'Am I really tempted if I do not, however briefly or tentatively or slightly, consent? Have I been really tempted if I have rejected only that which entirely repels me or that from which I stand entirely aloof?'[9] But this is simply a muddle. I must certainly feel a desire for the tempting thing—which after all usually has some good aspect to it. I may feel 'If this were not wrong I should do it'. And if feeling like this is what Knox contrasts with entire repulsion or aloofness, then all

---

[6] Weston (1907) (pp. 215–16) suggested that Satan wished to defeat Jesus, as he does with everyone, and also to discover the secret of His sinlessness, but had not realized what that secret was.

[7] Schleiermacher (1928), pp. 414f.   [8] Mark 14: 33; John 12: 27.

[9] Knox (1967), p. 47.

right. But this is not consent. To consent means to say—briefly, perhaps, or tentatively or slightly—'Yes, I will do it', and the desire may be felt without that. If Knox wants more than this desire before he will call it temptation, he is coming close to demanding that for temptation to be real it must be successful, or perhaps to saying 'Have I been really tempted if I have rejected only what I have rejected?', both of which are plainly absurd.

But the first of Schoonenberg's points is more difficult to answer. Did Christ have a will capable of sinning? When we were looking at the arguments in the last chapter, we concluded that His human will was indeed capable of willing sin unless one took into consideration, as one should, the fact that He was also divine. But this seems to be just what Schoonenberg finds objectionable; Jesus' incapacity for sin would have been determined before ever His human will could operate. He would no longer be 'consubstantial with us', for His actions would always have been predetermined before He chose; or rather, since that way of putting it brings God into time, His acts and choices would be causally dependent on something other than Himself.

One way to resolve this would be to say, like Schoonenberg himself or like Robinson,[10] that while Jesus was sinless in the sense of *impeccantia* (freedom from ever having actually done wrong), He was not sinless in the sense of *impeccabilitas* (incapacity for sin)— even, presumably, when we take His divinity into account. Despite the union with God, Jesus might have sinned; but He did not. Now neither Schoonenberg nor Robinson advocate a Christology like the one I have been advocating, but they could claim with some justice that their view of Jesus' sinlessness is as compatible with my position as with their own. If the point of union between God and Man is, as I have argued, the central self, and if this could not, so to speak, 'transmit' revelation on its own, is it not clear that it could not on its own transmit the divine *impeccabilitas* either?

This is so; but I am still not quite happy about relying on *impeccantia* by itself. We are left with a Jesus whose sinlessness is a matter of good luck; He might quite easily, it seems, have committed a few minor sins in the course of His life. But is it conceivable that God should have chosen to become incarnate in, or even to act decisively in, someone who might at any moment sin—i.e. *rebel*

---

[10] Robinson (1973), pp. 88ff.

against goodness and against God Himself? Surely not. Unless, indeed, we take the line of Forsyth and Mackintosh mentioned earlier,[11] of degrees of incarnation in Christ Himself, and extend it to a degree neither of them intended, so that God only became incarnate completely once it was clear that Jesus had resisted all temptations and was now by His own (grace-assisted) efforts immune to any further attack Satan might launch? I do not think either Schoonenberg or Robinson wishes to say this. Robinson quotes with apparent approval the statement of Theodore of Mopsuestia that 'it was not *because* Jesus was a good man that God united himself to him';[12] and of course it would make nonsense of the Gospels' portrait of Jesus and the nature of His ministry if there was, at least until Gethsemane, a perpetual uncertainty over whether the whole thing might not have to be called off. Yet this seems to be the only way in which we can dispense with *impeccabilitas*.

Suppose, then, that we do not try to dispense with it. Are there other ways in which to resolve Schoonenberg's problem? One possibility might be to insist that freedom to sin or refrain from sinning is a far lesser freedom than the freedom from sin. This is certainly true. And freedom *from* sin is possible without freedom *to* sin (despite Robinson):[13] for it is the kind of freedom which belongs to God Himself and to the Church Triumphant in heaven, the souls of just people made perfect, where freedom to sin is non-existent. The trouble is, this other and greater freedom is different from our ordinary human freedom to choose. Putting it in rather different terms, Meyendorff quotes Maximus the Confessor as distinguishing between natural will towards the good (θέλημα φυσικόν) and deliberative choice between good and evil (γνώμη or θέλημα γνωμικόν), and teaching that our Lord had the first of these like anyone else, but not the second.[14] Maybe so; but does not that destroy His full humanity?

Perhaps, then, we should take a line which Robinson seems to favour, and say that Jesus' freedom to sin, which He shares with the rest of us, nevertheless was not a matter of indeterminacy 'as if it were merely a matter of contingency which way he acted'.[15]

---

[11] Forsyth (1909), p. 495; Mackintosh (1913), p. 336.

[12] Robinson (1973), p. 95, quoting PG 66, 997.

[13] Cf. e.g. Rom. 6: 16, 2 Pet. 2: 19.

[14] Meyendorff (1975), pp. 137 and 149, quoting Maximus, *Disput. cum Pyrrho*, PG 91, 308d.

[15] Robinson (1973), p. 95.

Robinson quotes Tillich in support: 'The decisions of Jesus . . . stand under the directing creativity of God (providence). And God's directing creativity in the case of man works through his freedom. Man's destiny is determined *by* the divine creativity, but *through* man's self-determination, that is, through his finite freedom.'[16] If this means that God has the last word, but leaves us a certain amount of indeterminism in the process, Tillich is in effect agreeing with the 'stronger sense' of 'freedom' outlined earlier. But this is what Robinson is evidently rejecting. Perhaps what we are being offered is the view (which has certainly been held by many theologians) that our actions can be predetermined by God and still remain free. I confess that I cannot swallow this myself. But if I am wrong, then the whole argument against *impeccabilitas* collapses. I think that in fact predetermination of our actions by God would make God the author of sin, the vilest criminal merely a tool in His hands, and His the true responsibility. But if not, if causation by God is in a different category from causation by (say) our upbringing or environment, then Jesus could be sinless in the sense of being incapable of sinning, and yet be as free as any of us. For His *impeccabilitas* is caused by the providence or directing creativity of God, and as this does not (we are assured) diminish human freedom in us, no more does it diminish it in Jesus.

This would solve our problem. But it is not a solution I could support myself, as I do not think divine predetermination of this kind is compatible with human freedom in the second of our two senses, and as I think this second kind of freedom is both real and important. Readers, however, who find no difficulty in the position described may skip the next six paragraphs ('may' in the first sense of freedom, naturally): the rest of us must look for another way out.

A third possibility, then. God is altogether free from sin, utterly good. Now if Jesus is united to God not only by the central self but in a single person or πρόσωπον, it follows that any causal power exerted by the goodness of God upon the human life of Jesus is not external to Him at all, and therefore not destructive of His freedom. It is analogous, in a way, to the power exerted upon my present life by the habits I have acquired through free actions in

---

[16] *Systematic Theology*, ii (Welwyn, 1957), 149, quoted by Robinson (1973), p. 95.

my past. I cannot now escape responsibility for the litter on my desk by pleading 'I cannot do otherwise, as untidiness has become "second nature" to me'. Maybe it has, but this is no excuse if it did so through repeated indulgence in untidiness before there was any question of 'second nature'. The cause of my untidiness is not something external to me. So also with the sinlessness of our Lord. It was caused by God; but whereas God is 'external' (in the sense we are using that word) to you and me, He is not external to Jesus Christ, being united with the human nature of Jesus into a single Person. Jesus' freedom is that of the whole Incarnate Word, and is not impaired by any influence of part of the whole πρόσωπον on another part.

I am sure this is basically right. But is it enough? Is not Jesus' *human* freedom impaired even if His *total* freedom is not? And if the answer is 'No', is there still not the difficulty that it is God the Son with whom Jesus is one, whereas earlier I was arguing that the influence of God on Jesus' earthly life was that of God the Holy Spirit? Is that not 'external' causation after all?

Maybe: but consider the following approach. We are free to choose between good and evil, even if, thanks to original sin, we have an appalling bias the wrong way. Now why is this important? Because without it we could not be held responsible for what we did, praised for the good and blamed for the evil; nor, except in a purely utilitarian sense, could we be punished or rewarded. It is important for human responsibility. It is *not* important in itself as a constituent part of human nature. Indeed, it is our hope that by God's grace we shall one day have lost this freedom, having no more use for it. In one of his novels Charles Williams described a character who had at last won her 'freedom to yield herself': 'More and more securely the working of that Fate which was Love possessed her. For it was fatal in its nature; rich and austere at once, giving death and life in the same moment, restoring beyond belief all the things it took away—except the individual will'.[17] Rare indeed in this life, but is not this our hope for heaven hereafter and do we hope to cease in heaven from being human? Surely not; and if not, then this freedom is not an essential part of human nature.

Yet it is part of human nature now; and it is surely part of God's

[17] Williams (1954), pp. 124–5.

plan for human nature. Is not freedom a necessary condition before someone can be called good (or indeed bad)? And since God wishes us to be good—more than that, in fact, to be holy—has He not given us this freedom, and with it the attendant risk of sin? This is true. But it is only so because this is the only way in which *created* lives can become good and holy while remaining purely created lives. With Christ, if He is indeed God incarnate, His created human life is good and holy by His own will; even if the immediate agent of this be the Holy Spirit, that makes no real difference. Christ's human goodness is like that of the redeemed in glory, in that it is beyond being affected by the risks of moral freedom; it is also like that goodness in being the work both of its possessor and of divine grace; it is unlike it in that its possessor actually is God and is therefore in His divine nature good and holy without the need ever to have been liable to sin. But it remains clearly a human goodness.

Yes; but even so what of the principle 'What is not assumed is not redeemed'? We remember what Schoonenberg was saying: without freedom Jesus' will is not redemptive and our human will is not redeemed. Has that argument been answered yet?

Perhaps not; but is it in fact a sound argument? God the Son assumed a human body, soul, will, and all that is needed to be a human being, in order to redeem us. But the body, soul, and will are not in themselves 'redemptive'; they are so only because they are part of our redemption by the whole God–Man, Jesus Christ. Nor did they need to have every characteristic that human bodies, souls, and wills can have. The Lord did not need to be both left-handed in order to redeem left-handed people and right-handed in order to redeem right-handed ones. The will is, I suppose, that part of human nature most deeply corrupted by the Fall, and that part which most clearly needs redemption and, therefore, assumption by the Lord. But there is no disputing that it was so assumed. What Schoonenberg seems to be demanding (without of course intending to) is that the assumption of a human will should make no immediate difference to that will—in order that our wills should be redeemed, we are asked to suppose, Christ's will must itself be redeemed. Whereas in fact human nature is redeemed because God has shared it, and in so doing changed it.[18] His will was protected from sin; His body rose again from the tomb; in both He is the first-fruits, and we are, we hope and believe, to follow Him, who is the first-born of many brethren.

---

[18] I am not saying that we are saved by the Incarnation alone; I hope what was said earlier shows that. What Cabasilas said of the triple barrier (see p. 113) seems to me basically correct: it was needful not only that Christ should be born as one of us, but also that He should die for our sins and be raised again for our justification.

14

Divine Action

CRITICISM of incarnation as involving an impossible breach in the divine life fell, it may be remembered, into two halves. The first assumed a view of history—the history of the universe, that is, as well as of the human race—as a 'closed weft', to use a phrase of Bultmann's,[1] in which God never intervenes; His hand is to be seen in particular events only in so far as those events exemplify His purpose. And this applies to the life of Jesus as much as to any other event in the universe.

The main difficulties with such a view are (*a*) that there are strong reasons for believing it to be false and (*b*) that there probably *could* be no reasons for believing it to be true. Some element of discontinuity is, I believe, inescapable in a Christian view of the universe, however liberally we take the word 'Christian'—and indeed in almost any recognizably religious view of it. Oddly enough, Schoonenberg, whom I quoted earlier in support of the 'closed weft' line, realizes that this cannot be continued indefinitely: although anxious to stress the 'penultimate phase of salvation, the earthly', and that 'the breakthrough occurs of the final completion in Christ's parousia not merely from outside but also from within', he acknowledges that 'breakthrough' is the proper word to use, and that 'the final completion of the individual person passes beyond death'.[2] Let us see if we can give his insight logical form.

Discontinuity is implied if there is any kind of life beyond death. And this in two ways. First, because a life which exists in this world and is either continued in disembodied form or embodied in a 'resurrection-world'[3] is surely breaking the continuity of this world, and possibly that of the next as well; either it is a part of the pattern of this world which leaves it and is transferred to another, or it

---

[1] In Bartsch (1953), p. 197. [2] Schoonenberg (1972), pp. 174–5.
[3] I owe this expression to Hick (1964), p. 265.

is something not fully a part of the pattern of this world which was acting on it but is no longer doing so. Perhaps it could be argued that the first of these alternatives leaves the continuity of this world unaffected; the life ends (as far as this world is concerned) in accordance with exceptionless law, and the discontinuity is not within the world but within the life. But there is a second way in which survival of death breaks the closed weft. For it must have begun at some point. There must have been a first person who survived his or her death, before whom no one had done so. There must (to use old-fashioned language) have been a first immortal soul.

The same applies to our reaction to God, not just to His dealings with us. There must have been a first person to have any kind of experience of God, and a first person to realize the difference between right and wrong. The Bible depicts them as the same person, or rather people, but that is not essential. Experience of God might possibly be got round. A consistent 'continuist' will take the same line here as with actions of God; an 'experience of God' is simply an experience which is significant as an illustration of God's purposes. But I suspect that the point about moral experience is harder to get round. Ethical categories cannot be resolved into non-ethical ones.[4] If then ethical categories have any validity at all, there must have been a point when they appeared in human history, and not simply as a recombining of previous non-ethical ones (as happened when somebody for the first time combined the ideas of 'large', 'lizard', 'fire', 'breathing', and 'winged', and came up with the idea of a dragon). The discontinuity may or may not have been the result of divine action in the world, but it certainly broke the 'closed weft'.

I strongly suspect that *consciousness* is another example. I am aware of the world in a way in which a machine could not be: a robot might react to its surroundings in the same way as a human being, but it would not have those puzzling things called 'sensations', 'impressions', or 'sense-data' which have given rise to such prolonged philosophical arguments. There must have been a first creature (or several such) which did more than just react to its surroundings, which was actually conscious of them; and once again this gives us a discontinuity. Again, we may deny that God had

---

[4] The classical statement of this is in Hume's *Treatise of Human Nature*, iii. 1; it has been much debated in the present century, but the case for what has been called 'Hume's Law' seems to me to be really unanswerable.

a hand in this; but if there is a God who created and sustains the world, it is not easy to see how it happened without His having a hand in it—intervening, in fact.

It seems, therefore, highly probable that God has intervened in His world, to make His creatures (or some of them) aware of that world, aware of right and wrong within it, and capable of receiving life beyond it; and most of this on evidence that 'continuists' ought to find hard to deny. Accounts of miracles or incarnations they may brush aside as false. Perhaps they might wish to abandon belief in any life other than this one rather than relinquish the principle of the closed weft. But I doubt if many 'continuists' wish to deny right and wrong or their own awareness of the world around them.

Even if they do, there is the second argument I mentioned earlier: that their views cannot be known to be true. If the world does form a closed weft, how can one know that it is the work of God or discern His purposes within it? Not by revelation, clearly; for God to reveal something to people in the world by (say) prophecy would be just as much intervention as a miracle; indeed it would *be* a miracle. Granted, not all revelation has to be by prophecy. There is also, for instance, 'wisdom literature' in the Canon. But for God to have given wisdom to anyone other than by the normal means of heredity and environment would again break the continuity. (Wisdom that is given by these means we shall come on to in a moment.) Any 'revelation' within the closed weft is the product of preceding circumstances, and those in turn of others that preceded them, and so on; the supposed revelation has no link with the God whom it is supposed to reveal that it does not share with every other state of affairs in the universe, including false, pseudo-revelations. Isaiah is on a level with Hitler, as far as external inspiration is concerned.

(There is indeed one way out of this, but not one which I think will appeal to Christian 'continuists'. One Hindu tradition claims that the Vedas have always existed, from all eternity. If this were so, any revelation in them could be part of God's creation, yet distinct from all other parts; its causes would always include its own earlier existence. Revelation could then exist without any breach of continuity. But I have never known any Christian resort to this idea.)

Can we then see revelation as the insight of wise and intelligent people, wise and intelligent by natural (but God-given) processes?

The obvious catch is that there are insights and insights. What to me is a penetration into great mysteries may to you be pretentious rubbish. Of course, in some cases we can check what is said. If our wise sage tells us that pride goes before destruction, and a haughty spirit before a fall, we can in theory look for cases of pride and haughty spirits and see what really happens to them. But usually this cannot be done—especially where God is brought into it. We have already mentioned Wiles's instance of the prophet Hosea, and his statement that 'it was the pain of Hosea's continuing love for his unfaithful wife which gave rise to the distinctive emphasis in his oracles on the compassionate love of Yahweh for his erring and suffering people'.[5] Very likely this is so. But why should we think Hosea right? It has been suggested that the Norsemen's vision of Ragnarök was inspired by experience of the power of northern winters. Why not adopt this insight and take their winters as valid evidence of the ultimate defeat of heaven? Why is Hosea's love for Gomer a sounder basis for religion? Wiles's answer (not of course to this counter-example) is that 'such a conviction [as Hosea's] about God remains on any assumption an unproven judgment of faith'.[6] Well, on Wiles's assumptions, yes, though 'guesswork' might be nearer the mark than 'judgment'. (That is, as far as Hosea himself was concerned. We who read him are not so much guessing for ourselves as trusting in his guesses.) But 'on any assumption'? If there really is such a thing as revelation, then our 'judgment of faith' is unproven only because we cannot be sure whether Hosea's oracles were genuine instances of it; if God did inspire him, they are reliable enough. But if there is no such thing as revelation, they cannot be instances of it; they are purely speculative, applications of Hosea's marital problems to the history of the nation, just as Ragnarök is an application of Norse experience of bitter weather to history. Indeed, they are applications which Hosea himself seriously misunderstood, as he thought the Lord had spoken to him, and He hadn't. On the traditional view, Hosea's oracles may be true revelation, while the Prose Edda is splendid mythical speculation. On the 'continuist' view, both are speculation, and there is no reason to believe either.

Moreover, on the traditional view Hosea at least might have good reason to believe his own oracles, in the circumstances of receiving

---

[5] Wiles (1974), p. 71.   [6] p. 71.

his revelation; and he might find his ideas supported by the oracles of, say, Amos. 'If God inspired Amos, perhaps He is also inspiring me, for our messages have much in common.' But on the 'continuist' view the circumstances of Hosea's reception of his oracles, if they suggested that God was directly sending them, deceived him. While the oracles of Amos do not support those of Hosea at all; that two devout Hebrews in the same social circumstances should get partly similar ideas is not surprising.

Revelation, then, cannot be claimed as evidence for preferring a 'Christian-continuist' view to an agnostic one. What of religious experience, though? In an unguarded moment, Wiles asks the question: 'What kind of affirmation about God does Christian experience justify?'[7] He suggests that one answer is 'transcendence'; 'the "absoluteness" of Schleiermacher's feeling of absolute dependence and the "ultimacy" of Tillich's "ultimate concern" must be taken with full seriousness.' But on the continuity principle they must *not*. No experience can be of anything except an event or state of affairs within the world, the closed weft. If Schleiermacher felt absolutely dependent, or Tillich ultimately concerned, that is no doubt of psychological interest, but it tells us nothing whatever about God. He may be a transcendent Creator, certainly; but He may equally be a self-contemplating Prime Mover, as in Aristotle, or an eternally 'released' soul in unmoved bliss, as in the Yoga school of Hinduism—or a figment of the imagination. Tillich's experience is, on Wiles's principles, no more valuable as evidence than that of a cosmic pessimist like Schopenhauer or A. E. Housman. We cannot, as Wiles seems to think, experience 'that which makes ultimate sense of things';[8] if this is an item within the universe, it can hardly make sense of the universe, and if it is not, we cannot experience it without discontinuity.

The only possible hope is in natural theology. *Ad hominem* one can but point out that Wiles regards the traditional cosmological argument as 'invalid as a formal inference';[9] I think, though he does not say so, that he would take a similar line over the physico-theological arguments too. He thinks that the former covertly appeals to an underlying sense of wonder that there should be anything at all, which is fair enough. But if it is not a valid argument,

---

[7] Wiles (1974), pp. 32–3.   [8] p. 34.   [9] p. 34.

what help is it to us? Can a 'sense of wonder' get us beyond the closed weft? The physico-theological arguments are linked with the idea of purposiveness. 'Can we', Wiles asks, 'make the transition from the apprehension of divine purpose in the particular occasion to the concept of divine purpose as something to be understood in a general and universal manner?'[10] But if the arguments are formally invalid, and if we cannot have the original 'apprehension' (as on continuist principles we cannot), the answer is, simply, 'No'.

I should, however, in honesty admit that I myself think more of natural theology than this. I think the cosmological and physico-theological arguments afford strong (though not absolutely conclu- sive) reason for believing in a Creator God; and there may be some reason to think we can know more about Him, for instance that He is good, though this is less certain.[11] But natural theology alone can carry us no further than this; many would say, not that far. To get any further requires, I believe, the fact that revelation claims to be the testimony of this same Creator. But this step is forbidden continuists. The most they can say is that there is, probably, a God who created this world, and who is, possibly, good, in a sense of 'goodness' which allows Him to leave the world He made strictly alone and do nothing for it once it is made except keep it from falling into non-existence.

So I am not seriously worried by the fact that the doctrine of the Incarnation clashes with a continuist view of God. This latter is so implausible as a Christian view that it can be ignored.[12] The charge that the Incarnation is incompatible with *traditional* views of God is more serious.

The argument was that God is *immutable*, and that an incarnation would involve a change in God; it is not therefore possible that God should become incarnate. The attempt to reply that the Incar- nation is only a real relation on the human side of our Lord, and not on the divine, seemed unsuccessful, unless it was accepted that both creation and incarnation were a kind of inner necessity to God, which did not sound convincing. But why should we think God to be immutable? Aquinas[13] gives three reasons: first, that

---

[10] p. 36.   [11] Cf. e.g. Swinburne (1979).
[12] I have dealt with this question at greater length in *The New Deism* (Bristol, 1990).
[13] *Summa Theologiae*, I. 9. I.

in God there is no potentiality (which is required for change); secondly, in change part of the thing changed persists and part does not (e.g. if an object changes colour from white to black the stuff it is made out of remains constant), whereas God has no parts; and thirdly, because God, being infinite perfection, cannot attain anything further.

Of these, the second is mistaken, for a thing can change by having something added to it, which is precisely what happened at the Incarnation, the 'taking of manhood into God'. The third shows only that God cannot become greater or more perfect, not that He cannot change in a way which neither increases nor diminishes His perfection. But the Incarnation, while exemplifying His perfect goodness and love, did not add to them (let alone reduce them). So only the first argument remains. But it is not obvious that it is true, except on the supposition that God is timeless, which I do in fact believe to be the case. If so, there is indeed a sense in which there is no potentiality or change in Him; as a matter of fact, we need not have brought potentiality into it at all in order to show that a timeless God does not change. (Other arguments against potentiality in God seem to me to be either mistaken or to apply only to certain kinds of potentiality—e.g. the ability to become greater.)

But He is only unchangeable *sub specie aeternitatis*. To us who are timebound He can and does change; and one of His changes could be an Incarnation. From God's point of view, or that of any other timeless beings He may have created, the Incarnation is eternal; it is simply the case that God the Son has, by His own will, a human side to Him. From our point of view, there was a change in God somewhere about 4 BC; but it is not a change *except* from our point of view. Unless, then, strong other reason can be found for saying that in God there is no potentiality, the traditional view of God is perfectly compatible with Incarnation.

15

Christ's Relationship to the Human Race

WE now come to one of the most difficult of all the problems posed so far. Are we obliged to assert a relationship of Jesus to the rest of the human race which is an impossible one, either by trying to make 'humanity' into a kind of *thing* which can be affected (with a real change, not a notional one) by God's entering into it, or by making Christ's individual human nature something which we can enter?

Let us take the latter first. St Paul and St John both insist that there is a sense in which the believer is 'in Christ'.[1] But this, however it be interpreted, is a relationship between persons; nothing is said about our being incorporated into Christ's 'human nature'. If anything, the implication of John 17: 21 ('that they may be in *us*', addressed to the Father) would be that it is the *deity* of the Lord that the redeemed are within. There is no need to pursue this matter any further.

The other is more tricky. In Chapter 3 we saw that a Platonist view of what constitutes the universal 'humanity' would not help us, and (we went on) while Platonism did at least allow universals to be a kind of individual entity, other theories did not even do that much. But was this in fact correct? and if it was, can we perhaps see how the Incarnation might affect humanity collectively without bringing in universals at all?

It is true that most theories of universals treat them as things which cannot undergo real (as opposed to notional) change at the hands of particulars. I think the one that perhaps comes nearest would be the Hegelian theory of the 'concrete universal', according to which the universal is not an abstract property but an actual ('concrete') object existing in the world, whose parts are what we should normally call *instances* of the universal. 'Whiteness' actually

---

[1] e.g. Rom. 8: 1, John 17: 21.

consists of all white things. Hence it is really true that I am a part of humanity, and that 'any man's death diminishes me'. And since this is so, it might seem possible that an incarnation affecting the universal 'humanity' in one of its parts would *ipso facto* affect the other parts as well. There are problems here, though. Universals, whether concrete or abstract, can be linked by contingent relationships. It may be that all mice are timid, but inspection of one mouse will not tell us this; all it can tell us is that *this* mouse is timid. In certain cases we may be able to move from one specific instance to a generalization because we already know that this *sort* of move is reliable. If we find that in a particular mouse such-and-such a nerve has such-and-such a function, it is a safe bet that it has the same function in other mice; but this is because we have previous generalizations about the uniformity of anatomical systems to go on. And there are also *necessary* relationships, which, once grasped in a single instance, can be seen to apply to all: in seeing that one thing which has colour also has size, we realize that anything which has colour will have size too. Now clearly if we found a way of training a particular mouse to be courageous, this would leave all other mice unaffected; and similarly, while the Incarnation would yield one human being who was one with God and in no way alienated from him, it would not affect the rest of us. Nor would diversion of the nerve to some other function in one mouse affect any others. It seems, then, that the Incarnation, if it is to affect all humanity, must set up a relationship of the third, necessary kind, so that, given that in Jesus Christ God and man are reconciled, we can move to the general statement that all people are so reconciled (at least potentially), by some kind of necessary inference. But this inference would rest on a relationship between concepts (as with the concepts of colour and size), and it is hard to see how an event, even the event of the Incarnation, could bring about such a necessary relationship. The most it could do would be to *show* that union with God was possible despite the sin and fallenness of our race; it could not by itself bring about that possibility. (And of course it has normally been supposed that it did not in fact bring it about by itself; there was a Cross as well as a Stable.)

It may be—I put this forward as no more than a suggestion—that one major aspect of the Incarnation was precisely to show the true state of affairs; that Cabasilas' 'barrier of nature', like the 'barrier of death' (though not that of sin), was a barrier in our minds rather than in the structure of reality. If men and women were made in God's image and intended for fellowship with Him, then the facts that we quite obviously are not in such fellowship, and that the image is horribly marred, are (to put it mildly) disheartening. The gap might seem unbridgeable. It might well need the example of one whose closeness to God was even greater than we dared to imagine, and yet who was unquestionably one of us, sharing it may be even our 'original sin', to restore hope and show us that the barrier could be broken down, the gap bridged—because they actually had been. If *union* between God and us is possible after all, how much more must fellowship be! There was more to be done than this, because of the 'barrier of sin', a 'more' of which the Incarnation was a necessary condition, though not a sufficient one; but this much it could do by itself.

There are two other possibilities that should be mentioned at this point, two other suggestions about how Christ could have the effect of being a 'common person', affecting all our race, without our needing impossible manœuvres with universals.

The first was hinted at by W. R. Matthews in a book already referred to more than once, *The Problem of Christ in the Twentieth Century*.[2] He mentions Sanday's suggestion that Jesus' subconscious was the 'location' of the Divinity, and points to developments in the Freudian, and, still more, the Jungian schools of psychology. Jung talks of a 'collective unconscious'. Now if, Matthews points out,

the hypothesis of the racial unconscious is confirmed by psychological investigation, we shall have a strong suggestion, on empirical evidence, that our normal way of thinking about humanity is too individualistic, and that our separateness is true only on the level of consciousness while, below that level, we are linked together ... If we all partake in the same racial unconsciousness, a new meaning lights up the phrase 'in Adam all die'.

Redemption must somehow affect the unconscious, including the racial unconscious if there really is one, though Matthews is understandably not sure how this is to be managed. Telepathy, too, suggests a linking of minds beneath the level of consciousness; this might, Matthews suggests, be connected with Jesus' 'knowing what was in man' and hence with His bearing of our sins.

The 'telepathy' element is not, I think, of great significance.

[2] Matthews (1950), pp. 43ff., 50ff.

Christ's mind certainly affects the lives of His followers on the conscious level; if it also affects them on the unconscious, that is a thing to be very thankful for, but it does not make a major theological difference. The suggestion about the 'collective unconscious' is more important. For if this is a reality, then very probably indeed the Incarnation would affect it, and thereby affect the whole of the human race who share in it. 'Humanity' really would be a single unity (with many 'conscious' outcrops from that unity), and it could be affected by one human being's union with God.

Unfortunately, the catches are obvious. By no means all psychologists accept the teachings of the 'Viennese' school, and of those who do by no means all are Jungians. It is also possible that even if Jung is right, the 'collective unconscious' is simply a handy way of describing universal patterns in the functioning of the human brain, genetically transmitted no doubt, and should not be treated as a real entity any more than 'the bloodstream' should. The idea is an interesting one, but it would be rash of the Christologist to stake too much upon it.

The second suggestion is to see Christ as what I might call a socially 'common person'. William Temple expressed this in the form of a development of the idea of the 'concrete universal' alluded to a little while back.[3] There is no such thing as human nature apart from all individual human beings. But there is a perfectly real thing which we may call Mankind or Humanity, which is a unit and not a mere agglomeration. Each of us is largely constituted by the influence of others. 'I *am* mankind—England—my school— my family—focussed in a point of its own history. Mankind— "Adam"—has made me what I am. If similarly Christ makes me something else—the participator in His own divine freedom (St John viii. 36)—then indeed "there is a new creation".' For Christ's Incarnation 'was not merely the addition of another unit to the system ... it was the inauguration of a new system of mutual influence, destined to become, here or elsewhere, universally dominant'. This seems to me absolutely right. It will not do, not quite, as an explanation of the 'common personhood' of Jesus in terms of the Incarnation alone, because the inauguration of the new system called for more than just incarnation—the whole of Christ's ministry, death, and resurrection was involved. But it does look as if this, in combination

[3] Temple (1924), pp. 151–3.

with what was said earlier about the necessity of a demonstration of the possibility of human fellowship with God, could give us something near to what was wanted, a way of understanding the corporate significance of the Incarnation for the whole of humankind. (Not a complete understanding, of course; but enough to be going on with.) And we must keep in mind a fact that is sometimes forgotten by those who stress the 'corporate Christ'—the fact that it is not said that all human beings are automatically incorporated into Him, but only that believers are. It is never suggested that Herod or Caiaphas was automatically 'in Christ' simply by being human. Christ made it *possible* for them to be 'in Him'; He did not make it inevitable. It is the Christian of whom it may truly be said that he or she is a member of Christ's Body. And of course whatever the nature of this incorporation may be, it is quite certainly nothing to do with universals, Platonic or otherwise. The objections raised in Chapter 3 were probably valid criticisms of some incautious theologians; they have no weight at all against the doctrine of the Incarnation as long as its defenders keep in mind what the Bible actually says.

16

Ethical Considerations

WHAT of the charge that the traditional view is in some way uneth-
ical, immoral, or unspiritual? Some versions of this charge are,
frankly, rather hard to make sense of (which is why Chapter 4 contained so many quotations), and there is some risk that one may
miss their point. When as distinguished a theologian as Mackintosh
tells us that 'non-ethical realities admit of no true unity', one is
inclined to wish one could ask him whether he means his own body
is not a unity, or whether perhaps his hands and feet are ethical
realities. There is some justice in some of the claims made—that
our Lord's humanity was overshadowed in much traditional Christology is perhaps the greatest weakness in that Christology, and the
strongest card in the revisionist's hand. Yet surely the traditionalists
have learned their lesson by now; indeed, many of them, throughout
the centuries, have given the lie to the apparent bias in their theoretical Christologies by a passionate (some might even say excessive)
devotion, not to God the Word, but to the human figure of Jesus.

Forsyth's accusation, that 'Chalcedonism' stood things on their
head by requiring that one somehow descend, from a 'scientific
theology' accepted by most ordinary Christians in uncomprehending
obedience to an authoritative Church, to 'such personal experiences
as may thereupon be open' would be serious indeed if it were true.
But surely it depends on a misunderstanding of what the analytic
Christologist is about? His own expression 'scientific theology' ought
to have given the clue to his error. Astronomers do not tell the
public: 'First understand my theories about the normal sequence,
the origin of red giants, the occurrence of pulsars and the like,
and then, if you really must, you may go out on a clear night and
look up at the sky.' Biologists do not demand a knowledge of the
processes of digestion and the role of individual enzymes before
they will allow us to eat our breakfast. On the contrary: the astronomers themselves very likely began by gazing at the stars and feeling

within themselves a wonder which was intellectual as well as aesthetic, and the biologists, lured perhaps into their science by
curiosity about what happened to their breakfasts when they were
eaten, were not thereby prevented from enjoying them. It is possible
that as their studies proceed they may come back to us and tell
us to avoid certain easy but dangerous mistakes which their discoveries have unmasked. Long ago astronomers told us that the
earth is not the centre of the universe after all, and that we were
ill-advised to guide our lives by columns in the papers headed 'What
the Stars Foretell for You'. Biologists are apt to come up with warn-
ings about cholesterol and the proportion of polyunsaturated fats
in our diets which are mildly alarming even if not always fully understood. But the beauty of the stars and the pleasure of good food
are not vetoed by any scientist, to themselves or to others.

It is not very different with theology. There may be some Christologists who really did begin with the abstract definitions and debates
and then try to work out a suitable devotional life on this basis.
A consistent revisionist might well feel obliged to do so, fearing
that traditional patterns of devotion were infected by the errors
of the past; as I said earlier on, if some of the more extreme revisionists are right, the vast majority of Christians have been and still
are guilty of idolatry. But with most this has not been so—not even
with the revisionists. Most Christologists began as Christian believers, worshipping and trusting and trying to obey the Son of
God who loved them and gave Himself for them. Later, indeed,
they came to wonder how this glorious salvation came about, and
sought to construct their 'scientific theology'. But there can be few,
and those poor unhappy souls, who did not remember all along
that the fact, not the theory, was what counted, that we are saved
by God's grace and not by theology, however accurate. 'Thoughts
are but coins', wrote C. S. Lewis;

> let me not trust, instead
> Of Thee, their thin-worn image of Thy head
> From all my thoughts, even my thoughts of Thee,
> O Thou fair Silence, fall, and set me free.[1]

And God forgive us and rescue us all if we are so far gone as not
to echo those words. The astronomer who forgets the beauty of

---

[1] 'The Apologist's Evening Prayer' (Lewis (1964), p. 129).

a starlit night, the biologist for whom the salt has lost its savour, are to be pitied for their loss; but the theologian who forgets the Christ who saved us is close, not to losing anything, but to being lost.

I doubt if the Church, or even the Church's theologians, have normally expected their theories—even their dogmas—to be the basis of everyday faith. Christians have indeed been asked to believe that Jesus Christ was truly God and truly human; but the refinements of 'scientific theology' have only been for those who wanted to know or speculate more, like the refinements of scientific astronomy.

The other main complaint of Mackintosh and Forsyth was that while the traditional theology taught that the *motive* of the Incarnation was love, and in this was admirably correct, the method by which this love was supposed to achieve its end was not spiritual or moral. This is where I become seriously bothered. Surely a spiritual method of achieving a goal must be one that uses spiritual means, that is, means which are located in the spiritual side of human nature rather than the physical: but the union of God and Man in Jesus has surely been seen as just that, except possibly by Apollinarians. 'The flesh would not have been capable of assumption', wrote Aquinas, 'except by its relation to the rational soul.'[2] And if by a moral means we mean one which involves goodness on the part of those redeemed as well as on that of the Redeemer, no one has doubted that sanctification is part of God's purpose for us, though as a goal rather than merely as a means. On the positive side, their stress is laid on the will. We quoted Mackintosh's words, that 'Jesus Christ is identical with God in will': and it looks as if this is really what was meant by a 'moral' or 'spiritual' method. Now if it is held that the will is the 'organic centre of personality' (again Mackintosh's words) one can see why this position was held—but even so, not why we should accept it as true. It looks like yet *another* mitigated Apollinarianism. Certainly the two theologians we are considering did not see God as 'taking over' the will of the man Jesus, or substituting His own for it, but it is hard to see what else their views could lead to, even if it was God in kenosis who was doing the taking over. And would this be particularly 'moral'? Surely not. On any view of the Incarnation (except those which treat it as merely a myth or an allegory) it was a tremendous act of love and compas-

---

[2] *Summa Theologiae*, 3, q. 6, art. 2.

sion; to seek to make it somehow 'more moral' is to gild refined gold.

I find almost equal difficulty in doing justice to Cupitt's objection. His reference to 'Jesus' emphasis upon ... the disjunction of things human and divine'[3] is especially puzzling. Elsewhere, Cupitt himself has said that 'there is no insuperable barrier between man and God. God is close to man and offers forgiveness freely ... Where Jesus taught his disciples to pray directly to Our Father, the church of Jesus prays to Almighty and Everlasting God through Jesus Christ our Lord'.[4] 'Disjunction' seems an extraordinary word to use; Cupitt apparently wants to accuse Christendom *both* of having made God too familiar and 'human' *and* of making Him too imperial and remote. And to do so he alters his view of Jesus' teaching as is needed.

Of course, it is quite true that at times Christians have erred in both these directions. In stressing the majesty and power of God and His Christ, in conformity with many sayings of Jesus Himself,[5] the Church has all too often arrogated that power to herself, and claimed, in the name of the God of love, the right to imprison, to torture, and to burn; or, less vilely but more subtly, made herself and her institutions into yet another mediating layer between us and God, under the control of the sinners who (because there is no one who is not a sinner) inevitably form her leadership. It is also true that God *has* been presented far too often as 'the Old Man in the sky', and made out to be the kind of being who will be bound to pardon us because *c'est son métier*. Yet one would have thought it was the idea of the Incarnation that both these errors offended against, by ignoring the fact that there is *one* mediator,[6] whose kingdom is not of this world,[7] and who found the way of reconciliation very costly. Cupitt says it is 'really very confusing' to find a mediating religion focused around a man whose own religion was immediate;[8] but it only confuses him because he does

---

[3] In Hick (1977*b*), p. 195.
[4] Cupitt (1979), p. 80. It is only fair to remember the speed with which Cupitt's views change.
[5] e.g. Matt. 25: 31ff.; Mark 14: 62; Luke 22: 29f. Of course, there is the difficulty that Cupitt may reply that such sayings are inauthentic.
[6] 1 Tim. 2: 5.   [7] John 18: 36.   [8] Cupitt (1979), p. 81.

not believe in the Incarnation, and therefore has to suppose that within twenty years of Jesus' death His followers had completely reversed the whole thrust of His message without anybody's noticing and complaining. Whereas if Jesus really was whom the Church has supposed Him to be, His religion *would* be more immediate than ours, and we *could* both address God as our Father and meet, work, or pray in the name of the Son,[9] believing both in the loving forgiveness of God and in the means and proof of that love, which we call the Cross. Take away the keystone of the arch, and yes, the resulting ruin does look a little confusing.

Driver's desire to subject Christology to ethical judgement is well-founded. Ethical truths are as solid ground as any others, and can be used like other facts to test the validity of a theological position. Christianity is ethically 'vulnerable' just as it is historically. And ethical arguments have been used before now in theological debate. It is a standard charge against the idea of double predestination, whereby God was supposed to have assigned some people to heaven and others to hell before ever they were born, on no basis other than His own choice, that it means either that God was less than just (which was scripturally intolerable) or that arbitrary damnation was perfectly just, which was contrary to a plain ethical truth. Similarly, it has been argued in criticism of some theories of the Atonement that they require that human sacrifice be morally acceptable, or that it be right to punish the innocent for the sins of the guilty, and that these too are morally intolerable ideas. Whether these particular arguments are decisive or not is not our concern here; the point is that this *kind* of argument is certainly legitimate in theology. If, then, a particular kind of Christology leads to an ethical falsehood, such as racism, that kind of Christology is mistaken. (We are not running counter here to Driver's claim that we ought not to 'develop a christology first and inquire into its ethical consequences later', even if that claim is justified. He was referring there to constructive work, not critical, as his approach to existing Christologies shows.)

The problem is, what do we mean by 'leading to'? If we meant 'logically entailing' the case would be clear. This is what was alleged in ethical criticisms of double predestination or substitutionary atonement—that they logically entailed untenable ethical positions.

---

[9] Matt. 18: 20; Mark 9: 38ff.; Luke 10: 17; John 14: 13; etc.

But this is not the case with Christology and the rendering 'weak, invisible or ashamed' of most of the human race, of which Driver complains. Nor, to be fair, does he claim that it is. Obviously there is no valid move from 'Jesus Christ was male' to 'All females should be treated as inferior to males'; if there were, there would be an equally valid move from 'Jesus Christ died in His thirties' or 'Jesus Christ was born in a stable', let alone 'Jesus Christ was a Jew'. What Driver does claim is that Christology provided 'powerful rationalizations' for evils like racism and sexism. And this claim must be treated with some care.

A rationalization is an argument developed to defend a position or prejudice which is really held for quite different reasons, probably non-rational ones. Christians are no less likely than others to develop such, and if they do they will often be rationalizations that claim a Christian basis, maybe one in the person of Christ. The most infamous example in Church history is of course anti-Semitism: Jews had prosecuted Jesus, therefore were guilty of His death, and so hatred of (other) Jews was justified. It can hardly be claimed that anti-Semitism *originated* in this way, but, having come into existence, this is the way it was rationalized. Again, in controversies over the ordination of women, the fact that Jesus was male has often been used against such ordinations, although it is unlikely that any of those advancing this argument would otherwise have supposed that the clergy had to resemble Jesus (except in the holiness of life to which all Christians are called). But, however misguided such rationalizations are, they do not affect the facts on which they are supposedly based. Certain Jews did prosecute Christ, and He was in fact male. It is simply that the attitudes supposed to derive from these facts do not really do so. There is no rational (as opposed to rationalizing) connection. Of course, if a rationalization of some ethically objectionable view were really implied by some theological position, then it would indeed cast doubt on that position. But this is not the case. If there were a real connection, we should be anti-masculinists on the grounds that all who prosecuted, condemned, and executed Jesus were male, and deny ordination to Gentiles because Jesus was Jewish. The prejudices are there, and an excuse to hold them is sought. Indeed, often these same prejudices have sought rationalization in terms of science; but that is hardly reason to abandon the scientific enterprise.

It may be, however, that Christianity has been, in Driver's words,

'easily invaded' by objectionable views—that the link is not so much
rational as psychological. This may well be true, to some extent.
That there are dangers to which Christians are exposed, more so
than many others, has long been known, at least since some suggested 'Let us sin more, so that grace may abound',[10] if not since
James and John asked for the best places in the Kingdom.[11] Maybe
some of the evils Driver lists are among these. But dangers attach
to any set of beliefs, any occupation, any way of life, and the cure
is not to abandon the beliefs, occupation, or way of life, but to
know the dangers for what they are and avoid them.

It is worth quoting an avowedly feminist theologian (with views
in some ways quite like Driver's own): 'Theologically speaking . . .
the maleness of Jesus has no ultimate significance', and if it has
some symbolic significance, it manifests the 'kenosis of patriarchy,
the announcement of the new humanity through a lifestyle that dis-
cards hierarchical caste privilege and speaks on behalf of the lowly'.[12]
This is surely true; and I suspect it applies to all Driver's
dangers. Incidentally, it is hard to read what Driver says about
Jesus as the 'male beholden to nothing that is not male' without
rubbing one's eyes, when one recalls that He was born of a virgin,
with no human father. John Donne's saying, that 'He came of
woman so, as that he came of nothing but woman; of woman, and
not of man',[13] seems nearer the mark. Driver does indeed treat
of the Virgin Birth,[14] which he tries to depict as a reduction of
the mother to nothing (as in creation *ex nihilo*). In the light of
the great, even excessive veneration that has been paid to the Blessed
Virgin during the course of the Church's history, this is almost
equally bewildering. But this is all *ad hominem*.

What, then, of the charge of moral *unhelpfulness*? The argument
here was that we cannot be called upon to imitate the example
of someone who had the decisive advantage over us of being God;
and that even the effect of the Passion is diminished by the realization
(or should we say merely 'belief'?) that this man being crucified
was really the Son of God all the time. The latter point is not all
that difficult to meet. I quoted Sydney Carter in support of this,

---

[10] Rom. 6: 1.   [11] Mark 10: 35ff.   [12] Reuther (1983), p. 137.
[13] Sermon on Easter Day, 1630, in Donne (1953–62), ix. 192.
[14] Driver (1981), pp. 140ff.

but deliberately refrained from giving the last verse of the ballad, saving it till now:

> If you are a son of man
> Then you can be mistaken;
> You hang upon the cross of doubt,
> You feel yourself forsaken,
> And whether you will rise again
> Is more than you can tell—
> And if you were the son of man
> You've tasted that as well.

So He did. Christ's human knowledge was limited, and therefore He was open to uncertainties, and could cry 'Why hast Thou forsaken me?' (though still, as George MacDonald pointed out, addressing the Father as '*My* God'). But this does not meet the first point, that He cannot be a helpful example to us unless we are able to imitate Him, and we cannot imitate Him if He was God.

Perhaps we can, mind you. Paul does tell his readers to be imitators of God,[15] and Paul's Master told His followers to be perfect as their Father in heaven was perfect.[16] But if we can be called upon to be like God in heaven, surely *a fortiori* we can be called upon to be like God incarnate on earth?

Divine or not divine, Christ's life can be an example to us (though the society in which He lived was of course very different from that in which most of us have to follow His example). But an example is more than just a thing to be imitated. It is supposed to be an encouragement to us, a stimulus to effort. Can Jesus Christ give us that if He is more than human? 'It gives me no encouragement in facing the world's temptations to be told that they were overcome by a Being, whose human weakness was reinforced by combination with omnipotence ... Is there not something futile in the thought of a finite being straining after resemblance to infinite perfection?' But John Caird, from whom this quotation was taken, went on to give what is surely the decisive reply: 'Not a finite but an infinite ideal is what we want ... Our aim as spiritual beings is not likeness to man but likeness to God, participation in a divine and eternal life. The goal of spiritual attainment ever recedes as we advance.'[17]

---

[15] Eph. 5: 1.
[16] Matt. 5: 48. The parallel passage in Luke 6: 36 has 'merciful', not 'perfect', but the idea of being like God is of course there just as much as in Matthew.
[17] Caird (1899), ii. pp. 115–16.

Two sorts of encouragement can be given to us: that of the equal and that of the ideal. An aspiring athlete may be encouraged by the example of a contemporary with the same training as herself who has done rather well; she may also be encouraged by the example of the world record-holder, even though she knows that the latter had advantages she herself lacks. It is the same, only more so, with examples for life. It is true that I may be encouraged by the story of someone like St Augustine, whose sanctity was achieved after long failure and doubt; it is also true that I may be encouraged by that of Jesus, who, though He too knew temptation and uncertainty, was held to the ideal by the strength of His union with divinity. To demand that one life should give us both kinds of example is unfair. (And yet the life of Jesus comes close to meeting even this unfair demand. For we do not achieve holiness by our own unaided efforts; we say that we depend upon the aid of the Holy Spirit. Jesus' 'human weakness was reinforced' by God; so is ours.)

We are now faced with those criticisms which suggest that orthodoxy is itself objectionable in a moral or quasi-moral way. The first, Hick's accusation of a 'pre-Copernican' mind on the part of traditionalists, is not one that can easily be dismissed. The parallel that he draws between Christian and Ptolemaic 'epicycles' has a horrid plausibility about it. Yet has he not to some extent misrepresented the history both of astronomy and of religion? The appalling complexities of pre-Copernican astronomy were due more to the fact that the planets move in ellipses than to the fact that they move around the sun. The scheme proposed by Tycho Brahe, in which the sun and moon move around the earth and the planets around the sun, produced no particular problems except those which arose from insistence on circular paths (which as a matter of fact it shared with Copernicus' own original scheme). It was a passion for aesthetic symmetry that led to the complexities, more than geocentricity.

But that of course is by the way. More serious is the fact that the position Hick justifiably criticizes in the Council of Florence was itself a *development*—one whose germs can indeed be found much earlier, but only as germs. Christians had never believed that you had to be a Christian in this life in order to avoid hell-fire. The existence of the patriarchs and prophets of the Old Testament made that impossible; no Christian would hold that Abraham and Moses were lost souls (though their salvation might have been delayed until the Harrowing of Hell). And of course many were quite willing to extend this to those outside Israel. They could quote St Peter to the effect that 'in every nation anyone who fears God and does what is right is acceptable to Him',[18] or St Paul's description of Epimenides as a prophet.[19] Justin Martyr could call Socrates and Heraclitus 'Christians before Christ' on the same basis as Abraham or Elijah.[20] Yet Peter went on to baptize Cornelius, with the assurance that 'everyone who believes in [Jesus] receives forgiveness through His name';[21] Paul went on, after saying 'The grace of God has appeared for the salvation of all men' to call Jesus not only Saviour but (almost certainly) *God*,[22] who gave Himself to redeem us; and Justin said that though the Logos had been in the philosophers, yet He had been made man to share our sufferings and so bring us healing; 'for it is one thing to have the germ of something and imitate it as best one can, but quite another to have the thing itself'.[23] Salvation for all of them was by Christ, yet not only visible Christians were savable. If by the time of Florence the second half had been overlooked, that was a change, whereby one view present in earlier centuries had been swamped by another also present then. There has since been a shift in the other direction.

What is one to say of the 'epicycles' that have been introduced into Christianity to avoid the conclusion drawn by Florence? The 'invincible ignorance' one is of doubtful value here. It is a vital principle in moral theology, for it is quite true that no one is blamed for doing something wrong when the only reason was that they did not realize what they were doing and could not have avoided the mistake. If you hang your coat over mine, which it exactly resembles, and I take yours by mistake, I am not guilty of theft! But does this apply to the receiving and rejection of salvation? On the normal understanding (and I imagine this applied at the Council of Florence too), one who accepts Christ as Saviour is saved, but not because this is a meritorious deed; and one who rejects Him is lost, but not because this is a wicked thing to do. Both were

---

[18] Acts 10: 35.
[19] Titus 1: 12. (The authorship of the Pastorals is not of course relevant here.)
[20] *First Apology*, c. 46 (PG 6, 397c).
[21] Acts 10: 43.
[22] Titus 2: 11, 13–14.
[23] *Second Apology*, c. 13 (PG 6, 467a).

originally lost because of their sin; but one has accepted the salvation offered (which is not a particularly virtuous act, though it is certainly a wise one) and the other has not. Invincible ignorance excuses overlooked blame, guilt, and punishment; but the unbeliever is not being blamed, held guilty, or punished for failure (through ignorance) to believe, but only for having sinned *without* the excuse of invincible ignorance in the rest of his or her life.[24] If I miss my train through an unavoidable mistake over the times, I am not blamed for doing so; my ignorance was invincible; but that does not mean that I catch my train after all.

The strong point of the 'baptism of desire' approach is that this concept was there in Roman Catholic theology already. It was absurd to regard as outside the Church someone who was awaiting baptism but died before receiving it. If, then, someone who would have been baptized had circumstances been otherwise (i.e. had he or she lived a few days longer) is to be regarded as a Christian, should the same not be said of others who would also have been baptized had circumstances been otherwise (i.e. had they realized the truth of the Christian gospel)? The weak points are: First, that this is an *extension* of the concept from a clear case (where someone actually did desire the sacrament) to one far from clear (where someone perhaps would have desired the sacrament if circumstances had been very different indeed, but in actual fact did *not* desire it).[25] Secondly, that it would often require knowledge of a non-existent free act (the decision whether or not to be baptized that 'would have' taken place if the person had been properly informed). Although some Arminian and Molinist theologians did think this sort of knowledge possible (to God), it seems to me a logically incoherent idea, though to demonstrate this would lead one into the very difficult terrain of the logic of counterfactual conditionals. Thirdly, that it seems to demand a sacramental theology which rates baptism higher than faith, since faith is accepted only as a kind of substitute for the sacrament. Theologies which hold that it is faith in Christ which admits one to the Church will not really *need* the idea of 'baptism of desire', and will have difficulty in extending

---

[24] John 3: 18 notwithstanding: 'because he has not believed' *explains* the judgement, it does not *justify* it, as the tense makes clear ('has not', not 'did not').

[25] An unkind critic might suggest that even the most hardened villains normally desire their own good, and since their good lies in Christ, they too 'really' desire baptism.

some other doctrine in the way that 'baptism by desire' might conceivably be extended.

These two 'epicycles' are, as Hick says, more characteristic of Roman Catholic theology than of Protestant, and perhaps that is why the present writer (being a Protestant) has more sympathy for the third (though it too is found among Roman Catholics, I should add). It is to all appearances biblical; though the passages usually cited[26] have been the subject of much dispute, the most natural interpretation does seem to be on the lines of the 'harrowing of hell' and the preaching of the gospel even to those already dead. Furthermore, as we saw just now, *whatever* line was taken on the interpretation of these verses, there had to be some way to account for the salvation of the saints of Israel under the Old Covenant, and it would be difficult (even 'epicyclic') to account for this without letting in some of those who were not Israelites. If Abraham was saved by Christ without having known of Him in this life, why not Melchizedek to whom Abraham paid tithes; why not, indeed, Socrates or Heraclitus? And of course there are many passages which suggest that God's purpose is to have mercy on *all* people through Jesus Christ.[27]

An 'epicycle' should be an idea introduced *ad hoc* to explain an awkwardness, as was the case with the actual epicycles of Ptolemaic astronomy; no one would have thought in terms of epicycles if the planets had not been observed to move in a different way from the other stars. An 'epicycle' should not be something which was there in any case to serve some other theological purpose—which is the case with all three of the views Hick considers epicyclic. It is surely the mark of a good theory, in theology as well as science, that it turns out to account for facts other than those it was originally based on. If any of these three will in fact, besides doing its original task, explain why the Council of Florence was wrong, so much the better for it. Would it not be *more* of an 'epicycle' to abandon the doctrine of the Incarnation in order to be able to disagree with Florence? (Though, to be fair, Hick has undoubtedly other reasons for not believing in the Incarnation, and might plead, much as I have, that his view accounts for facts other than those he first based it on.)

---

[26] 1 Pet. 3: 19, 4: 6; John 5: 25–9. Matt. 27: 52 and Eph. 4: 8–9 might reflect a similar idea.

[27] e.g. 1 Cor. 15: 22, 2 Cor. 5: 14, 1 Tim. 2: 3–6; Titus 2: 11–14. This does not mean that God's purposes may not be frustrated by human perversity; only that they are His purposes, and unlikely to be frustrated by God Himself.

Next, what of the Christs of other worlds than this? Can we say—
Sydney Carter again—

> Who can tell what other cradle
> High above the Milky Way
> Still may rock the King of heaven
> On another Christmas Day?[28]

or do we regard this as impossible, with Puccetti and the characters
in Smart's dialogue?[29] Could God become incarnate more than
once? Opinions differ. Carter (and Alice Meynell before him) say
'Yes', and have the weighty authority of St Thomas Aquinas behind
them;[30] so does Dr Morris;[31] Puccetti says 'No, not at the same
time anyway';[32] Mascall says 'Yes, in different species, but not twice
in the same species'.[33]

It is perhaps worth remarking that the figure of 10^{18} planets with
'personal life' suggested by Puccetti would not meet with universal
acceptance. Some scientists have thought that the odds against life
appearing at all upon the earth were overwhelming.[34] Attempts
to use these figures as the basis for a theistic proof were almost
certainly misguided, and the calculations are to some extent flawed.
Nevertheless, they do do something to make it look doubtful whether
life can often have appeared elsewhere in the visible universe. Furthermore, even given life's appearance, the likelihood of its evolving
intelligence is not great. It has only once done so on Earth (whereas,
for instance, a bipedal stance evolved not only in human beings
but in birds and more than one line of dinosaurs, and eyes, I understand, in some forty different lineages[35]). And if the appearance
of intelligence was the result of many a priori improbable events,
it would presumably take longer to appear elsewhere—very likely
so long that the planet was no longer able to sustain life at all

---

[28] Carter (1969), p. 7.

[29] Smart (1960), pp. 95–6. The dialogue characters do not of course represent
Smart himself; yet the Christian spokesman in the dialogue never actually refutes
them.

[30] *Summa Theologiae*, 3, q. 3, art. 7 (not of course with other planets in mind).

[31] Morris (1986), pp. 170 ff.

[32] Puccetti (1968), p. 139.

[33] Mascall (1956a), pp. 40 ff.

[34] For a critical discussion of these see Bartholomew (1984), ch. 3.

[35] I owe this to Barrow and Tipler (1986), p. 132, quoting Ernst Mayr.

by the time it would have appeared.[36] So the figure of 10^{18} may need to be reduced—maybe even to 1.

But let us suppose that it is in fact correct. What exactly are Puccetti's arguments? As summarized in Chapter 4, they were in effect these: (1) If there are two simultaneous incarnations, as given this figure there would surely have to be, we have two corporeal beings, with each of whom the Son of God is numerically identical, yet who cannot be identical with each other. (2) If this were neverthe-less the case, we should have as good reason to worship these other 'Christs' as to worship Jesus. (3) We should have, in order to allow all these incarnations, to accept a Quaternity—and indeed more than that—instead of a Trinity.

Now the last is not correct unless the first is. If a Person of the Godhead can only be incarnate once at a given time, and if there are more than three incarnations at once, then certainly there would have to be more than three Persons in the Godhead. But if God the Son could be incarnate more than once at the same time, we do not need any more Persons. And the second point need not bother us much either. Undoubtedly if God has become incarnate on some other planet, and if we learn of this, we should have good reason to worship Him in that form. Not *quite* as good reason as we have to worship Jesus, for Jesus is *our* Redeemer, whereas the 'X-Christ', as Puccetti calls Him, is the Redeemer of the people of planet X; but still good reason. But why is this a problem? Our worship would, then as now, be directed to God the Son, except that we should know more about His saving work in the universe than we do now. (I might point out, for what it is worth, that many Hindus actually *do* worship more than one incarnation of Vishnu, though not from different planets.)

No, Puccetti's first point is the main one. The trouble lies in a certain ambiguity in the expression 'numerically identical'. Jesus Christ is numerically identical with the Son of God, agreed, but not in the sense in which Cicero is numerically identical with Tully. For there is more to the Son than the humanity of Jesus, and more to Jesus than the deity of the Son: whereas there is nothing more to Cicero than Tully or to Tully than Cicero. If a hand appears waving to us from a window, and I tell you 'That is Professor Puc-cetti'; and if later a face appears, and I say 'There is Professor

---

[36] See Barrow and Tipler (1986), pp. 556ff.

Puccetti again': I should take it hard if you disbelieved me on the grounds that a hand cannot be identical with a face. There is one total πρόσωπον of God the Son and Jesus of Nazareth—and, it may be, of the 'X-Christ' and many others. But that does not mean that all φύσεις within that πρόσωπον are identical with each other.

St Thomas went further, and said that God *could* have assumed two human natures, had He chosen; which Dr Mascall denies. It may be of some help in answering Puccetti to look into this point too, though strictly speaking we do not need to. Mascall's argument is that the human nature which the Word assumed had no 'personal individuality' of its own, only that given it by the assuming Word. 'If *per impossibile* he assumed, and conferred his personal individuality upon human nature twice over, there would not after all be two individuals but only one.'[37] Now there would only be one ὑπόστασις, agreed; but, as Aquinas says, 'there could still be multiplicity on the part of the nature on account of the division of matter'.[38] Two people usually have different ὑποστάσεις and also occupy different volumes of space; we can call them 'two' on either account—usually on the second! If God did become incarnate twice over, the two would be one person in the sense of having one ὑπόστασις, one central self, but they would be two in the sense of being in different places (and/or times). One might be a male Jew and the other a female Gentile, for example. And this would apply also if one of the two were not human.

I can see no objection, then, to there being more than one Incarnation, provided of course that one is possible. It should be worth adding, too, that not all who have considered the theology of life on other planets have thought that multiple incarnations would be necessary (though to me this seems the most natural opinion). Mascall cites E. A. Milne as suggesting that we should *inform* the rest of the galaxy of the Incarnation here.[39] This is not convincing: many races might have become extinct long before we managed to contact them. C. S. Lewis speculated[40] that salvation might be possible for other races without any need to follow the pattern of

[37] Mascall (1956a), pp. 40ff.

[38] Aquinas, *Summa Theologiae* 3, q. 3, art. 7.

[39] Mascall (1956a), p. 37, citing Milne, *Modern Cosmology and the Idea of God* (Oxford, 1952), p. 153.

[40] 'Perhaps—who knows—not even a second incarnation ... some act of even more appalling love, some glory of yet deeper humility' (Lewis (1953), pp. 135–6); cf. Lewis (1959).

Incarnation/Passion/Resurrection that it followed here; but until another pattern is discovered, or at least imagined, this remains doubtful. Or again, other planets might never have known a Fall—also an idea Lewis embodied in his novels. And Karl Rahner, noting that we cannot dismiss the idea of other Christs simply by appealing to 'God's decree', nevertheless thinks that it is a more promising approach to ask:

How are we to understand the inner connexion and unity of the cosmos as a whole, the nature of man and angel [and presumably other corporeal persons too] in such a way as to make it comprehensible that the Logos became 'only' man, and yet that as such he is Head and End of the whole cosmos ... in respect of a real function which he exercises with regard to the angels as well?[41]

If indeed we can understand the unity of the cosmos in this way (and perhaps there is biblical authority for this[42]) then one Incarnation might be enough; but I confess to doubts.

We may heartily agree with those who dislike orthodoxy for being 'static' that the picture of God given us in the Bible most certainly is not that of a remote and static Ineffability, to whose fixed serenity we might possibly aspire but who never steps out of it into life and action. That is the God of Aristotle, not of Abraham—nor of Jesus. The God of the Bible is a living God, a devouring fire, a loving Father; all images of action, energy and life. And it is sadly true that at times theologians have tended to forget this, and to use formulae to describe God or Christ which, however unintentionally, suggest the static rather than the dynamic. The question is whether to suggest is necessarily to *imply*; is the 'suggestion' really bound up with classical Christology?

I should judge that there is no necessary implication. It all depends less on the formulae themselves than on the beliefs and presuppositions of those who use them. Take the idea of the 'two natures'. 'Nature' can certainly be taken to mean something static. But it can equally well be taken to mean something very far from static—the nature, say, of a hurricane, a waterfall, a thunderbolt. We must not forget the remark of Fr. Schoonenberg quoted earlier, that 'divine and human nature quite simply indicate everything

---

[41] Rahner (1961), p. 198.
[42] Rom. 8: 19ff. But perhaps this refers only to the 'lower' creation, not to our equals or superiors; cf. Mascall (1956a), pp. 38–9, 44–5.

pertaining respectively to the divine and the human'—whether, be it noted, the items included under that 'everything' are static, or dynamic, or a mixture of both. If I call an aeroplane 'twin-engined', is my description to be faulted because it suggests something static, which an aeroplane is not? Hardly, I think; but in that case no more ought earlier generations of Christians to be faulted for saying that Christ shared in the divine and human 'natures'. They may have had too static an idea of God (or even of man); or they may have combined a static idea and a dynamic without fully realizing the difficulty of such a combination: but that does not affect the validity of their formulae.

It may be objected to my own proposed analysis that it does not in fact use the term 'nature'—indeed, was at some pains to avoid it—and that if, as I have already said I believe, God is the creator of time, not an inhabitant of it, He cannot be called 'dynamic', seeing that the activity of anything dynamic must be 'in time'. The latter of these objections is certainly a mistake. If God is outside time because He created it, He is not indeed dynamic in the usual sense, but then neither is He static. For a static thing is one which endures through a period of time without doing anything or changing at all, and God does not endure through any period of time. A writer may write something which is bad grammar, but cannot *be* bad grammar, or good grammar either. If we call the writer 'ungrammatical', it is by 'analogy of attribution' as the Scholastics called it, as being the cause of something ungrammatical in the proper sense of the word. And by that analogy God is both dynamic and static, but far more the former: the creator of the furnaces of the stars and the falling snowflake, the thunderer on Horeb and the bearer to Calvary of a cross.

The first objection is more serious at first glance. But although I tried to avoid using the word 'nature' as one of the key concepts in my attempts at analysis, I did so because I was concerned more to analyse the union of God and Man in Jesus Christ than to describe what God or people were. As was said at the time, 'Human nature consists of those qualities or disjunctions of qualities which are had by all men and women and are had in their entirety by nothing else, and similarly with divine nature ... Orthodoxy says that the incarnate Lord had both sets; which, if the unity described above is the true one, is in fact the case.' And to the extent that those qualities are dynamic (which I entirely agree is a *large* extent, seen *sub specie temporis*), my description is perfectly compatible with a 'dynamic' view of what was happening in Christ.

There is one interesting possibility which has not so far been raised but which belongs, I think, in this section. In his discussion of the 'progressive Incarnation' Christologies of Dorner, Forsyth, and Mackintosh, Dr G. S. Hendry suggests that it is a mistake to think of these as putting forward 'a view of the incarnation as a result achieved by a gradual process ... [with a] precise point at which the result was achieved'. In actual fact these theologians wanted 'to present a view of the incarnation as having its reality in the process as a whole ... as a dynamic reality which could only be interpreted in the dynamic character of *genesis* (becoming) and which the static category of *physis*, employed by the ancient church, could not grasp without distortion.'[43]

Whether this is a correct interpretation of the theologians involved is not our concern here. What does concern us is that here we have an analytic Christology which it really would be difficult to express in terms like *physis*, even in the sense we have been explaining just now. For even in that sense we were saying that the incarnate Lord had both sets of qualities, the divine and the human, including dynamic ones. But here it is being claimed that 'had' or 'has' are not the right words to use, nor even 'will have'. The Incarnation is not a state (like Jesus' being Jewish), not even a dynamic one (like Jesus' being alive); nor yet is it a process leading to a state (like His journeying to Jerusalem).[44] It is a process which has to be described in its own terms, like the wanderings of a gypsy who has no particular destination. If we say that a certain gypsy is 'a nomad', we are not describing a state of the gypsy, present or future, but an ongoing process with no goal except itself. (Actually *genesis* is no better a category than *physis*; the gypsy is not becoming anything by being a nomad, or if he or she is, then that 'anything' is perpetually changing.)

The trouble with such a view (and it should be made clear that I am not saying anyone has ever held it—I may well be fighting a Christological chimera!) is, oddly enough, that it has lost contact

[43] Hendry (1959), p. 98.
[44] It is significant that Barth, whom Hendry sees as supporting this view, though he stresses humiliation and exaltation, ties these in with the 'two states' of Christ, and sees these as completed; 'Where in Paul, for example, is He the Crucified who has not yet risen, or the Risen who has not been crucified?' (Barth (1956–8), IV/1, pp. 132ff.)

with history, the history in which the dynamic life and activity of God is shown. For it would usually have been said that the processes involved in the Incarnation were those of the humiliation or kenosis of the Son of God in becoming one of us and dying in obedience on the Cross, and the exaltation or 'plerosis' of the Son of Man through His growth in wisdom and stature and in favour with God and man,[45] the life in which He learned obedience through suffering,[46] and the resurrection and ascension in which He was once more glorified. But these lead to results; the Son of God is not perpetually becoming more and more humbled, beyond even death or the Descent into Hell, nor is the Son of Man usually supposed to become more and more glorified. (The latter is perhaps defensible. Some have thought that heaven itself is a perpetual growth in the love and knowledge of God: 'The Bride will always discover more and more of the incomprehensible and unhoped-for beauty of her Spouse through all eternity'.[47] And I suppose that this might apply to the humanity of our Lord, though I doubt if anyone has ever said so. But I do not see how it could be applied to the humbling of His divinity.) A process which is its own justification and does not lead to any final result, though perfectly possible, hardly seems to square with what we are actually told of the Incarnation. There is what looks like an intolerable choice between possibilities: either the process of God's becoming man is over, and, presumably, so is the Incarnation, or it is still continuing. If it is still continuing, then either it is progressive (as with Gregory's concept of heaven) and the Word is not yet fully incarnate, nor indeed ever will be: or it is not progressive, and we had better drop Forsyth's 'kenosis/plerosis' language, for we have little or nothing on this view that was not already there in views which see the Incarnation primarily as God's activity in Christ. So all in all, there seems nothing to be gained by adopting this line.

[45] Luke 2: 52.   [46] Heb. 5: 8.
[47] Gregory of Nyssa, *Commentary on the Song of Songs* (PG 44, 1037c).

17

The Questions of Christologists

OGDEN's attempt to eliminate the 'empirical-historical' Jesus, on the grounds that it is the 'existential-historical' Jesus who is the real subject of Christological assertions, seems to me utterly misconceived, and to have far less to be said for it than his other objections to traditional Christologies. He insists on treating the historical and existential Jesuses (if we may abbreviate his terms) as if they were two distinct things, rather than two aspects of or approaches to the one Person. We may readily agree that in affirming that Jesus is the Christ we are not affirming it because this Jesus was born in the reign of Herod the Great and lived most of His life in Nazareth; but this is not to say that the Jesus of whom we say that He is the Christ is not identical with the Jesus who was in fact born at that time and did in fact live in that town.

There are of course cases where we do have to separate two 'persons' who are ostensibly the same. The King Arthur of Malory is clearly not the same as the historical Arthur (assuming that there was one). But here of course Malory's Arthur is not 'existential-historical' but fictitious, and I do not think this is what Ogden wishes to say about the Jesus of Christology. It is interesting and instructive to examine a parallel Ogden uses to illustrate his point.[1] In the Gettysburg Address, Abraham Lincoln referred to the bringing forth on the American continent, fourscore and seven years earlier, of a nation dedicated to the proposition that all men were created equal. Unquestionably Lincoln meant an actual happening—the Declaration of Independence. 'And yet', Ogden goes on, 'it is just as clear that the only event the patriot means to refer to is the existential-historical event.' Maybe; but if anyone were to say 'The real subject of Lincoln's allusion was not the actual Declaration of Independence in the past by the founding fathers

[1] Ogden (1982), pp. 56f.

of the United States', they would leave their hearers baffled. Certainly there were many facts about the Declaration which were not relevant to Lincoln's patriotic concerns. It would have made no difference if the Declaration had been drafted by Hancock rather than Jefferson, or if it had been signed fourscore and eight years before, not fourscore and seven. But it was of course absolutely vital to Lincoln's citing of it that it should, as Ogden says, have originated the American nation and that it should have stated that all men were created equal. Had it been known to be a fake, or had it stated that all men were not created equal, he could no more have cited it as authorizing his patriotism than a modern Roman Catholic could cite the Forged Decretals as authorizing his attitude to the Papacy. The 'existential' and 'historical' Declarations are one and the same; the difference lies in the attitude to or use made of them, or rather of it. Similarly, there is a difference between the scholar seeking to reconstruct the historical facts about our Lord and the believer putting faith in Him (though they may be the same person); but the subject of facts and faith is one and the same. It is possible that Ogden was misled by his own language into the sort of 'imperceptible glide' we mentioned earlier. He describes the 'empirical-historical' Jesus as 'the actual Jesus of the past in so far as he is knowable to us today'.[2] This is not quite correct. The historical Jesus about whom Christological assertions are made is not the Jesus of the past in so far as He is knowable, but simply the Jesus of the past. (And, many would add, of the present; for He rose again and lives.) By adding his qualification, Ogden has slipped into a different region of thought—from facts about the past to people's ideas about the past today, ideas about what the past was like. And of course there is a real difference between our historical ideas and our 'existential' ideas about Jesus, even though there is no difference between the Jesuses they are about. Hence Ogden is able to drive his wedge between the two; if he had said 'the actual Jesus of the past, who is to some extent knowable to us today by historical enquiry' it would not have been so easy.

I remarked earlier that many recent Christologists seemed to assume that revelation ceased with the Ascension. This cannot be said of Ogden. He is driven by his own dichotomy between the historical and existential Jesuses to the weird conclusion that revela-

[2] Ogden (1982), p. 43.

tion (not that he would use that word) flashed briefly just after (and perhaps during) the ministry of Jesus, among his followers though not himself, and never reappeared. The 'Christ-kerygma' of Paul or John is not the norm of Christology, as Bultmann had supposed:[3] but no more is the teaching of Jesus himself; 'what our sources do or do not permit in the way of inferences concerning the empirical-historical Jesus is simply of no theological consequence'.[4] 'Not even an implicit christological claim by Jesus is needed'.[5] It is the earliest witness of the apostles that is 'the normative witness of faith by which the appropriateness of all christological formulations must be justified';[6] the early Church was right to regard apostolicity as the criterion for admission to the canon, but wrong to regard anything as apostolic except 'the earliest stratum of Christian witness that we today can reconstruct'.[7] This position, which one might well incline to dismiss out of hand as absurd, derives as far as I can see from Ogden's dichotomy. If the existential Jesus is a different thing from the historical one, and if he or it alone is the Jesus of Christian faith and witness, then he or it appeared for the first time when people began to witness to the existential Jesus—perhaps during the historical Jesus' lifetime, perhaps later. And all later witness must be judged by that, for if the existential Jesus really does the job ascribed to him, 're-presenting the meaning of ultimate reality for us', presumably a differently witnessed-to Jesus would not do so.

One must conclude that Ogden's attempt to eliminate the historical Jesus is both illogical in its starting-point and incredible in its conclusion. That our Christological evidence need not be confined to the historical sources for Jesus' life we may agree; God can reveal His truth where He chooses: but the historical Jesus is one with the Jesus of our faith, and if *per impossibile* the two were incompatible, then our faith would be in vain. Fortunately, they aren't, and it isn't.

The complaint of 'parochialism' *could* be dealt with very briefly by answering 'So what?' But perhaps we ought to put a bit more flesh on to that rather skeletal reply.

---

[3] p. 51; but cf. pp. 108ff. with their reliance on Paul and John.
[4] p. 56.   [5] p. 60.   [6] p. 62.   [7] pp. 102–3.

It is doubtless true that to millions of people the arguments of Christian theologians are of no great moment. (It always has been so.) To many devout Christians theology is an intellectual frill; what matters is faith, hope, and love. (The second part of this is certainly correct.) But this of course is not what the complaint means. The idea is that the arguments of Christian theologians are unimportant to *non-Christians*, and of course they are. No doubt the arguments of physicists were for many years unimportant to the citizens of Hiroshima and Nagasaki; that something is felt to be of no moment does not mean that it *is* of no moment.

The question is not 'Do Christians put immense weight on one person at one point in history and one particular area?' They do. The question is 'Are there good reasons for or against their putting the weight where they do?', and the mere fact that it is only one person, one point in history, and one area is by itself irrelevant. If it does not make sense to suppose that God might act and suffer in one person, then by all means scrap the idea of Incarnation; parochiality does not enter into it. If it does make sense, then the Incarnation may be true after all, and we are not in that case being parochial in the least (unless thinking about God is parochial).

Of course Christian theology can and should take account of whatever truth is available from outside its own past. It has habitually done so, from the time of St Paul onwards. With the enormous growth in science and scholarship of recent years, and the understanding, or at least knowledge, of other cultures that has come about at the same time, there is far more to take account of than there used to be. But there is no need to begin discarding the Christian's own past—or if there is, it has got to be demonstrated, not just asserted or assumed. It may seem parochial, even arrogant, to suppose that ours is the true tradition. So it is, if we are unwilling even to consider the claims of others; *any* opinion, however broad and liberal in form, is arrogant if it refuses to recognize that it may perhaps be mistaken. But if there is a special work of God somewhere, and a tradition springing from it, someone has got to be in that tradition, and to call this arrogance is to try and suppress God's truth. I am reminded of the objection brought at one time against theories of planetary origins which made the solar system depend on an unlikely event like the passing of another star close to the sun, that by making planets (and therefore *a fortiori* intelligent life) almost incredibly rare, they implied that the human race was

quite possibly unique, which was arrogant. Apparently the universe
had somehow to be designed so that life was either very common
or non-existent, all to save any intelligent life that did exist from
arrogance or parochialism. Better reasons were in fact found for
abandoning these theories, and better reasons may be found for
abandoning traditional Christology; but they have got to be *reasons*.

It is always worth remembering the difference between the *cause*
of a belief and the *reasons* for it. It is true, as Dyson says, that
'because he is more or less central to our history, we tend to regard
Jesus Christ as central to the history of others'.[8] (Although of
course if this 'our' means 'our culture's', it is to be kept in mind
that He was not central to the cultural history of Christians for
many years, during which it was stoutly maintained that He was
indeed central to the history of the world.) But this states merely
a cause which disposes us to regard Jesus as central to all history;
it does not affect any reasons there may be which would justify
us in so regarding Him, to make them stronger or weaker. The
most that it means is that we should be cautious, aware of possible
bias in our thinking, and open-minded when new ideas are presented
to us; but ought we not to be all these things anyway?

Nor is the variety within the tradition a serious reason for abandoning it. That there are varieties within Socialism is no reason
(by itself) for us to favour Capitalism; nor vice versa. In fact, as
far as variety within the New Testament is concerned, the Chalcedonian Christology, and indeed its main rivals, were intended to take
account of that variety; believing as its framers did that Scripture
was inspired by God, they were reluctant to disregard any of it.
I cannot do better than quote Moore here:

There are times when some big new idea is trying to emerge, when some
unprecedented spiritual experience is flailing around, trying to find words.
When this is happening, there will be a notable gap between the available
images and the new idea ... All that can then be done, until some intrepid
spirit produces some startling new image, is for the people involved to
use the language of the accepted images and stretch it, try to use it to
point to more than it normally does ... The intrepid spirits were the members
of the Johannine community whence came the Fourth Gospel and the
Johannine Letters ... The images afforded by the Johannine people gave
to the people who had been getting along with a Son of Man Christology

[8] Dyson (1969), p. 14.

what they saw they needed to give clearer expression to the faith they already held.[9]

Wiles's statement, that at the outset 'incarnation was one of a number of ways in which Christians thought and spoke of Jesus, but it was the one which (in developed form) was to establish itself',[10] describes the same fact but less perceptively. The point is that while incarnational Christology could accommodate the other truths, they could not by themselves accommodate it; rather as Einstein's physics will account for Newton's, but not Newton's for Einstein's.

As regards later variety, and the influence of the environment, these need not bother us much. Of course Christians are partly creations of their culture (though also of their Christian past) and of course this affects their thinking. It may affect it for ill (as indeed I believe has happened—with the growth of anti-incarnationist Christologies); we must all be on the alert for this. (Which, as C. S. Lewis once pointed out, is one reason for reading old books. 'People were no cleverer then than they are now; they made as many mistakes as we. But not the *same* mistakes ... Two heads are better than one, not because either is infallible, but because they are unlikely to go wrong in the same direction.'[11]) But it hardly proves that what is *distinctive* about Christians and not found in their environment, such as belief in the Incarnation, is mistaken, or is excessively parochial.

It is what people have in common when they say something—whether it be the Creeds that they are saying, or 'The train leaves at 9.15'—that gives it meaning. No doubt Professor Houlden is right to say that his imaginary instrument would show all reciters of the Creed to mean different things by it, but only in an artificial sense of the word 'mean'. 'When I think in language', said Wittgenstein, 'there aren't "meanings" going through my mind in addition to the verbal expressions: the language is itself the vehicle of thought'.[12] There may be differences in associations or emotional overtones between reciters of the Creeds (as there may be between a train-spotting enthusiast and an irritated commuter over 'The train

---

[9] Moore (1980), pp. 153–4. 'Son of Man' may perhaps be a misnomer here.
[10] In Hick (1977*b*), p. 4.   [11] Introd. to Athanasius (1944), p. 7.
[12] Wittgenstein (1953), para. 329.

leaves at 9.15'), but these do not affect its meaning. An actual mental reservation or a complete misunderstanding might, but that is not what Houlden meant.

It may be remembered that there were four main subheadings to the objection that traditional approaches to Christology have been too narrowly Western and Hellenistic: first, that the patristic vocabulary and concepts did not and could not cover all the ground needed for discussing the person of Jesus Christ; second, that the risk in tying ourselves too closely to Hellenistic concepts is great, since even if these have not yet become meaningless, it may well be that they will at some time in the future; third, that these concepts cannot be transferred to other cultures without impeding the Church's evangelistic and pastoral work; and fourth, that no single philosophy is divinely revealed truth, so that it is wrong to tie our Christology to one, as the traditional formulae in effect do. Of these, the first is quite justified, and cannot be disputed. There are many questions the Fathers did not raise, nor their Councils settle. This does not of course mean they were *wrong*: no more than the statement that X was born in 1909 is wrong because it does not say *where* X was born.

The second and third are really one: they deal with the difficulty of maintaining Hellenistic concepts in environments changed by time and space respectively. But to what extent are the old formulae really chained to Hellenistic concepts? They were of course written in Greek; yet they have been translated often enough, and Chalcedon approved the Tome of Leo, written in Latin. It is partly a matter of philosophical terms. (See Excursus VI below.)

It seems wrong to accuse the traditional formulae of being narrowly Hellenistic. They were drawn up in a Hellenistic (and Roman) environment, of course, but it is not at all clear that the philosophical outlooks peculiar to that culture were built into them. It is interesting and instructive to look at some of the writings on the person of Christ which have emerged from non-Western Churches. There is often an asking of questions which the Fathers did not ask—as was said earlier, the patristic concepts did not and could not cover all the ground needed for all time. But I am not sure that there is any notable contradiction of the traditional Western views on those questions that the West *did* ask. Let me take a few instances. Dr Mbiti suggests[13] that three pictures of Christ are of particular relevance in many African cultures. One is that of *Christus Victor*; Africa has many myths of the origin of evil, but none of redemption from it. '*Christus Victor* at once reminds our peoples of the loss of immortality which he now restores; of the loss of the resurrection, which he now brings about in his own life and in the promise that those in him will be resurrected; and of the loss of rejuvenation, which now in Jesus begins to take place.'[14] Another is that of the perfect man who has gone through the *rites de passage*, with the interesting consequence that the death of Christ is not seen primarily in sacrificial or soteriological terms: these 'are the effects rather than the causes of the cross'. Jesus died because this is part of humanity. 'It was as an ordinary man that Jesus died, and the great Christian *differentia* comes obviously from the fact of the Resurrection.'[15] And a third is that of the Redeemer who 'opens the way and possibility for men to ... become akin to God ... In Christ, through the new relationship or kinship which he makes possible, the individual discovers his true individuality and simultaneously loses his individuality in order to gain the new corporateness without which he cannot exist.'[16] These are fascinating approaches, none of them—save possibly the first, and I am not too sure of that—natural to modern Western thought, yet all plainly valid Christian teaching. But so far are they from requiring us to abandon traditional Christology that, one feels, if Chalcedon had never taken place, Africa would one day have invented it. With the perfect man who has conquered not only His own death but the death of the world and who, being human, is also Son of God and makes us God's kindred, are we so far from Chalcedon after all? Will anything less do?

India has of course a great metaphysical tradition of her own; and though a good deal of Indian Christological thought has concentrated on questions of how far, if at all, traditional Indian concepts like *bhakti* and *avatāra* can be used by Christians, there have been approaches by way of metaphysics as well. Usually these have been concerned with the doctrine of God, not of Christ. But the Roman Catholic lay theologian Brahmabandhab Upādhyāya (1861–1907)

---

[13] 'Some African Concepts of Christology', in Vicedom (1972), pp. 51ff.
[14] p. 55.   [15] p. 57.   [16] pp. 61–2.

did discuss both. Christ to him was 'Nara-Hari', the man-God; but how was He both? His answer is, interestingly, quite like the one suggested in the present work. 'According to the Vedānta human nature is composed of five sheaths or divisions (*kośa*) ... presided over by a personality (*ahampratyayi*) which knows itself' and is but a reflected spark of the Supreme Reason. 'The time-incarnate Divinity is also composed of five sheaths; but it is presided over by the Person of Logos Himself and not by any created personality (*aham*).'[17] Boyd, to whom I owe this information, feels this is moving in the direction of Apollinarianism. But the 'sheaths' include the human mind (*manomaya kośa*) and intellect (*vijñānamaya kośa*); and *aham* is simply the Sanskrit for 'I', for 'ego' if you like. It is the centre which presides over human nature, not part of human nature itself. Upādhyāya seems to me to be perfectly consistent with Chalcedon, even though he is approaching the Person of Christ from a quite different metaphysical standpoint to that of the Western Fathers.

There are undoubtedly problems for anyone who wishes to develop a Christology within the framework of Indian metaphysics. Are we to use the Advaitin (non-dualist) system, the best-known in the West, in which the ultimate Reality is indescribable, without qualities, yet one with each individual self? or some other, perhaps the Visitādvaitin ('qualified non-dualist'), where the ultimate Reality is seen as a personal God, and individual souls as part of the universe which is His body?[18] Are we to make the distinction which most Indian philosophies make between the self, *ātman*, and the ego, *ahamkāra*? Are we to use the common Hindu conception of an *avatāra* (as we shall see Appasamy did, or V. Chakkarai, but not Upādhyāya)?[19] But the specific problem that the Fathers of Chalcedon were facing, and their solution of it, does not seem to be particularly alien to Indian thought. 'Greek christology has not exhausted the mystery of Christ', writes Klostermaier, 'though it has helped the Church the better to see some aspects of Christ.'[20] To agree with him is not to reject the wisdom of either India or Greece.

I should add in honesty that some Indian Christian theologians

---

[17] Quoted from *The Twentieth Century*, 1901, p. 7, by Boyd (1969), pp. 79–80.
[18] Or of course some third position; cf. Panikkar (1964), pp. 129–31.
[19] Cf. also Klostermaier's vigorous rejection of the term (Klostermaier (1969), p. 115).
[20] p. 118.

have strongly criticized traditional Western theology. Boyd mentions Appasamy as 'attacking the Chalcedonian formula'—because it was too close to Hindu patterns of thought! Actually, it was Nicaea rather than Chalcedon that he attacked. The moral rather than metaphysical union between Father and Son that he taught is just that—union between Father and Son in the Trinity, not between God and Man in Christ.[21] Appasamy is clear that Jesus is the Incarnation of God, and compares this to the Hindu idea of *avatāra*.[22] The main differences between the two are that *avatāras* are often held to be of only a part of God; that their purpose is less noble than that of Christ (at the best God becomes incarnate to destroy the wicked, not to help them), and that they are many, whereas Jesus is unique. (This, Appasamy holds, is not because God could not become incarnate in others besides Jesus, but because there simply is no one comparable to Him.) Also that in some Hindu schools no incarnation is possible except a docetist one. It is hard to wring any criticism of Chalcedon out of this. More to the point might be Pandipeddi Chenchiah, who certainly did criticize Chalcedon (and Nicaea) as 'not in accordance with Indian or Asiatic genius'; but his reason for saying this was that they 'weave a temporary philosophy round the permanent facts of Christianity', a straightforward objection which could (and has) come as easily from European pens as from Asiatic, and which we have seen reason to believe is based on a misunderstanding.[23]

Not very much Chinese theological writing is readily available in Britain: but in the symposium *Christ and the Younger Churches*, already referred to, there is an essay by Principal C.-S. Song which is of interest.[24] Song clearly writes under Western influence, discussing and repudiating the dichotomy between the 'Jesus of history' and the 'Christ of faith', and suggesting that Baillie came close to adoptionism. But he makes the strong claim that if Chinese religion undergoes 'a real Christological transformation' 'the Chinese will be able to intuit the meaning of the Incarnation in a most vivid and personal way. In Chinese the words "love" and "pain" are mutually exchangeable. Moreover these two words are combined

---

[21] Boyd (1969), pp. 120–1; Appasamy (1942), pp. 35ff.

[22] pp. 251ff.

[23] For Chenchiah see Boyd (1969), p. 162.

[24] 'Christian Encounter with Eastern religions' (in Vicedom (1972), pp. 63–82); cf. also Song (1979).

into making a verbal expression which expresses human love in its highest degree. A mother "pain-loves" her child for example.' In non-Christian Chinese religion this is not associated with Heaven, which may help explain the appeal of Mahāyāna Buddhism in China, where something like this 'pain-love' is ascribed to the Bodhisattvas. 'But Jesus Christ', Song continues, 'is not a Bodhisattva. He is God's pain-loving *enmanned*. When we see Jesus Christ we see God who acts for us, who does not spare himself in the Being and Act of his own Son.'[25] This is well said, and this concept of 'pain-love' is certainly not in the Western idiom: but it turns out, once again, to entail the *vere Deus vere homo* of traditional Christology.[26]

It must be acknowledged that in recent years a number of serious and severe criticisms have been made of Christology in the name of the 'Third World', or, as one symposium[27] prefers to describe it, in less West-centred language, the 'Two-Thirds World'. These have about them something of the moral approach that we have seen in Western form in Driver (see Chapter 4 above), but are directed specifically to the *Western* characteristics of current Christ-ology, and therefore belong best in this chapter. They come from those who have actually suffered from the defects criticized, and for that reason even if for no other would demand our attention and respect; and, though less 'radical' than some of the approaches we have been considering, they have a force and conviction of their own. For example, Professor Orlando Costas, of Costa Rica, declares that 'God's Incarnate Word has been, by and large, pro-claimed in a foreign language'—foreign, that is, 'to the cultural reality and social experiences of the hearers'. Jesus has acquired a disfigured face in the Two-Thirds World. In South Africa He has been identified with the ruling ideology and power structure, 'a projection of the Afrikaaner . . . who has established a harmonious universe where each part can develop separately'. British rule left the West Indies with a 'British-type Christ'. Where the United States has dominated, He has been distorted into 'an overpowering, prag-matic saviour with a plastic face', an image reinforced through the

---

[25] In Vicedom (1972), p. 80.

[26] Professor Kitamori's essay in Vicedom (1972) (pp. 83–90), 'The Problem of Pain in Christology', is explicitly Chalcedonian; but it is also more 'Westernized' than most of the other contributions, and may be thought suspect for that reason. Yet it is significant that he finds no difficulty in reconciling his Japanese culture with orthodox Lutheranism.

[27] Samuel and Sugden (1983).

'consumeristic religiosity' that infects much American missionary work and theology. Spain left Latin America with a 'baby Jesus' and an impotent dying saviour—and Protestants in the same area could only replace impotence and innocence with power and impressiveness. Swings to opposite extremes—a 'Guevara' Christ in Latin America or a 'guru' in India—are equally distortions of the actual facts. 'Whether by imposition or reaction ... we are hard pressed to recognise the true face of Jesus of Nazareth as described in the New Testament.'[28]

The indictment could be paralleled in many other writers,[29] and must be at work in far more Christians (and non-Christians) who have never put their thoughts on paper. And it is a devastating indictment, for there is great and terrible truth in it. But it is an indictment of what in my introduction I ventured to call 'proclamatory Christology'. *Analytic* Christology does not really enter into it. 'Black people', writes George Cummings, 'have never had any abstract theoretical difficulty in affirming the unity of divinity/humanity in Jesus ... Our problem with Christology has been much more concrete, because of our desire as black people to see the empirical reference points in our experience which would support the claim that in Jesus Christ God has performed a decisive act on behalf of our liberation.'[30] Even Sobrino, one of the most radical of these writers, ends up with an avowed acceptance of Chalcedon—though by a route which would have startled the members of that Council. It is '*proclaiming* Christ in the Two-Thirds World', as Costas's title explicitly puts it, that has been so defective. And there is no reason to suppose that any revisionist analysis would improve the proclamation. Indeed, it is surely more likely that it would worsen it, by weakening the identity between God and the Jesus whose life-style would today be labelled 'Third World'—and so between the ground of all hope and the people who most need hope.

We can take this point further. For the truth of the matter is that it is contemporary 'radical' theology that is most often narrowly Western and twentieth-century, and that is most likely to be dated by time and unassimilable by other cultures. It is not of course

[28] 'Proclaiming Christ in the Two-Thirds World', in Samuel and Sugden (1983), pp. 6–9.
[29] Cf. e.g. Sobrino (1978); and several other contributors to the Samuel/Sugden symposium.
[30] 'Who do you say that I am? A North American Minority Answer', in Samuel and Sugden (1983), p. 334.

homogeneous, and doubtless a great deal of it is not open to this sort of criticism, but equally a great deal *is*. The passion for continuity mentioned in Chapter 14 above is a good example, based as it is *not* on contemporary science (which is Western in origin, but is good sound exploration of truth) but on a non-scientific philosophy derived from habits of thought vaguely associated with science. Wiles is absolutely right to say that the idea of a special act of God in particular events is not to be ruled out 'simply on the ground that it would offend against an understanding of the world which is already known to be comprehensive'.[31]

The extreme scepticism about the historical value of the Gospels associated with many 'radicals' is of similar origin.

We need to determine most carefully [writes Dyson] whether negative historical judgments are reached by these scholars *qua* historians or *qua* theologians. There is evidence to suggest that those who have come to the gospels as historians have in fact been far less sceptical about the basic trustworthiness of the sources than those who have been predisposed in their enquiry by an explicit theological, philosophical or even literary attitude.[32]

This is surely correct. Perhaps there are other factors at work too: a limited range of texts to work at, which encourages the spinning of elaborate theories with (of necessity) very little actual evidence, and (a very twentieth-century Western feature) the unconscious feeling that since Science progresses by ever new theories, and originality is what makes the really outstanding scientific genius, Theology must do the same, and new theories must be constantly developed, or at least those of the last generation but one revived. I suspect that in fact very few original theologians have ever actually set out to be original. Science has to keep up to date, because new evidence is always being fed into it; but much less is fed into theology. Sometimes it is; indeed, sometimes this happens by way of science (the geological discoveries of the early nineteenth century, the rise of Darwinism, the development of psychology); but on nothing like the same scale as with the natural sciences themselves. If, then, theologians feel an obligation to make new advances in the same

---

[31] Wiles (1974), p. 36. His only reply is that there is too much divine guidance and providence in the world for these to be special acts and yet allow for 'the relative independence of causation within the world'. This needs arguing; such acts would still be a tiny minority of all events.

[32] Dyson (1974), p. 25.

way as the scientists, they are very likely to theorize in advance
of their data, to be both destructive of what has gone before and
wrong. And they are almost certain to be narrowly Western and
twentieth-century. When, for example, we find Küng assuring us
that 'since in modern man's environment cultic sacrifices are no
longer offered ... the concept of sacrifice is not related to any experience and has thus become largely misleading and unintelligible',[33]
we may not notice that he means modern *Western* man—not modern
Ghanaians, Indians, or Australian aborigines. (Though, to be fair,
by 'modern' he does not presumably mean 'twentieth-century', as
cultic sacrifices have not been offered in most of Europe since the
Dark Ages.) Note, too, that the other possibility (that we have lost
something valuable in shedding the concept of sacrifice) is not even
considered; the 'modern man's environment' is decisive. Again,
when we read Bultmann's celebrated aphorism 'It is impossible to
use electric light and the wireless ... and at the same time believe
in the New Testament world of demons and spirits',[34] we have
moved beyond even modern Western man to modern *secularized*
Western man—a common phenomenon, I agree, but not a universal
one even in the West, and far from it elsewhere (even among users
of electric light and wireless). Of course, it may be true (indeed,
I think it *is* true) that cultic sacrifices ought no longer to be offered.
It may be true that we ought not to believe in demons and spirits.
But this is a different matter. There are *reasons* why we should
not do these things; and the mere habits of thought of present-day
Europe are not reasons. Küng and Bultmann are assuming, not
arguing, that a twentieth-century Western secularized viewpoint is
ipso facto the true one; and I have a feeling that a lot of radical
theologizing, less explictly perhaps, does the same.

It has long been recognized that the main purpose of most of
the early Councils was not so much to lay down an orthodox line
as to rule out lines which were *not* orthodox. Provided that these
were unambiguously repudiated, language could be, and was, used
which allowed other ambiguity, or at least a certain latitude of interpretation. What Lonergan says of the Nicaean όμοούσιον applies
also to Chalcedon: 'It leaves the believer free to conceive the Father'
(or, in our case, the Son) 'in scriptural, patristic, medieval or modern
terms; and of course contemporary consciousness, which is histori-

---

[33] Küng (1976), p. 425.   [34] In Bartsch (1953), p.5.

cally minded, will be at home in all four.'[35] He may have been a little sanguine in that last sentence, but the first seems to me entirely correct—and one might add to it 'in European, African, Indian, Chinese or most other terms'.

[35] 'The Dehellenising of Dogma' (Lonergan (1974), p.23).

18

The Matter of Evidence

WE now turn to those objections which are based, not on the concepts or the inner consistency of traditional Christology, nor on its coherence with other truths, but on the alleged evidence for it. Of these, the first was that Christianity was in a peculiar way vulnerable to historical discoveries, in a way that other religions for the most part are not.

We must surely accept that this is true, and that we cannot seek to avoid this vulnerability. The question is, is it really an *objection* to traditional Christology, or merely a *description* of it? Can we not live with this vulnerability? Does orthodoxy really require the falsifying either of faith or of historical enquiry?

'Even if we recognise an element of risk in faith', writes Knox, 'it cannot be the kind of risk involved in assuming the accuracy of an historical fact'.[1] Now I can see that there is perhaps another element of risk besides the historical one. Some people who saw Jesus' miracles refused to take the risky step of becoming His followers, preferring to ascribe the miracles to Beelzebul.[2] It is certainly possible to believe that there is a God without taking the risky step of faith in and obedience to Him; millions do do precisely that. There is an element of risk in faith; we may be wrong to take those steps. Agreed.[3] But why should not the other element be present too? Historical facts are to some degree uncertain. Some are so well documented that to doubt them can only be a rather futile intellectual exercise: to doubt whether Queen Anne is dead or whether the American Revolution ever took place would be ludicrous. Others are much less certain: the date of Themistocles' flight

[1] Knox (1963), p. 17.
[2] Matt. 12: 24 par.
[3] Knox's own picture of the risk is a dark one: the risk is 'that the God of heaven and earth will . . . fail to justify our trust in him' (p. 17).

to Persia, for example, or the existence of King Arthur, are familiar cases from European history. If we plump for one particular answer to these questions, we may well be wrong: perhaps there was no 'real' Arthur at all. Apparently the idea is that no fact which is less certain than the death of Queen Anne or the historicity of the American Revolution can be a basis for faith; and unarguably the details of the life, death and resurrection of Jesus are less certain than these.

But why should this make much difference? Suppose that the facts are roughly as stated in the Gospels. To a contemporary they might be as certain as the death of Queen Anne to us. But as the years go by the possibility of checking the Gospel accounts will diminish; it seems almost inevitable that if our redemption did take place at the time it is said to have done it would eventually become less certain than it was. From a purely historical point of view there is nothing very surprising here. But the theological point is presumably that God would not allow our salvation to depend on something that grew steadily more and more uncertain. He may be willing to allow us a leap of faith into His arms, but He will certainly provide us with a solid jumping-off position. Since the life of Jesus does not afford this, it cannot be the jumping-off position provided.

Now all reasoning on the basis of 'what God ought to have done' is tricky. But in few cases can it be of more questionable value than here. History or no history, we do *not* have a solid jumping-off point. Knox thinks we run the risk that God may fail us. But to have the jumping-off point for this risk we must know that there is a God; and though I do myself think that there are good reasons for saying we do know this, still many, perhaps most, of those who have considered the matter think either that there is no God or that we do not *know* that there is, we *believe* it, in faith. Again, Knox, if I understand him correctly, holds that 'the historical Event to which all distinctively Christian faith returns' is not the Incarnation, Death, and Resurrection of Jesus but the coming into being of the Church (in which of course the figure of Jesus played an important part). But this is just as vulnerable historically as the other. Admittedly the Church now exists. But perhaps her coming into being was quite different from that suggested by the New Testament. Perhaps she was founded by a group of confidence tricksters, 'upsetting whole families by teaching for gain what they have no

right to teach'.[4] Such people did exist; Lucian's portrait of Alex-
ander of Abonouteichos is a fascinating example, though Alex-
ander's missionary movement faded with his death. If the Church
arose from such men, then present faith in the Church is not well-
founded. Again, when Knox says 'The Church reflected in the New
Testament documents is not the primitive Church only, but is the
Church I know',[5] he is, I am sure, absolutely right: but *which*
Church that we know? The Anglican (to which I believe he belongs,
as I do)? the Methodist? the Armenian Apostolic? the Fire-Baptized
Holiness Church of Independence, Kansas? Is 'the Universal
Church' the proper answer? But what is the Universal Church?
Rome, and the Eastern Orthodox too, have been known to claim
that they are identical with the Universal Church; so perhaps would
the Jehovah's Witnesses. If I know of God through the memory
of the Church, I must know which version of the Church to know
Him through; but how can I know this without an element of risk
(into which historical questions will almost certainly enter)?

Faith, then, is bound to be vulnerable. But it need not worry.
Unless we accept the scepticism of some scholars, which, as has
already been suggested, may well not be based on strictly historical
considerations, we have a perfectly reasonable basis for the real
leap of faith. It may turn out that the whole thing was wrong. That
is the way we have to live most of our lives. I set out to catch
a bus not knowing whether it will run, only believing it will; I bring
up my children not knowing whether political or economic folly
will leave them a world to live in. I am far more certain than I
am of either of these that Jesus Christ lived and rose again; and
it is far more likely that evidence will turn up to overthrow the
first two beliefs than that it will turn up to overthrow the third.
At all times I live, and must live, with the possibility that, being
human, I may be mistaken; but this does not falsify faith.

What of falsifying history? Do we have to say, with Harvey's
imaginary objector in Chapter 5, that 'it is intolerable to honest
inquiry if the New Testament critic or believer decided in favour
of one historical judgement rather than another because it is more
compatible with his religious beliefs'? Surely not. Religious beliefs
may be true, after all, and we may have good grounds for believing
them true; and if so, why should we not use them in forming our

⁴ Titus 1: 11.   ⁵ Knox (1963), p. 30.

historical beliefs? If a 'Believe it or Not' column tells me (as one I once saw did) that a woman once gave birth to 365 children at once, I reject it, not on historical grounds, but on scientific ones, and no historian will blame me. Why not bring religious grounds in too? As S. W. Sykes has said, 'the preoccupation of modern post-enlightenment theology with the threat of historical disproof has led to a certain overlooking of the fact that, in the absence of historical disproof, a doctrinal argument may carry considerable weight'.[6] His example is Jesus' sinlessness. This can never be proved historically (we should need to know everything that Jesus ever did, said, or thought!); it might be *dis*proved historically, but in fact has not; so in the absence of such disproof we are quite entitled to believe it on doctrinal grounds.

Let us see what happens if we apply this reasoning to the Resurrection. Putting things simply, we do not have just two possibilities, namely, that Jesus did literally rise from the grave or that He did not. We have four: (A) Jesus was the Son of God, and He rose again; (B) He was the Son of God, and He did not rise again; (C) He was not the Son of God, and he did rise again; (D) Neither was he the Son of God, nor did he rise again. Now historians by their normal criteria (scientific perhaps rather than strictly historical?) may say, quite correctly, that (C) may be ruled out. The theologians may say for theological reasons that (B) can also be ruled out. (That is up to them. Some theologians would not rule it out.) The choice then lies between (A) and (D). Now the theological evidence for Jesus' being or not being the Son of God is none of the historian's business. Let us suppose that it does point to His being the Son of God. The question then arises, which way does the historical evidence point—the historical evidence, that is, *apart* from the general principle that the dead do not rise, which is enough to eliminate (C) but not (A). If this historical evidence points strongly to the conclusion that the Resurrection never took place (if, for example, all early accounts assumed that Jesus never rose at all, and only later writers included resurrection narratives), it might well lead us to conclude that our theological reasons for believing in Jesus' Sonship were after all wrong, or that (B) ought not to have been eliminated. Historical evidence would be pointing to theological conclusions. But if the evidence is inconclusive, or

---

[6] In Sykes and Clayton (1972), p. 96.

if, as is in fact the case, it points on balance to the reality of the Resurrection, then the theological evidence is plainly relevant, and makes the Resurrection virtually certain (to the Christian who is willing to accept historical evidence, that is). I cannot see that this is in the least destructive of 'honest inquiry'. We cannot help but allow our belief (or unbelief) to affect our historical judgements. What we must not let it do is so to prejudice our minds that we pervert the facts. The believer must not let belief, nor the unbeliever unbelief, affect their assessment of the historical data; we must not (for instance) defend the authenticity of Mark 16: 9–20 just because they would provide further evidence for the Resurrection. We have to be honest in our judgements (and indeed in our interpretation, in so far as these can be separated), and that means we must be on the look-out for even *unconscious* dishonesty. But once the historical evidence has been honestly assessed, our conclusion may quite legitimately be affected by our non-historical beliefs or unbeliefs, and vice versa.

We now have to look at the actual historical evidence. It is not of course possible to do this in detail in a few pages of a book concerned with analysis rather than with biblical criticism and interpretation; but a few remarks may be in order, directed as much to the logic of the arguments described earlier as to their content.

Of the extreme views professed by some about the Gospel accounts of Jesus something has already been said. Intensive study by a large number of ingenious minds of a small quantity of material, especially when those minds are anxious to produce something new, is virtually certain to give rise to weird suggestions, including extreme scepticism. There are far more ways in which a story about Jesus can be false than ways in which it can be true, and it is often easier to attack its credibility than to defend it. (The attacker has the initiative; the defender is, naturally, 'on the defensive'.) One can usually think up a situation in which someone might conceivably have invented the story; and then how is anyone to tell whether they actually did invent it or not? But practically the only way of doing the reverse is to argue that the story goes against everything that people would have wanted to say about Jesus, and obviously, as we are dealing with things which people *did* want to say about Jesus, and indeed actually said about Him, there are going to be very few passages where this can be done. (Even these few are not immune to the sceptic: some of Schmiedel's 'pillar-sayings'[7] have been shaken by would-be Samsons before now.[8]) So startling claims are a priori to be expected, and are in fact made.

What is more, in the making of them serious errors of logic can easily occur. Perhaps an illustration may be helpful. I mentioned earlier the scepticism of some scholars about the designation 'Son of Man', and the fact that (for instance) Vielhauer, Conzelmann, and Perrin do not believe Jesus ever used it of Himself. Now Vielhauer's main argument for this, is, I understand,[9] that the expression never occurs in the same saying as the expression 'kingdom of God'. The two sets of sayings therefore come from different sources; and as it is undisputed that Jesus did preach about the kingdom of God, it is the 'kingdom' set which is (on the whole) authentic, and the 'Son of Man' set must be regarded as the creation of the early Church.

Now one useful test of the validity of an argument is to see if the same logical form can be shown to lead to absurd conclusions from true but different material. Suppose, then, that we had a collection of sayings ascribed, let us say, to the late Mr Aneurin Bevan, and that it turned out (as might well be the case) that the National Health Service and disarmament were never referred to in the same saying: would we conclude that, as Bevan certainly did mention the National Health Service at times, he cannot ever have mentioned disarmament? Surely not. Of course, if it were true that in no full-scale speech or writing ascribed to Bevan, even in one setting out the whole range of his political thought, were the two ideas both mentioned, we might begin to wonder; but short sayings might well fail to combine the two. And it is of course short sayings that we are concerned with in the Gospels. If we allow ourselves to look at the contexts in which the Evangelists set the sayings, 'Son of Man' and 'Kingdom of God' do occur together.[10]

The argument is not, then, formally valid. But it might still be correct. It seems to be based on Sherlock Holmes's maxim, 'When

[7] See Cheyne and Black (1899–1903), ii, cols. 1881ff. Schmiedel is in effect the father both of the 'criterion of dissimilarity' and of that of 'coherence' sometimes used to supplement it.

[8] Notably Mark 13: 32.

[9] Vielhauer's essay is not I think available in English; I have relied on accounts in Fuller (1963), pp. 47–9, and Jeremias (1971), pp. 267–8. I hope I have not done Vielhauer injustice as a result.

[10] e.g. Mark 8: 38, 9: 1; Luke 21: 31, 36; John 3: 5, 13.

you have eliminated the impossible, whatever remains, however improbable, must be the truth'. Sheer coincidence is presumably an impossible explanation of the separation of the ideas; so the explanation that they come from different sources, however improbable, must be true. Readers of Conan Doyle, however, have long realized that Holmes, to be correct, must either by 'impossible' have meant all that is *untrue*, or, more likely, have meant that whatever remains must *include* the truth. In fact Holmes himself seems to have said this latter on one occasion: 'When the impossible has been eliminated the residuum, however improbable, must contain the truth.'[11] To eliminate one impossible solution does not automatically leave you with just one possible one; indeed it hardly ever does. Ironically, Holmes himself, on the occasion of his more careful formulation of the maxim, overlooked a hidden alternative which was in fact the true one. Are there alternative explanations to Vielhauer's apart from sheer coincidence?

The answer is that there are. Jeremias, for instance, suggested that 'kingdom' sayings belonged to Jesus' public preaching and 'Son of Man' ones to His private teaching of the disciples.[12] This is possible enough; I am not sure that it is correct, but its mere possibility is enough to show the flaw in Vielhauer's argument. (In favour of Jeremias's suggestion it might be noted that on two occasions in the Fourth Gospel the phrase 'Son of Man' is used outside the circle of disciples—and bewilders the hearers;[13] but this is not always the case.[14]) Another possibility: the separation might have been caused by the fact that very few 'kingdom' sayings involve the first person singular, for which 'Son of Man' is usually an equivalent (whether or not it has additional significance). Only a handful of such exist,[15] and it would not be surprising if by coincidence none of these had 'Son of Man' rather than 'I'.[16] No doubt this particular piece of scepticism is an extreme one, and even those who hold to it do not necessarily use the argument I have been

---

[11] Doyle (1981), p. 106.
[12] In Sykes and Clayton (1972), p. 96.
[13] John 9: 35, 12: 34.
[14] For public 'Son of Man' sayings, cf. Mark 2: 10, 28; Matt. 8: 20 (par. Luke 9: 58); Matthew 11: 19 (par.Luke 7: 34); some of these are discussed by Jeremias.
[15] I have noted Matt. 12: 28 par., 16: 19, 26: 29 par., Luke 4: 43.
[16] To confuse things more, Matt. 16: 28 (though not the parallels) and 25: 31–4 have 'the kingdom of the Son of Man'; for the kingdom of *Jesus* see also Luke 22: 30, John 18: 36, and cf.Luke 23: 42.

criticizing. (Conzelmann only mentions it briefly, though approvingly; Perrin mentions it but does not himself use it.) But the point is not whether Jesus did or did not describe Himself as 'Son of Man', though I am sure He did; the point is the logical failure of the argument to prove anything.

The 'criterion of dissimilarity', again (the idea that only those sayings of Jesus should be accepted as genuine which have no parallels in rabbinic sayings or in the teachings of the early Church): if that were applied to our 'Sayings of Aneurin Bevan' we should accept as genuine only those sayings which had parallels neither among earlier Socialists nor among the 'Bevanites' of the 1950s. And this too seems going a bit far. Of course, many of those who use this criterion realize that it is absurd—yet they somehow are reluctant to abandon it. Perrin, after admitting the obvious defects in the criterion, continues: 'We have no other choice. There simply is no other starting-point.'[17] But starting-point for what? Not for 'rediscovering the teaching of Jesus' as it really was, for Perrin agrees that the criterion can exclude perfectly authentic material.

As a matter of fact, the situation, it has been pointed out, is even worse than it appears. For any material that seems inconsistent with first-century Palestinian Judaism must clearly be eliminated, while the 'criterion of dissimilarity' calls for the elimination of anything paralleled in that Judaism, so that there is 'no wonder ... that our knowledge of the historical Jesus is scanty; it is all eliminated before we start'.[18] This is of course an exaggeration, as the writer goes on to admit; but it does show the dangers of a priori scepticism. The criterion of dissimilarity is of some use against the few eccentrics who still try to prove that there was no such person as Jesus (as it yields a minimum collection of acts and sayings which are virtually inexplicable except in terms of a real Jesus); and it is of some use if we wish to find out what surviving teaching of Jesus was original to Him or of little use to the early Church. But this is not saying much. 'Our Lord', said George MacDonald apropos of Matthew 22: 39, 'never thought of being original. The older the saying the better, if it utters the truth He wants to utter.'[19] And the Church

---

[17] Perrin (1967), p. 43.

[18] Barbour (1972), p. 6. Paradoxically, the closer the early Church kept to the teaching of Jesus, the less we are allowed to trust what it says of Him, for only where His teaching was not reproduced are we allowed to recognize it as His.

[19] MacDonald (1976), p. 295.

has habitually made the most of what sayings of His she possessed. Morna Hooker is right to see 'serious faults in the logic' of using this criterion (even coupled with that of 'coherence') to establish Jesus' authentic message, in that they 'offer us only those sayings which the church treated as peripheral'.[20]

The attempt of Ogden to discard even the criterion of dissimilarity rests on another piece of mistaken reasoning. All we can know of the Jesus of the past, he argues, is what the earliest witnesses tell us; how then can we distinguish between the Jesus of the past and the Jesus of whom they speak? To the extent to which the witnesses are reliable, we cannot, but of course where they are reliable it does not matter, because there is no difference between the two. Yet even if to some extent they are not reliable, we know something of these early witnesses besides what they tell us of Jesus, for we have other records of early Christianity in the rest of the New Testament. We can therefore distinguish between elements in the Gospels which fit the known interests of the earliest witnesses and those which do not. If all I know of Juliet is what Romeo tells me of her, I can still, if I know he is passionately in love with her, take as pretty reliable anything unfavourable he says about her. What is true and worth remembering, though, is that we cannot *both* use the criterion of dissimilarity to detect possible early-Church material *and* reconstruct the views of the early Church from the material in the Gospels. That would involve circularity.

It is worth remarking that even if doubt is cast on individual items in the Gospels, this need not affect their reliability as a whole. 'Not a single line from the gospels', we quoted from Cupitt earlier, 'can be taken as certainly historically reliable', and he goes on: 'The portrait of Jesus that emerges is a mere web of conjectures'.[21] No doubt this is true of some 'radical' pictures of Jesus which supplement what remains of the Gospels after treatment by stressing the themes they find in these remains, or the more congenial of them (forgetting that the more meagre the remains the less likely they are to be typical). But even if Cupitt's first assertion were true we should not have to accept his second, as a short piece of simple arithmetic will show. Consider a set of five stories about Jesus. Let us suppose that, so far from being certainly reliable, they have as high a chance as one in three of being false. We do not, it seems,

[20] Hooker (1970–1), pp. 481–2.   [21] Cupitt (1979), p. 70.

have a reliable account of Jesus in these stories. But in fact there is a chance of more than one in eight that all five are true; a chance of more than 40 per cent that no more than one is false; odds of almost 80 per cent that most of the stories are true; and only one chance in 243 that all are false.[22] In other words, even if we have doubts over individual items, the general impression may be quite reliable, not a 'mere web of conjecture' at all. Paradoxically enough, we may know a good deal about Jesus without being able to say in detail and with absolute certainty what exactly we know. The evidence as a whole may be adequate even if no one item taken alone is indisputable.

It could be that even if extreme scepticism about the Gospels is unjustified, nevertheless among individual items that are doubtful are to be included all those passages in which Jesus is depicted as calling Himself the Son of God or implying a claim to divinity. The argument is that all the more extreme claims are to be found in the Fourth Gospel and are to be ascribed to the Evangelist himself, not to Jesus; that the same applies to most of the 'Son of God' passages; and that the few Synoptic examples are probably inauthentic too.

We cannot embark here on a full-scale discussion of the nature of the Fourth Gospel and the traditions behind it. We might, however, note briefly that a surprisingly strong case can be made out for the authenticity of the two most 'extreme' sayings in that Gospel, 8: 58 ('Before Abraham was, I am') and 20: 28 ('Thomas said to him "My Lord and my God"'). Consider 8: 58. It begins with the 'Amen', a turn of phrase which is widely regarded as a genuine practice of our Lord's,[23] and one which is not paralleled in early Christian practice or contemporary Judaism. It looks interestingly as if John used it only in passages where he was quoting Jesus directly, and not in those where he may have been elaborating an idea of Jesus' in his own words. (Some of John's 'Amen' sayings in fact bear close resemblance to 'Amen' sayings in the Synoptics: compare 3: 3 with Mark 10: 15; 8: 51 with Mark 9: 1; 13: 21 with

---

[22] The actual figures are: 32 out of 243 that all are true; 80 out of 243 that just four are; 80 that just three are; 40 that just two are; 10 that one is; and 1 out of 243 that none are.

[23] Cf. e.g. Jeremias (1971), pp. 35 ff.; Lindars (1972), p. 48.

Mark 14: 18; 13: 38 with Mark 14: 30.)[24] If this is the case—if, that is, John did not introduce this solemn opening into his own material, but used it only when it was there in the material as he received it—it lends considerable support to the idea that 8: 58 is dominical, especially as 8: 51 (another 'Amen' saying, and one with Synoptic analogues) leads naturally into the hearers' retort which eventually elicits the 'Before Abraham was, I am'.[25] The development of the argument from 8:31 onwards is ascribed by Lindars[26] to 'the methods of a preacher'; but while this is quite plausible in the Johannine *discourses*, it is much less so with a heated argument such as we have here (and one quite lacking in the repetitions and mysterious vaguenesses of the discourses proper). There are sentences that look 'Johannine', such as verses 54–5; but these can be excised if we wish without affecting the structure of the passage. I find it hard myself to believe that the last part of the dialogue (vv. 51–3, 56–9) is not a genuine reminiscence; if it is artificial it is most unlike John's usual artifices. I should add that Bultmann holds that the sentence does not identify Jesus with God;[27] but his reasoning turns on the supposition that such identifying would have to be expressed by straight grammatical assertion, whereas in fact it is done by allusion. Surely John could not have written it, or described its results, without realizing what he would be taken to imply? And indeed Bultmann himself adds that for John 'in Jesus' words God speaks the ἐγώ εἰμι'. I suppose it is just possible that Jesus Himself spoke the words without any thought of Exodus 3: 14, but no more than just possible; not likely.

20: 28, Thomas's recognition, introduces a minor disciple for no very obvious reason. Dodd regards the passage as 'a dramatization of the traditional motive of the incredulity of some or all of the disciples'.[28] Yet it fits Dodd's own outline of the typical resurrection-appearance pericope,[29] and I am not sure that there is a 'traditional motive of incredulity' after the Resurrection. (Matthew 28: 17 seems to refer to uncertainty rather than incredulity, perhaps failure to recognize the risen Lord, as in Luke 24: 16, John 20:

---

[24] Also John 13: 16 and 20 with Matt. 10: 24 and 40, though the latter lack 'Amen'.
[25] Naturally, that most 'Amen' sayings are authentic does not mean all are; but it makes it more likely.
[26] Lindars (1971), pp. 45ff., esp. p. 47.   [27] Bultmann (1971), p. 327 n. 5.
[28] Dodd (1963), p. 145.   [29] p. 143.

14; if these 'doubters' disbelieved, why had they come to Galilee at all? while Luke 24: 41 has the disciples disbelieving for *joy*, a very different reaction from Thomas's.) I can see no real reason for rejecting this story and its 'high' Christology, unless all Resurrection stories, or all stories with a 'high' Christology, are rejected on a priori grounds. It is not of course about a claim by Jesus, but He accepts the salutation (in words which seem to be echoed by Peter in 1 Peter 1: 8). I am therefore inclined to wonder whether these 'extreme' passages in John may not be based on genuine tradition, whatever the nature of the main Johannine discourses. A similar analysis of other passages (including the less extreme 'Son' ones) might well yield several more convincing-looking instances. But let us turn to the Synoptists.

The sceptical case would, I think, be that although the Evangelists themselves certainly regarded Jesus as the Son of God, they hardly ever depict Him as using the expression. It is used in addressing Him by the Father (Mark 1: 11 parr., 9: 7 parr.), by Satan (with an 'if') (Matt. 4: 3, 6 par.), and by demons (Mark 3: 11, etc.); it seems to be a title that supernatural agents know of but mortals do not, until, according to Matthew at least, Peter comes out with it—by divine inspiration (Matt. 16: 16)[30]. Jesus is depicted as calling Himself 'the Son' in a context where 'the Father' is also used (Matt. 11: 27/Luke 10: 22, Mark 13: 32/Matt. 24: 36; Matt. 28: 19), but doubts have been expressed over all these. The last of these (the baptismal formula) one can understand being doubted, as the early baptisms described in Acts seem to have been in the name of Jesus, not of the Trinity. But what of the others? The main reason for doubting Matt. 11: 27 par. ('All things have been delivered to me by my Father', etc.) seems to be its notorious resemblance to Johannine language; but this is hardly enough. Even if none of John's uses of 'the Son' were genuine, it could be that he was echoing this saying or something like it; certainly this is far more likely than that 'Q' was echoing some sort of proto-John. Jeremias[31] strongly defended the authenticity of the saying, but doubted whether 'the Son' was here a title, thinking rather that what we have here is a parable, which in English would properly be rendered 'Only a father knows his son, and only a son knows his father'. The trouble with this is that what the 'parable' says would not

---

[30] The centurion's use of the title in Mark 15: 39 hardly counts.
[31] Jeremias (1971), pp. 56ff.

be true! it seems far more likely that it was a genuine titular use. (Even if it was a parable, it was presumably intended to apply to Jesus and His heavenly Father.) Mark 13: 32 par. is of course one of Schmiedel's 'pillar sayings', and a pretty convincing one. Nineham has indeed suggested (without committing himself) that it might have arisen in the early Church 'in an attempt to deal with the non-fulfilment of (real or alleged) prophecies of Jesus about the End.'[32] Now the obvious examples of such prophecies would be Mark 9: 1 and Mark 13: 30 (and parallels). But these would not have given rise to the invention of a 'saying' of Jesus to deal with them until the last hearers of Jesus were near death, and this would not be until too late a date for the saying to be accepted by Mark unless he wrote his Gospel much later than is usually supposed. Not that it would have been much of an answer even then. If Jesus was thought to have predicted an imminent End, the natural 'answer' would have been to say 'No, He didn't', not to devise a saying implying ignorance in the Lord of the Church *and let the unfulfilled prediction stand*, only two verses away. Surely either Mark did not think 13: 30 was unfulfilled (in which case he did not need 13: 32) or he was writing too soon to know it would not be fulfilled (in which case again he did not need 13: 32).

To the above passages we should add the parable of the Wicked Husbandmen (Mark 12: 1–9 parr.), where the 'son' of the story is naturally taken to be Jesus Himself. Nineham,[33] adopting a suggestion of B. T. D. Smith's, proposes simply to excise the figure of the son altogether as an addition by the later Church to enhance the allegory; but the same reply can be made to this as to the even more drastic proposal to declare the whole parable inauthentic, namely, that if it, or the figure of the son, were not dominical, we should expect a reference to the Resurrection. 'This conclusion', as Jeremias says, 'makes it impossible to see in the parable an allegory which the primitive Church would put into Jesus' mouth, since his resurrection had such a central importance.'[34] This is the sort of case where the 'criterion of dissimilarity' is genuinely useful.

But perhaps the most difficult piece of evidence for the use of the title 'Son of God' in Jesus' own lifetime is Mark 14: 61–2, where the High Priest asks Jesus 'Are you the Messiah, the Son of the

---

[32] Nineham (1963), p. 361.   [33] p. 310.   [34] Jeremias (1966), p. 59.

Blessed?' and is answered (in almost Johannine tones) 'I am'. It has been contended that contemporary Judaism did not use 'Son of God' as an equivalent to 'Messiah'. This may be so. But that simply means that Caiaphas was not using it as an equivalent to 'Messiah'; he was using it (and 'Messiah' too, for that matter) *because Jesus was reputed to use it or accept it.* (Cf. Matt. 27: 43.) And it was presumably Jesus' acceptance of this title that allowed Caiaphas to declare him guilty of blasphemy.

It seems to me therefore far more likely than not that Jesus did accept the title 'Son of God'. And I cannot resist mentioning two concealed presuppositions which tend to creep into the thought of those who use Jesus' alleged silence over the title as an argument for a revisionist Christology. First, it seems to be taken for granted that Jesus never did anything *rarely*. Thus Matt. 11: 25–7 par. 'are very different in style and content from the main body of his teaching', says Cupitt.[35] Agreed, at least as far as the Synoptic accounts are concerned. But unless we also know that Jesus never said anything that did differ much from the main body of His teaching as it has come down to us, this does not get us very far. The second is the assumption (already alluded to) that revelation ceased at the time of the ascension (or before); that if Jesus did not say something, it cannot have been revealed to Paul or John or the writer to the Hebrews. Forsyth put it rather well when he said: 'There is more inspiration in the Epistles than in the Gospels, as Luther truly said. That is to say, in the total revelation the inspirational element predominates in the Epistles and the exhibitory element in the Gospels. It is in the Epistles the heart of the fact ceases to be dumb.'[36] Jesus Himself never spoke—according to the Synoptists, that is—of the grace or the love of God; yet few revisionists, as far as I know, would conclude that we ought not to believe that God is gracious or loving to us sinners. It is not otherwise with Jesus' sonship. It would seem prima facie quite likely that Jesus would not go about proclaiming His divinity in so many words as a general rule. When, according to St John, He did so, the result was an attempt to stone Him before His hour had come. (When His time had come, and the question was put to Him directly, He accepted the title.) But notoriously a good deal of what He said makes far better sense in the light of His divinity than without it, as if, in Austin Farrer's

[35] Cupitt (1979), p. 98.   [36] Forsyth (1909), p. 169 (cf. also p. 103).

phrase, He knew *how to be* God rather than *that* He was God,[37] and this knowledge emerged from time to time almost 'of its own accord'. Not only in the claims to override or intensify the Mosaic Law,[38] or to forgive sins,[39] but also, I should say, in some of the sayings in which He describes Himself as 'coming',[40] and in some of those in which things are to be done 'in His name'.[41]

E. M. B. Green argued in rather similar vein (it is of course a standard line of orthodox apologetics) in *The Truth of God Incarnate*;[42] and it is interesting to see how Cupitt answers this.[43]

> The Bible itself sees these powers, sufferings and glories as having belonged to many before Jesus, and as becoming general in the future. His death is in a line of such deaths, his power of bestowing divine forgiveness is a power which he transmits to his followers ... Is it not strange to argue from Jesus' perfect continuity with his background to his absolute discontinuity?

If Green had spoken of absolute discontinuity, this might have made sense *ad hominem*. But of course Green never denied that Jesus' death shared characteristics with other deaths, e.g. the characteristic of being a martyrdom. What he said was that it had certain other characteristics peculiar to itself, such as being the bearing of our sins or tearing apart the curtain that kept us from God.[44] The power to forgive sins was indeed transmitted to His followers (according to the Fourth Gospel![45]) but this in itself suggests an unprecedented authority. The Queen can not only give a command to a soldier in her army, she can give a commission to an officer empowering him to give such commands; but does this imply that he is as much Head of State as she?

The argument from 'filial consciousness' also appeals to something better explained by Jesus' divinity than otherwise. The address 'Father' or 'Abba' is the most celebrated basis for this argument.

---

[37] 'Very God and very Man', in Farrer (1976), p. 135.
[38] Matt. 5: 21, etc.
[39] Mark 2: 5ff. parr.
[40] e.g. Matt. 10: 4–5; Mark 10: 5; Luke 12: 49; Mark 1: 38 (but not Matt. 11: 3, 19).
[41] e.g. Matt. 7: 27; Mark 9: 38–9; Luke 10: 17 (but not Mark 9: 37).
[42] See esp. pp. 42 f.
[43] In Goulder (1979), pp. 38–9.
[44] Green (1977), p. 51.
[45] John 20: 23; but I agree that Matt. 18: 18 probably means the same.

In *all* Jesus' prayers (unless the quotation from Psalm 22 on the Cross be counted) He addresses God as 'Father' or 'My Father', and there is no serious doubt but that the actual word He used was the Aramaic 'Abba'. The usage is attested by all four Gospels and, indirectly, by St Paul.[46] And, it has been pointed out, this is unique; no one among His contemporaries used the word.[47] Mr Cupitt, indeed, thinks that Luke put in his references to Jesus at prayer just to edify his readers[48] (and probably he would say the same of John); but even if this were so, the interesting thing would be that Luke took it for granted that Jesus at prayer would call God 'Father', even to the extent of inserting the word into a verse from a Psalm.[49] Cupitt also adds two other points (apart from the quite irrelevant one that there have been many great saints who were not divine): that 'there is a big jump between "unique sonship" and "divinity"', and that the son–father view of man's relationship to God is deeply embedded in Jewish tradition; 'Israel in general and the King of Israel in particular were in a unique relation of sonship to God.'[50] Both points are correct. The first means that the 'filial consciousness' argument could not be used against an Arian of old, or a modern Jehovah's Witness; it does not, however, in the least help any other anti-incarnationist view. The second would be fair enough if Jesus were Israel in general, or the King of Israel; and Christians, like Nathanael or the Palm Sunday crowds, have certainly called Jesus 'King of Israel'. So it is possible that Jesus' filial and Messianic consciousnesses were linked. But on the whole it seems unlikely: His 'Father' language seems more one of intimacy than of royal privilege, and his 'Messiah' language (notoriously infrequent) is not as a rule linked to the Son/Father

---

[46] Romans 8: 15; Gal. 4: 6.

[47] Vermes (1976), p. 211 cites a passage in the Babylonian Talmud (bTaan.23b) to show that 'for the charismatic, as for Jesus, God is *Abba*'. But Hanan there is simply echoing children who had called *him* 'Abba', and the passage does not show that Hanan himself usually thought of God in this way.

[48] Cupitt (1979), p. 112.   [49] Luke 23: 46.

[50] p. 112. In Goulder (1979), pp. 166–9, Cupitt admits the superhuman and pre-existent status given Jesus in the New Testament, but holds that his view of Him as prophet and teacher is closer to this than orthodoxy is. This startling claim is justified by slipping in the word 'metaphorical' before 'pre-existent'. The New Testament could and did use metaphors for Jesus (e.g. 'stamp' in Heb. 1: 3, or 'Lamb' in John 1: 29), but there is not the slightest suggestion that they meant His pre-existence to be metaphorical.

relationship. (By Jesus Himself, that is: Nathanael, Peter and Caiaphas are all reported as juxtaposing the two in speech.[51])

I think, therefore, that there is quite adequate reason to think that Jesus' own words provide evidence for His exalted status, and therefore, provided no intermediate 'Arian' status be introduced into the debate, for His divinity. This is not to say that if there are other strong reasons for thinking that Jesus was not divine, or that He could not possibly have said anything that implied that He was, we could not work out ways of getting round these words. It *is* to say that we cannot use His alleged silence as evidence *against* the idea of His divinity.

One would naturally expect that the next question to be discussed would be 'is there "theological evidence" for Jesus' divinity?' But this question has already been answered, in effect, in our constructive analysis, and answered 'Yes'. There is really no need to go over this ground again.

The '*necessary* absence' of evidence alleged by Young is another matter (see above, pp. 65f.). The contention was, it may be recalled, that if any action of Jesus calls for Him to be more than human, we are faced with a modified form of docetism; if, on the other hand, it does not, it cannot be evidence for His divinity. Cupitt formulated a similar argument to show that the '*aut deus aut homo non probus*' defence of orthodoxy could be stood on its head, but his formulation is inferior to hers: all he has shown is that Jesus' language was not that of an ordinary good and sane human being. But to move from this to say that the defence is docetist is to beg the question; on the incarnationist view Jesus was not an ordinary human being but a very unusual one indeed! No ordinary good and sane human being will claim to be the Prime Minister of Britain—except the Prime Minister, who is in this respect not ordinary but unusual.

In point of fact the same kind of answer can really be made to Young, though her formulation does not beg the question quite so obviously. 'If Jesus was an entirely normal human being', she writes, 'no evidence can be produced for the incarnation.'[52] To this Professor Lash replies that exactly the same can be said for evidence for the reality of God if (as is accepted by the majority

[51] John 1: 49, Matt. 16: 16; Mark 14: 61.   [52] In Goulder (1979), p. 62.

of theologians). He does not appear as a fact in the world.[53] This
is fair enough *ad hominem*, but not of course conclusive, as an
atheist could take up Young's cudgels without any worry over such
a reply, and there is also the minority of theologians who do think
that God appears as a fact in the world. Lash goes on, however,
to point out that the same sort of objection could also be made
to the idea of a prophet or holy man: if it is part of the definition
of a perfectly normal human being that there can be no evidence
that he discloses the presence or character of God in a way most
of us do not, then either prophets and holy men are not perfectly
normal human beings or there can be no grounds for asserting their
existence. Again, the atheist will be unmoved; but Lash has, I think,
got close to the weakness in Young's argument. What exactly is
meant by '*normal* human being'? There are millions of people who
are not 'normal' people in *some* sense of the word: some are abnormally tall, others abnormally short, others again abnormally intelligent, stupid, fair, dark, good at tennis, knowledgeable about
computers, skilled at hunting, or devout. And clearly in many ways
Jesus was *not* 'normal'; He was better than the rest of us, for one
thing, and wiser, for another. And according to orthodoxy He was
also divine, which makes Him abnormal in a third way. Now this
third kind of unusualness might well affect His life in other ways—
enabling Him, for instance, to forgive sins or to give His life as
a ransom for many. Similarly, being abnormally good at tennis may
affect, indeed has affected, the life of Mr Ivan Lendl, making him
richer and more famous than most of us and with a lot more tennis
trophies on his shelves. But these trophies are of course perfectly
good evidence that Lendl is abnormally good at tennis, without
in the least suggesting that he is not human. Similarly, there is
evidence in Christ's life that He was divine as well as human; but
unless we already know that the two are incompatible, this is not
evidence for docetism.

I must add that Young seems not only to have begged the question
in the way described, she seems also to have fallen into the trap
mentioned a few pages back, that of assuming that revelation ended
at the ascension, only she has gone further than most. She has
(unconsciously, of course) taken it for granted that there could be
no revelation to and through Jesus Himself either. Suppose for the

---

[53] p. 63.

sake of argument that Jesus really did say 'Before Abraham was, I am' and thereby claim divinity. The act is a purely human one: I could say the same, and so could Young, though neither of us would be telling the truth. But it remains possible that Jesus was inspired to say it. And in that case it could be, and would be, evidence for His divinity. Young has overlooked the fact that much of our knowledge comes at second hand—that we are *told* it—and that according to a very widespread view this is true of most, or even all, of our knowledge of things divine. Even Jesus Himself, I argued earlier, did not know all things of Himself, but learned them; and indeed the Bible depicts God as telling Him things: 'Thou art my beloved Son', or 'I have glorified it, and will glorify it again.'[54]

---

[54] Mark 1: 11 par., John 12: 28—though the latter was not, we are assured, really for Jesus' sake.

19

Concluding Remarks

THE writer of a work such as the present one must almost inevitably feel at the end of it a sense of clumsiness and even of guilt. Is it right to treat the holy mystery that we call the Incarnation with the tools of a very limited human reason? Are we not in reality merely juggling with our own concepts, words, and formulae, spinning webs out of our own brains that do not in any way strengthen the walls from which they hang, but only disfigure them? The spider taketh hold with her hands, and is in kings' palaces; but does the King want her there, and is it not absurd for her to think that she is in some way doing the King service?

It may all too easily be so. If it is so, may God forgive me for writing what preceded, and you for having read it. But I hope it is not so. Refusal to use the tools of the intellect in the contemplation of God made man is invitation to the unbeliever to deride the whole of our faith, not unnaturally supposing that what is claimed to be beyond comprehension is in fact beneath it. Refusal to analyse is licence to revise; and though analysis is likely to go wrong, revision is still more so, being just as much the creation of one mind, and lacking such support as the wisdom and piety of the past can give. The persecution of heresy has brought shame upon the Church of Christ that must never be forgotten; yet heresy is a genuine peril for all that. We are justified by grace through faith, and though faith is not a matter of the intellect, it is possible for there to be beliefs in the intellect which are incompatible with those that make faith possible. By the mercy of God, we are most of us muddle-headed, and a soul may have utter trust and love towards Christ even while it holds false beliefs which if they were true would make that trust and love ridiculous. But it is unwise to rely all the time on human inconsistency; better to correct those beliefs before they become cancers to eat away at faith and in the end destroy it.

Revision is an attractive idea, attractive both to the adventurous in mind who seek something new, and to the unadventurous who seek something easy; and there will always, I think, be a need for defenders of orthodoxy to try and show that, new or old, easy or difficult, it is nevertheless the truth.

That orthodoxy has its own perils is no less true. All theology does; there is the permanent danger of supposing that intellectual assent, even intellectual understanding, is a substitute for saving faith; but orthodox theology carries with it perhaps a peculiar temptation to pride, to contempt of one's adversaries—to thinking of them as adversaries and not as brothers and sisters for whom the Lord Jesus gave His life, and who may well love Him better than one does oneself. The work must no doubt be done, but in a desire for humility, in an awareness of the dreadful possibility of being wrong, in a constant returning from words about the Lord to the Lord and Word himself. If anyone reads this book, and finds in it a help in keeping the mind directed towards the Christ who loved us; if anyone reads this book and finds its faults and errors a hindrance to faith that calls not for praise but for forgiveness; either way, pray for me, please.

Excursus I

Myth and Metaphor

IN an earlier passage I said that it did not seem satisfactory to treat Jesus Christ as a 'helpful symbol'. But this expression was my own, and did not perhaps do justice to the many anti-incarnationist thinkers who have not used it. Some have used language which suggests that they would prefer to describe the Incarnation as a *metaphor*;[1] more frequently it is called a *myth*.

Metaphor need not concern us long. The nearest I can get to a view that really does regard the Incarnation as a metaphor—as an idea, that is, which is not literally true but describes something which is, like calling God a Rock instead of saying that He is unchanging and utterly reliable—would perhaps be a view like Donald Baillie's,[2] where we have the 'becoming flesh' of John 1:14 replaced by an activity of God which is best understood in the light of the 'paradox of grace' as it operates in other human lives. God did not literally become incarnate, but that is an appropriate metaphor to describe something which He really did do. This would be an example, then, of a 'metaphorical' incarnation—except that Baillie would not, I am sure, have liked the name; he regarded himself as explaining the meaning of the Incarnation (in our terms, analysing it), not as denying its literal truth. Another possible example would be Ritschl, with his rejection of the idea of using metaphysics in theology. Since the function of Jesus Christ in establishing the Kingdom of God is a divine function, He has for us the value of God, and may be, indeed ought to be, called divine; but since we cannot analyse this divinity without the forbidden metaphysics (if then), the divinity of Christ might just possibly be called a metaphorical one. But I am not sure that Ritschl would have accepted the description any more than Baillie.

What, then, of *myth*? It has often been pointed out how loose

---

[1] Cf. Hick (1977*b*), p. 175.   [2] Baillie (1961).

and elastic this term is when theologians get their hands on it; it has been said (and justly) of Bultmann, for one, that he 'neither offers a satisfactory definition nor abides by the definition he does offer'.[3] Its commonest use among the unsophisticated is to mean 'an untrue story of great antiquity, probably about gods or heroes', and this has been used in theological circles. For there was at one time a 'Christ-myth' school which used the word quite straightforwardly to indicate their belief that no such person as Jesus of Nazareth ever existed; but none of the contributors to, say, *The Myth of God Incarnate* wanted to say that. Let us look, however, at some other suggested definitions or understandings of 'myth', and see whether they will help us.

Here, then, is Professor James Mackey: 'Images which evoke a certain depth and universality of human experience may be called symbols . . . Myth, finally, is a symbol or series of symbols developed in the form of a story.'[4] He adds a little later:

Myth is a perfectly valid way of apprehending and expressing reality in all its depth and breadth, and of probing whatever person, thing or event is thought to be of great significance in our world . . . So if the New Testament is myth to its very core, that tells us something about the point on the spectrum of human perception and expression at which it operates; not whether it is right or wrong, but how to interpret what it has to say.[5]

Here, again, is C. S. Lewis:

The first hearing [of a myth] is chiefly valuable in introducing us to a permanent object of contemplation . . . which works upon us by its peculiar flavour or quality, rather as a smell or a chord does . . . The experience is not only grave but awe-inspiring. We feel it to be numinous. It is as if something of great moment had been communicated to us. The recurrent efforts of the mind to grasp—we mean, chiefly, to conceptualise— this something, are seen in the persistent tendency of humanity to provide myths with allegorical explanations. And after all allegories have been tried, the myth itself continues to feel more important than they.[6]

Both these writers see myth as best understood in the light of its impact on us: it 'evokes a certain depth and universality of human experience', 'works upon us by its peculiar flavour'; but both are

---

[3] R. Hepburn in Flew and Macintyre (1955), p. 229.
[4] Mackey (1979), p. 78.   [5] p. 82.   [6] Lewis (1961), pp. 43-4.

also agreed that its effect is to convey 'something of great moment' or 'express reality in all its depth and breadth'. And I think it is obvious that the story of the Incarnation (especially if its continuation to the Cross and Resurrection be included) fits both descriptions very well. It does evoke depth and universality; it does work upon us by a peculiar flavour of its own; it does purport to convey something of great moment, and maybe even to express reality in all its depth and breadth. (I am not sure of this last; has not Mackey been a little too sweeping in his language? It evokes a sense of reality in all its depth and breadth, but not *all* of reality, so that 'express' seems doubtfully appropriate; 'apprehend', Mackey's alternative word, is better, provided that it is only *partial* apprehension that we are thinking of.) As far as I can see, incidentally, on either basis a myth might be literally true—a true story conveying a true meaning. That is certainly the case with Lewis's version: we could hear a true story with the same effects as a fictitious one. God might be the Author. And of course it is by no means unknown for Christians to see the story of Christ as just this, a *true* myth, literally true as well as true in what it evokes.[7] Mackey, indeed, writes[8] of the myth as 'woven' about the events of Christ's life and death. This rather suggests that what he has in mind is that later thought has interpreted these events with the aid of images and symbols in such a way as to express its significance for them; the myth is woven about the events, not incorporated into them from the start, and God, while He may have inspired His people to frame the myth, has not built its significance into His world. It remains the fact, however, that as far as Mackey's actual definition goes, a myth could be literally true, provided that the terms needed to embody it were not simply words but could be called 'images' or 'symbols'— terms which evoke depth and universality. And of course terms like 'God', 'came down from heaven', and the like are capable of evoking depth and universality. Mackey does not, I think, develop this approach himself; he seems to write as if myths in general were not literally true. To this extent his view is perhaps closer to that which I have ascribed to Ritschl, and it is significant that, when he comes to list some of the 'symbols' (i.e. depth-evoking images)

---

[7] Cf. e.g. Tolkien (1964), pp. 62–3; or Chesterton (1955), pp. 172–4.
[8] Mackey (1979), p. 83.

used to describe Christ's work by the New Testament, he picks
out many which could equally well be called 'metaphors', such as
renewed access to God ('the symbol here is the opening of a road
after an avalanche, or the discovery of the North-West Passage')
or the paying of a ransom.[9] (That he is absolutely right to see
them as more than just metaphors I entirely agree.) Nevertheless,
as I said, as far as his initial definition of 'myth' is concerned, the
Incarnation could quite well be both a myth and an actual fact
of history. Someone who heard it would be apprehending reality,
and someone who told of it would be expressing reality; and this
in a double sense, in that they would be hearing and telling a true
story, but also hearing and telling a story of immense significance—
the more so precisely because the story was true.

If an orthodox Christologist still feels a little unhappy over calling
the story of the Incarnation a myth, even in Lewis's or Mackey's
senses, I think it may be for this reason: In all other myths, so
far as I know, the meaning of the myth and the story in which
it is conveyed are two different things. The story of Ragnarök is
one of a battle between gods and giants; the meaning—well, Lewis
has warned us against trying to conceptualize myths, but it is at
least something to do with the heroic facing of inevitable defeat.
This is the case even where the myth is a literally true one. To
me (I cannot of course speak for anyone else) the story of the Byzantine Empire has long had something of the quality of myth about
it (and, now I come to think of it, a myth not at all unlike that
of Ragnarök). Byzantium really existed; but the myth, or the meaning of it, is clearly something distinct from the history that conveys
it. Could it be, then, that the story of the Incarnation, even if true,
should be seen as something distinct from what the 'myth' conveys?

Moreover, is not the relation between 'myth' and 'meaning' really
that between the story of Jesus, from the angel's message to Mary
till the Ascension, and the doctrines of the Incarnation and the
Atonement? Is it not the story of Jesus on earth, with its 'images'
resonating in the mind—the stable and the Christ-child, the teacher
by the lakeside, the prisoner before the guilty judges, the cry of
dereliction on the Cross, the empty tomb, and the cloud that received
Him out of their sight—is not this the 'myth' (a true one, mind

[9] Mackey (1979), p. 74.

you), and are not the doctrines attempts to conceptualize it? Can the doctrines really be mythical *too*?[10]

With a good deal of hesitation, I am inclined to say 'No'. What can perhaps be 'mythical' is a kind of *picture* of the Incarnation, in which a rather anthropomorphic God the Son is thought of as *literally* coming down from heaven, descending through the sky. Put thus baldly, it sounds, and is, ridiculous; but it may well be that it forms part of the half-conscious background to the thought of a lot of us when we recite the Creed, and it may on such occasions have something of the power of a myth to move us.

It seems, then, that the definitions of 'myth' suggested by Mackey and Lewis, while they help us to see how the story of Jesus (or even the doctrine of the Incarnation) may greatly move us, do not say anything about the analysing or revising of the doctrine. Wiles, however, in his handling of the idea of myth,[11] intends that it *shall* say something about this, and to Wiles accordingly we turn. He operates, in effect, with an ostensive definition of 'myth'. There are four basic Christian myths (or one myth with four principal 'moments'): Creation; Fall; Incarnation and Atonement; Resurrection of the Dead and Judgement. Most people will accept that the first two and the last are 'myths', and not literally true. Why not the third as well?

Pittenger (whom Wiles quotes at this point) had argued that while the Creation, the Fall, and the Judgement could well be called myths, since myth deals either with 'ultimate and unique "events" such as the creation of the world or the end of history' or with 'universal and general truths, such as the unpleasant but universally observable fact of man's estrangement from God', yet 'the Incarnation and Atonement are tied up with a specific historical event ... On the one hand they are not *outside* history, and on the other they are not true of *all* history ... Of course they are told to us ... in language which has a metaphorical or "mythical" quality'; but that is inevitable if we talk of God. We must not suggest that the life and work

.

---

[10] Wiles (in Hick (1977*b*), p. 153) quotes the nineteenth-century scientist F. Baden Powell (*The Order of Nature*, 1889, p. 341) as saying: 'Every dogma is more or less a myth, as it is necessarily conveyed in analogical language and anthropomorphic action'; but this is clearly using 'myth' in another, and far too wide, a sense. We already have the word 'analogy' for this sort of job.

[11] In Hick (1977*b*), ch. 8.

of Christ are just 'helpful representations of what is universally true'; our faith is about what God does in the world for man.[12]

Wiles finds this untidy.[13] To straighten things out: there must be 'some ontological reality corresponding to the central character of the structure of the myth'. ('Character' here of course means 'nature' or 'quality'—he does not mean Jesus!) The traditional interpretations of course provided just such an 'ontological reality'. Could there be 'less direct interpretations which would still retain ... the ontological correlation?' He suggests that the answer is the union of the divine and the human at the heart of the human personality in the experience of grace; *this* is the 'ontological truth' symbolized in the myth,[14] the 'universal truth' that Pittenger had denied existed. Why, then, the link with Jesus of Nazareth? Partly because his life embodied just this openness to God; partly because his life was 'a parable of the loving outreach of God to the world'; partly because of the historical connection between Jesus and our own experience of grace.[15]

This is a fairly complex argument, and requires fairly detailed consideration. First, are the four myths Wiles mentions all on a level? are even the three which he thinks are agreed to be 'myths'[16] (in the nontechnical sense) on a level? I doubt it. Consider the myth of Creation. Elsewhere[17] Wiles has pointed out, quite correctly, the correspondence between this myth and the 'cosmological argument' for the existence of God. There is a world: but why? Because, says the cosmological argument, it depends for its existence on a God who depends on nothing and no one for His. The Myth states the Argument's answer without explicitly posing the question; it states it in a different form, partly for the sake of mythical power, partly because the conceptual apparatus for the argument was not available when Genesis was written. (As a matter of fact, the causal form of the argument did not take shape until well into the Christian era, very possibly under pressure from Christian theology.) Myth was virtually the only tool available. But consider the position where the third 'myth' is concerned. Was the conceptual apparatus for describing the union of divine and human in the work of grace

---

[12] Pittenger (1959), pp. 39–40.   [13] In Hick (1977*b*), p. 155.
[14] p. 161.   [15] p. 162.
[16] Many Christians do not of course agree; but that is another matter.
[17] Wiles (1974), p. 34.

undeveloped when the New Testament was written? On the contrary;
the conceptual apparatus for this task was readily available, and
indeed the apparatus we use today is largely derived from Paul
and John. (I cannot resist the temptation here, purely to set Wiles
and Cupitt at variance, to point out that the word 'grace' is never
found on the lips of Jesus in any of the four Gospels. For that
matter, the idea of God's loving us or the world is never mentioned
in the Synoptic Gospels at all: it is a notion put into words only
by incarnationists like Paul and John.) The Apostles were perfectly
able to speak of grace without using a myth, because that is just
what they did; to them, grace and Christ's work were inseparable
but not identical.

Consider, again, the myth of the Fall. *Is* this altogether a myth?
Wiles supposes it to reflect a universal truth, which he expresses
in the form 'men fall below the highest that they see and that they
could achieve' (an astonishingly restrained description of human
evil from the age of Pol Pot and Belsen).[18] The relationship between
myth and truth is not the same as in the case of Creation, for human
badness is obvious to anyone and the dependence of the universe
is not. (Even theists, outside the 'Abrahamic' tradition, have often
failed to see it.) Moreover, a strong case can be made out for saying
that something *like* the biblical Fall *must* have happened. Our
remote ancestors—not Adam and Eve, we shall assume, but merely
moderately advanced hominids—were not guilty of moral wrong,
nor of rebellion against God; an animal cannot be either. There
must have been a first ancestor, or group of ancestors, who went
wrong—'the Adam', as Charles Williams called them.[19] Ten million
years ago, there was no sin on this planet; at present there rather
obviously is. There was therefore a time at which it began, the first
time a human being rebelled against God and conscience; in other
words, there was a Fall. The only point we need to concede here
is that there might have been more than *one* Fall. (I do not mean
that more than one of the Adam may have fallen at different times,
though that too is possible; I mean that rebellion against God and
rebellion against conscience might conceivably have been separate
events.) If, then, the account in Genesis is to be labelled 'myth',
it was not written in mythical form because the conceptual apparatus
was lacking for anything else, nor because the thing described was

[18] In Hick (1977*b*), p. 160.   [19] Williams (1950), pp. 17ff.

logically inaccessible to the writer, but because the historical facts were, contingently, unknown to him, and to ascribe the Fall to an actual known historical person would obviously be out of the question.

The myth of the Last Things is in a different category again: it partakes of the character of both the others (though it is nearer to that of the Creation). There will be an end of the human race, that is for certain. To that extent, the Last Things resemble the Fall. But naturally they are logically inaccessible to us, not by a matter of mere contingent fact; and to that extent they are more like the Creation. Once again, the conceptual apparatus may not have been available to the biblical writers—the only thing is, we cannot be sure that it is available to *us*. (Is the Resurrection of the Body to be taken literally, despite 1 Corinthians 15: 35? If not, what does it represent? Do we have the conceptual apparatus to answer?)

The Incarnation and Atonement clearly are far closer to the 'myth' of the Fall than to either of the others. But in this case there is no question of the historical facts' being beyond reach. They might have been. I think C. S. Lewis said somewhere that if *per impossibile* it were shown that Jesus had never lived, this would mean only that the Incarnation had not *yet* happened. In that case, the gospel would be a myth of the same kind as the fall—giving an alternative concrete form to a truth which actually had such a form but where this was not available to us for some reason. However, this is not the case. The historical facts *are* available to us. Of course, the interpretation of them, in terms of God and sin, is not a historical event. But if this is 'myth', so equally is Wiles's 'union of the divine and human at the heart of the human personality'. That too is interpretation.

The movement from 'these other stories are myths' to 'the story of the Incarnation is a myth' is not therefore as plausible as it looks. That does not of course entail that it *cannot* be a myth, only that things will not be rendered any 'tidier' if we treat it as one. It could still be the case that the real meaning of the story was the union of the divine and human in the experience of grace. But there are two or three comments to be made here.

One is basically *ad hominem*. Wiles, as we have already noted,[20] dislikes the idea of a God who intervenes in the world He has made. If we talk of God's activity, we are really speaking of events within nature or history in which God's purpose 'finds clear expression or special opportunity'. Such a view of God's activity 'refrains from claiming any effective causation on the part of God in relation to particular occurrences', though it still sees Him as 'source of [the world's] existence and giver of purpose to the whole'.[21] But in that case, can we speak of any 'union of human and divine' in the experience of grace? The events we call 'experiences of grace' are not experiences of anything which is not purely natural; their only link with God is with Him as Creator, which they share with every other experience. There is no union of divine and human; all there is is an event which expresses God's purpose or gives it special opportunity. (How we can *know* even that is another problem, which I have discussed in the body of the text.[22])

This comment is, as I said, *ad hominem*; it is perfectly open to anyone who does not share Wiles's quasi-deism to ignore it. The remaining ones, however, are more general in their applicability. In the first place, I think attention should be drawn to the curiously second-hand nature of the Wilesian interpretation of the 'myth'. It is not an interpretation of the life of Jesus. That life tells us little or nothing about the union of human and divine in our experience of grace. It is only when the life of Jesus has been interpreted in terms of Incarnation that the Wilesian interpretation can even begin. I do not say this is a fatal objection to it, but it makes me wonder whether it would be a viable theology for long without belief in a real Incarnation to keep it in being.

The third point is in a way related to this last one. I think it is highly misleading to call the story of Christ, if its true 'ontological correlate' is the union of human and divine in the heart of human personality, a *myth*. The proper word is *allegory*. I do not mean the deliberate composing of an allegorical story to convey a non-literal meaning in, it may be, a more vivid or entertaining way, as with the *Roman de la Rose* or the *Pilgrim's Progress*. I mean the attaching of a non-literal meaning to an already existing story, in the way that Philo and Origen handled the stories of the Old

---

[20] See Ch. 3, above.   [21] Wiles (1974), p. 38.   [22] See Ch. 14, above.

Testament (as did of course many later writers[23]). Thus Dante, considering Psalm 114: 1 ('When Israel came out of Egypt'), says:

if we consider the literal sense alone, the thing signified is the going out of the children of Israel from Egypt in the time of Moses; if the allegorical, our redemption by Christ; if the moral, the conversion of the soul from the grief and misery of sin to a state of grace; if the anagogical, the passage of the sanctified soul from the bondage of the corruption of the world to the liberty of the everlasting glory.[24]

On this scheme, Wiles's understanding of the Incarnation is clearly an instance of the 'moral sense', which we today would doubtless speak of as one particular class of allegory. And notoriously the trouble with allegorizing texts which were not originally meant as allegories is that with ingenuity you can read quite different meanings into them. I have on my shelves a translation of a letter of St Gaudentius[25] (d. 410) on the parable of the Unjust Steward (Luke 16: 1–9), admittedly a very difficult parable to interpret, in which he takes it first as teaching 'that in this world nothing is really ours, but that instead we have been entrusted with the steward-ship of the goods of our Lord, either to use them, with giving of thanks, according to our needs, or to distribute them to our fellow-servants according as they have need', and then as about the devil (the steward) who wasted his master's property by seeking the ruin of mankind, and now wants to retain his grip on us by inducing us to disown our debts to God. Of course, the 'myth' school do not go into such detail in their allegorization of Christ; normally they concentrate only on the Incarnation, Passion, and Resurrec-tion. But allegorizing is what they are doing. And, not surprisingly, different allegories are drawn out of the story. Wiles's is not that of Bultmann. That of Paul van Buren in *The Secular Meaning of the Gospel*[26] was different again, being seen largely in terms of 'contagious freedom'. Such a variety among the consequences of an objective act of God in Christ would be natural enough; so tremendous an event would be almost bound to have great and varied effects; but as different claims for the true ontological reality behind a myth they are, simply, incompatible. 'Allegorizing' does seem the only accurate description; and not a complimentary one.

---

[23] And, once, St Paul (Gal. 4: 24).

[24] Letter to Can Grande della Scala, quoted by Williams (1943), pp. 56–7.

[25] Toal (1957–63), iii. pp. 332ff.; PL 20, 971.

[26] Van Buren (1963); this work does not represent van Buren's later views.

I think, therefore, that the whole enterprise of seeking a revisionist Christology or soteriology on the basis of regarding the Incarnation as 'myth' was misguided. But the quest for a revisionist Christology does not stand or fall by the usefulness of the concept 'myth', and most of the critics of traditional views have not tried to make use of that concept. Hence the fact that this is an 'excursus', a digression, not part of my main argument. It is for all that a digression that needed to be made.

Excursus II

'Central Selves' and the Trinity

IF what has been suggested in the preceding pages is correct, and the central self or ego of God the Son is also the subject of the acts and experiences of Jesus, it follows of course that God the Son has such a central self, and the natural conclusion is that the same applies to God the Father and God the Holy Spirit. Thus Galot says of the Son that he 'behaves to the Father as an "I" confronting a "You" '.[1] This in turn seems to lead on to something on the lines of 'social Trinity' theories. I do not propose to go into detail here, but only to submit to the reader a possible sketch for a Trinitarian theology suggested by what I have been saying about the Incarnation.

If the human soul consists (in part at least) of a central self which has a variety of experiences, thoughts, sensations, choices, and the like, and which is that which unifies all these; and if in the life of each Person of the Holy Trinity there is also a central self which unifies whatever in the divine life is analogous to experiences, thoughts, choices, and the like; how then are we to conceive of the unity of the three Persons? We are assured by Leonard Hodgson that

> there is in the Godhead the perfect instance of the kind of unity of which we have imperfect analogues on earth. When we have learned to measure by a scale of intensity of unifying power we no longer think that because the elements in the Godhead are ... complete persons, the degree of unity must be less than in the human self ... Seeing that the degree of unification demanded so far exceeds anything within our experience, how mysterious, tremendous and fascinating, we argue, must be the intensity of that unifying power which constitutes the unity of the Blessed Trinity.[2]

But can we not form even an imaginary sketch of what that unifying power might be?

[1] Galot (1980), p. 333. [2] Hodgson (1943), p. 96.

I think a *possible* approach (there may well be others far better, and the danger of pouring cold human rationalism over a divine mystery must not be forgotten) might be by way of 'experiences, thoughts, sensations, choices, and the like', which from now on, for brevity's sake, I shall call simply 'thoughts'. Could it be that thoughts of one Person are also thoughts of the other Two? I am inclined to think that this is possible; and if so, it would provide a unity which would indeed be more intense than any organic unity known to us on earth, yet one which could only hold between persons. There might of course be other forms of unity prevailing between the Divine Persons as well. Perhaps something like this was in Thornton's mind when he wrote of 'three personal centres of one absolute actuality'.[3] The difficulty that at once obtrudes itself is this: Surely my thoughts are by definition mine alone? We may talk about 'two minds with but a single thought', but of course what we mean is that both minds are thinking in the same terms—'let us go now to Bethlehem' or whatever it may be—and not that there is a *thing*, an event or an entity, which is in both minds at once. A universal can be in two minds at once, but not a particular. What goes on in my mind is necessarily my thinking, and what goes on in yours is yours; they may be exactly alike, but they cannot be numerically identical. Yet is this a logical necessity? There are indeed some things which are limited to one person by logical necessity; my awareness of my own identity cannot be anyone else's, or we should be the same person. But my house may also be yours; we may be joint owners. To which class do thoughts belong?

If thoughts really are entities in themselves, like the 'ideas' and 'impressions' of Hume or the 'sense-data' of more recent philosophy, then they belong to the second class. There is no reason, then, why one thought or sense-datum might not attach itself to two minds (if minds are also entities) or be a component part of two minds (if minds are to be analysed into bundles of thoughts). (In the case of embodied minds such as ours, there is one quite good reason why not, namely, the fact that our sensations and doubtless other 'thoughts' are mediated through our bodies, mine through mine and yours through yours; but this would not apply to God.) If, however, thoughts are to be conceived of more on the lines of the

[3] Thornton (1928), p. 415.

'internal accusatives' of the grammarian, as Berkeley supposed,[4] depending for their existence on an act of thinking or sensing, rather in the way that a race depends for its existence on being run, one's first reaction will be to say that they must belong to the first class, those items which by logical necessity must be either mine or yours. I cannot run your race, nor you mine. Yet a little reflection shows that this need not be the case. I cannot run your race, agreed; but we can both run the *same* race; indeed, a race actually requires at least two runners. It could be that the thoughts of God are like this, a kind of co-operative work of all three Persons. (Not necessarily *all* His thoughts: if, for instance, each Person of the Trinity knows and loves the other Two, then there would also be thoughts which were peculiar to each of the Persons.)

The usual alternative to a 'social' theory of the Trinity is one of 'modes of being', τρόποι ὑπάρξεως. But I am not sure how to combine this with a theory of the Incarnation which allows the Word to be aware of Jesus' experiences as His own; if the three Persons are modes of being of the One God, can one Person have experiences which are not also those of the other Two? Yet if the Incarnation is true, not only is the Second Person of the Trinity aware of Jesus' experiences in a way the First and Third are not, but He is also aware within His divine life of the fact 'These earthly experiences are mine', which the other Two are not aware of, because in Their cases it is not true.

Consideration of the Trinity in the light of the Incarnation also raises the question of Schoonenberg's deliberately startling suggestion[5] that we should replace the idea that the humanity of our Lord was 'enhypostatized' in the already existing hypostasis of the Word by the reverse idea—that the Word became enhypostatized in Jesus of Nazareth; that God became triune (by His own decision) through His 'salvific-self-communications'. There are serious difficulties in such a view quite apart from its novelty. Most obviously, in God there is no *time*; at least, both Schoonenberg and I believe there is none. How then can God 'become' anything, except from our point of view? This Schoonenberg fully realizes; that God becomes triune is 'what *we* know about God's Trinity ... On a Trinity in God from eternity and by necessity we as creatures cannot

---

[4] For a modern defence of this, cf. C. J. Ducasse, 'Moore's "The Refutation of Idealism"', in Schilpp (1952), pp. 225ff.

[5] Schoonenberg (1972), pp. 83ff.

make any statements, either in the affirmative or in the negative.'[6]
What Schoonenberg is therefore suggesting is not *quite* as paradoxical as it seems at first glance. God the Son and Jesus the Jew share one and the same hypostasis, which is human (being that of Jesus, who was human) and divine (being that of God the Son); but whether this hypostasis exists eternally in God, or rather (God being timeless) whether it would have existed in Him had there been no Incarnation, we have no way of telling. All we can say is that the Son and the Holy Spirit did not operate in history as separate hypostases until the Incarnation.

My chief difficulty over this, which has an irritating prima facie plausibility about it, is over the Holy Spirit. He is depicted in Scripture as active before the Incarnation and indeed as the agent of the Incarnation itself. He is not indeed 'personalized' in the Old Testament, but in the New, where He *is* treated as personal a good deal of the time, it is taken for granted that He is the Spirit mentioned in the Old Testament, who spoke through the prophets. It seems then that God was at least biune from (at the latest) the beginnings of His revelation to the world—very possibly from the beginnings of creation itself. Furthermore, the Father and the Holy Spirit are not enhypostatized in any created being as far as we know. Is there then only one fully personal hypostasis in the Godhead, namely, that of the Son? And what are we to make of the passages which ascribe to the Son a role in creation? On the whole it seems better (and more biblical) to retain our belief in an eternal Trinity, rather than accept Schoonenberg's modified Sabellianism.[7]

[6] p. 86.
[7] 'Modified', as Sabellianism denied the eternal Trinity; Schoonenberg is agnostic on this.

Excursus III

Kenosis

SOME form of kenoticism would clearly avoid the difficulty we were discussing earlier of there being two consciousnesses in the one Person after the Incarnation; so it would seem appropriate to discuss this sort of theory in a little more detail.

A major problem in doing so is that the word covers a considerable range of different theories. Brian Hebblethwaite uses it to describe any Christology that takes the humanity of our Lord 'absolutely seriously',[1] which strikes me as far too wide a definition. The modern Kenotic movement seems to have had its roots in Lutheran debates over the *communicatio idiomatum*. Lutheran orthodoxy held, not just that words could be used of the divine Son that belonged strictly to the Nazarene carpenter, and vice versa (so that we can say that God bought the Church with His own blood[2] or that He created all things through Jesus[3]), but that the attributes denoted by such words were really communicated from the one Nature to the other (so that Christ's body, like His Godhead, could be present in many places at once, as in the Eucharist). By some theologians the presence of divine attributes in the man Jesus was in practice reduced to a mere power of using them if He chose, which in fact He did not do; and this became the more prevalent view.[4] But if the divine powers were not shown in Jesus' earthly life, and if moreover the *communicatio idiomatum* applied in both directions, it was quite a natural step to say that the divine Word actually acquired human limitations, and therefore laid aside His divine attributes, in order to become man. The most celebrated defenders of this view were G. Thomasius and W. F. Gess; but the view was not confined to Lutherans, and we find, for example,

---

[1] Goulder (1979), p. 27.   [2] Acts 20: 28, *v.l.*   [3] Eph. 3: 9, *v.l.*
[4] I owe this account to Mackintosh (1913), pp. 237ff.

the Swiss Reformed theologian Godet following the Lutheran kenoticists in this, writing that 'Jesus no longer possesses on the earth the attributes which constitute the divine state ... It was necessary, first of all, that He should consent to lose for a time His self-consciousness as a divine subject.'[5]

The theory was taken up later in the century (and on into the twentieth) by a number of British theologians, but not always in its original form—nor indeed always in the same form as one another. The language of Bishop Gore could occasionally suggest that he was in sympathy with the Continental kenoticists: 'It will not suffice to say', he wrote, 'that the Son was limited in knowledge, etc., *in respect of His manhood*, so long as we so juxta-posit the omniscient Godhead with the limited manhood as to destroy the impression that He, the Christ, the Son of God, was *personally* living ... under the limitations of manhood.'[6] But more often he uses phrases like 'ceasing to exercise, at least in a certain sphere'[7] the divine functions, or 'refraining from the divine mode of consciousness within His human life',[8] which are more ambiguous. The idea that the Son ceased to uphold the worlds during His incarnate life 'could not be maintained unless the divine revelation positively and expressly forced it upon us. But it does not.'[9] So although the Continental kenoticists' position could not be ruled out altogether, it is clear that Gore did not in fact hold it. How exactly the problem was to be resolved was probably not to be known: 'We are asked how we relate this "limited" condition of the Son as incarnate with His exercise of all the cosmic functions of the eternal Word ... I think we had better give no answer.'[10] We should not 'attempt to "describe, beyond the Scriptures, the measure or the manner" of the divine condescension'.[11]

Weston was more explicit. 'The Lord Jesus chooses to measure some of His activities in a degree that we men can call our own ... Yet He is in no sense hampered in His own proper, eternal activities by the human measures He assumes.' 'If we like to put it so, God limited Himself in order to dwell in Mary's womb. But need we use such a term? ... Need we discuss which activity [upholding

[5] Godet (1876), i. p. 397.   [6] Gore (1895), p. 203.
[7] p. 90.   [8] p. 94.   [9] p. 206.
[10] Gore (1922), p. 226.   [11] Gore (1891), p. 163.

the worlds or being conceived] imposes the more self-restraint
on God? And if we discuss it, are we competent to find a solution
to the problem?'[12] The Son, therefore, continues to uphold the
world; He is one with the human Jesus, 'not by conversion of the
Godhead into flesh, but by taking of the manhood into God'. This
seems to have much in common with the position I was advocating
above. Why then is Weston usually reckoned a kenoticist? Perhaps
because he felt that without a 'self-emptying' the human life of Jesus
would be virtually impossible. 'It is an act of supreme divine power
that so orders the life of the Logos that within a certain sphere
He wills to have no consciousness of Himself that is not mediated
by His human soul.'[13] In order that Jesus' human soul should not
be swamped, so to speak, by the ocean of divinity, there must be
Kenosis. But this is envisaged as an eternal choice of God the Word.
The accusation of Knox and Vidler (echoed by Mascall) that Weston
'does not realize that in speaking of the Incarnation and the risen
and ascended Lord we are dealing not with changes in the eternal
nature of God, but with the relation of the timeless Being of God
to his manifestation in history'[14] is surely quite unjustified. Weston
is clear that the 'promulgation of the law of self-emptying which
He imposed upon Himself' was one of the 'unlimited activities of
the eternal Son for all time, activities from which He has never
ceased'.[15]

Mackintosh and Forsyth are more definitely kenotic. Mackintosh,
as we have seen, refused to predicate two consciousnesses or two
wills of Christ, and the context of the passage seems to suggest
(though he is not explicit) that he is not confining this to the
'lower state' like Weston, but is referring to the whole being of
the Incarnate Word. Like Gore, however, he avoided any conclusion on the question of the Word's cosmic functions, refusing to
support either Weston's belief that these continued or Godet's that
during Christ's earthly life the Father sustained the world directly
and without the mediation of the Word. 'Over all such problems
there hangs a curtain, alike for discursive knowledge and for
faith.'[16]

---

[12] Weston (1920), pp. 84–6.   [13] Weston (1907), p. 156.
[14] W. Knox and A. Vidler, *The Development of Modern Catholicism* (London,
1933), p. 219, cited by Mascall (1946), p. 31.
[15] Weston (1907), p. 321.   [16] Mackintosh (1913), pp. 483–5.

Forsyth depicted the kenosis as an act of 'condensing' the God-head: 'the divine energy was concentrated for the special work to be done ... The divine qualities were there; though their action was at once reduced, concentrated, intensified within the conditions of the saving work. The divine qualities were kept, but only in the mode that salvation made necessary.'[17] The position implied is clearly nearer that of Godet than of Weston; the 'concentration' evidently takes place in the continuing life of the Son, not just in a part of it.

Temple's famous question, then, 'What was happening to the rest of the universe during the period of our Lord's earthly life?',[18] was not *ignored* by any of the kenoticists we have been looking at (except perhaps Forsyth). Gore and Mackintosh are reluctant to give an answer, though Gore obviously *wants* to say 'It was sustained by God the Logos, as always'; Weston and Godet are both prepared to give an answer, though not the same one. Godet's, however (and probably Forsyth's), runs into serious difficulties after the Ascension. We seem to be driven to conclude either that our Lord ceased to be human after the Ascension or that His divinity has remained limited from that day to this, and will remain so for all eternity. Neither alternative is very attractive:[19] surely Weston must be right.

The question remains: ought his view to be called 'kenotic'? Weston was critical of theories which *he* called 'kenotic'; Temple presented a form of 'double-consciousness' view ('God the Son did indeed most truly live the life recorded in the Gospel, but added this to the other work of God'[20]) as an alternative to kenosis. It might be best to restrict the use of the word to theories which assert that the Son no longer possesses, or no longer uses, some of His divine attributes during the Incarnation—neither on earth nor in heaven. If, however, it is preferred to use it also for views which see the knowledge and power of *Jesus* as limited, but not those of God the Son, even during the earthly life of Jesus, well, that

---

[17] Forsyth (1909), p. 319.

[18] Temple (1924), p. 142; cf. Baillie (1961), p. 96.

[19] The former would be the easier. In that case the Son would no longer be consub-stantial with us (except *sub specie aeternitatis*), but He would have *been* such, and so still close to us, like (to use the well-worn simile) a king who had been a beggar, and retained sympathy for beggars after coming to the throne.

[20] Temple (1924), p. 143.

too is acceptable, provided it is made clear which usage we are
following; but it does seem the less convenient usage of the two.

If 'kenotic' is used in this latter way, a great number of patristic
sayings could be cited to show that in *that* sense the Fathers were
(many of them anyhow) kenoticists. It was (naturally enough) an
obvious way to explain Mark 13: 32 and its Matthaean parallel.
As we have seen, some, like Augustine and Eulogius, attempted
to get round that crux in other (and very unconvincing) ways; but
many Eastern Fathers thought differently. Gregory of Nyssa argued
against the Apollinarians 'How could "God in flesh" be ignorant
of "that day and that hour"?',[21] implying that if God assumed
a genuinely human *mind* as well as genuinely human *flesh*, then
there would be no difficulty; and Athanasius wrote that 'Just as,
having become a man among men, He hungers, thirsts, and suffers,
so also, as a man among men, He is ignorant ... He was right
to say "Nor the Son", speaking through the body in the flesh, so
that He might show that as man He did not know; for it is characteristic of humankind to be ignorant'.[22] And we have already quoted
Theodoret to similar effect. Later Fathers did indeed turn against
this kind of kenosis, but, Meyendorff has pointed out, this was
not because of some near-Docetism, but because of a tendency to
treat ignorance as a result of the Fall; since Jesus was not fallen,
He could not be ignorant.[23] Similar reasoning led some Byzantine
theologians, orthodox and monophysite, into 'aphthartodocetism',
denial that Jesus' body was corruptible, corruption too being a
result of the Fall.

The need to account for Jesus' ignorance was not the only reason
for modern kenoticism. There was also an entirely justifiable desire
to stress the Lord's full and genuine humanity; and a desire, too,
to stress the love and grace of the Son of God in so humbling
Himself. But the former can be stressed without a kenosis in the
first of our two senses; while the latter is not really a valid reason
on its own for believing the theory to be true. If it *is* true, then
indeed we have yet another reason to feel awe, gratitude, and love
for what the Lord has done for us. But if we do not know it to
be true, then we cannot use the greatness of the love involved as

---

[21] *Adv. Apoll.* 24 (PG 45, 1175a).   [22] *C. Arianos* 3. 46 (PG 26, 420).
[23] Meyendorff (1975), pp. 87–8. For a later linking of ignorance and the Fall,
cf. Schleiermacher (1928), pp. 415–16.

a reason to believe it true, any more than we can, like many Muslims, use the greatness and holiness of Jesus as a reason to deny the Crucifixion. It is a risky business, telling God what He ought to have done; we have ample reason for awe, gratitude, and love as it is, with or without first-meaning kenosis.

And I myself cannot believe in that kind of kenosis. Partly for the reasons given above; also because it is plainly impossible to state such a view without treating God as a *temporal* being, one to whom there is past, present, and future just as there is to us. But not only is this absurdly anthropomorphic, it surely entails denying that God created time as He did space. All the time we know of is the time of the material universe or of conscious beings within that universe; a being who is *not* within the universe, but, on the contrary, is One on whom the universe and all that is in it depend for their existence, is surely most unlikely to be Himself time-bound. But even if I am mistaken in this, the difficulty over the ascended Christ remains.

It is of course not a difficulty for the view I have been defending in recent pages. Are there others, though? Goulder and Cupitt think so. According to the former,

When it is asked, 'What then is in common between Jesus and God?' the reply advanced by modern kenoticists is 'Nothing as far as Jesus' human nature is concerned: but metaphysically he is the Word of God'. What this means, and what grounds there can be for accepting it (other than reluctance to allow that the church has been in error) remain obscure.[24]

If the prince in a fairy-tale, he has urged earlier, is turned into a frog, he retains his memory, his power of reason, his love for the princess, and so on; but if he 'becomes' a frog *completely*, with a frog's mind and individuality, and no memory of princely prior existence, we should say that the prince had been *replaced* by a frog. There must be continuity.

Now various replies could be made to this. One is to point out that if the prince later recovered his memory, etc., while retaining those of the frog-life in between, there would be no great difficulty. This actually happens in dreams. On Goulder's principle, I can never dream that I am a frog, since I should have the dream-frog's 'mind and individuality' during the dream, not Sturch's. Yet I *can* dream it, and remember the dream when I wake up. (Interestingly, I can

[24] Goulder (1979), p. 55.

also *forget* the dream and yet still have had it; but we can let that
pass.) Perhaps Jesus did not fully realize His own true nature until
the Resurrection or even the Ascension. I have doubts about this,
but some have taught something close to it. If so, and if, once risen
and glorified, He can say 'I am the first and the last and the living
one, for I was dead and now I am alive for evermore',[25] there
is an element of continuity.

But this is not the only possible answer. In fact, of course, the
aim of Chapter 10 was precisely to suggest another element of continuity. (It is one Hebblethwaite might be willing to accept: 'the
human subject Jesus', he says, '[was] not an independent human
subject'.[26]) And there is, on our second interpretation of 'kenosis',
yet another element of continuity; for although the Galilean
carpenter may not have known who in truth He was, the eternal
Word did.

This, however, is just what Cupitt finds an obstacle. His difficulties
are set out in a rather compressed but also rather important passage
in *Incarnation and Myth*.[27] Firstly, such a theory requires a *triple*
consciousness in the Lord. 'There is God the Son's divine self-
knowledge; there is Jesus's own awareness of himself as a human
servant of God; and there is God the Son's awareness of himself
in kenosis as being the true subject of Jesus's acts and experiences.'
He finds it unsatisfactory that Hebblethwaite only allows for the
first two. Actually, Hebblethwaite's words are 'God, *qua* God, is
aware of who he is and what he is doing',[28] which would naturally
be taken to include both His identity and actions as the eternal
Word *and* His identity and actions as Jesus of Nazareth. And
this is surely right. God the Son is aware both of His eternal
identity and of His human life, but this does not mean two consciousnesses in Him, any more than my own awareness of both sights
and sounds.

Cupitt even realizes this. 'It is as if a bit of my personality breaks
off in such a way that it believes itself from its point of view to
be an independent personality and agent. It is unaware of me, but
I am aware of it.' This is fair enough (except for 'breaks off', and
Cupitt does qualify that with an 'as if'!). Now we may readily concede

---

[25] Rev. 1: 18.   [26] p. 90.   [27] p. 45.
[28] p. 90.

that this is not easy to imagine. Dreaming that I am a frog may provide *some* analogy, but not a complete one, as the 'two conscious-nesses' in such a case are successive, not contemporary. But then I cannot imagine what it would be like to be God in any case; is there any extra difficulty in imagining what it would be like to be God and Man?

But, Cupitt continues,

the human Jesus' view of his acts and experiences as a servant of God logically must be different from God the Son's view of Jesus' acts and experiences as acts and experiences of himself in a state of kenosis. Mr Hebblethwaite's theory leaves no-one in the position of being able to say 'I am God in Kenosis, suffering in and for man': and if no-one can say that for himself, how can Mr Hebblethwaite say it of him?

The first sentence is true enough, but harmless; the second is quite mistaken. The idea seems to be that God the Son cannot say He is God in kenosis (as God the Son, He is *not* in kenosis) and Jesus of Nazareth cannot say it either (if He could, He would not be in kenosis!). So no one can say it. But this does not follow at all. Suppose I am wearing odd socks but am unaware of this (surely a logical possibility?). I cannot say 'I am wearing odd socks but am unaware of it' without being aware of it after all. But how does this stop Mr Hebblethwaite, noticing the clash around my ankles and my innocent lack of embarrassment, from saying it of me? Exactly the same holds of Christ. Jesus the man cannot of Himself know that He is God in kenosis, even if He is; but others can. God the Son can, for one. (He cannot say '*I* am God in kenosis', but He can say 'This man is I, the Son, in kenosis'.) Incidentally, even Jesus of Nazareth could in fact know and say it; for if His relationship with God the Holy Spirit is as was suggested earlier, it could be known to Him by inspiration. (We might compare Mark 1: 11/Luke 3: 22—where, admittedly, it is the Father who speaks, not the Spirit, though He too is present.) Obviously, to acquire the human knowledge that He was God in kenosis would not destroy the kenosis itself, which was more than just ignorance of His own heavenly identity.

If, then, this second type of Christology is to be called 'kenotic', then the present work is kenoticist, and I should be willing to defend the idea of kenosis. Whether this is really proper from the point of view of vocabulary is another matter; I should doubt it myself, as the Incarnation on this view is an adding (of something limited) to God, not an emptying out from Him; but there are enough debates among Christians already without adding another over etymologies and words.

Excursus IV

The Sinlessness of Jesus

I T is noticeable that even fairly radical Christologists like Schoonen-berg and Robinson are firmly, and rightly, convinced of the sinless-ness of Christ, at least in the sense of *impeccantia*. But two questions have been raised at times about this sinlessness which ought to be mentioned here: what caused Christ's sinlessness, and did it apply to 'original' sin as well as to individual sinful acts?

I have already suggested that the analysis of the Incarnation pro-posed in this book seems to imply that it was not simply by the union of divine and human in Jesus Christ that He was preserved from sin. This is not unprecedented. I found with interest that Duns Scotus, for one, held that 'the human nature of Christ was not rendered sinless by virtue of the union to the Word (as nature, it is no different from what it would have been had it not been united to Him) nor by virtue of its glory, nor even by grace (except indirectly) but by His *fruitio*' (that is, His 'enjoyment' of the vision of God, which is inseparable from the fullest grace).[1] The last part does not convince me; I can see no reason to doubt that grace, the work of the Holy Spirit on Jesus' life, was the direct source of His sinlessness. But it may be felt that in saying this I have come uncomfortably close to a position I was only lately criticizing. I objected to the idea that Christ was free to sin (even though in fact He never did) because this seemed to make His sinlessness a matter of 'luck'—He, God incarnate, might conceivably have rebelled against God. But it looks as if this were also implied by saying that His sinlessness was not the result of the Union but of the accompanying grace of the Holy Spirit. The Union might have taken place without that grace, and if so we might once again have God rebelling against Himself.

I am conscious of the difficulty, but not sure that it is fatal. The

[1] *Reportatio Parisiana*, I. 3. 12.

Incarnation was not a series of separate decisions on the part of God—'Let us join human nature to us. Oh, and let's have a soul as well as a body—and we might as well save the world while we're about it, and we'd better make sure we don't sin ...' It was a single purpose that brought it about that Christ was incarnate by the Holy Ghost of the Virgin Mary. There was therefore no question of an Incarnation by unity of central self without the accompanying grace; it was not a matter of luck that our Lord was good and holy, but a matter of the divine purpose.

But did this purpose also exclude the Lord from *original* sin? Until the nineteenth century, as far as I know, almost everyone would have said 'Yes'.[2] But since then there have been voices raised to the opposite effect. Mackintosh quotes Edward Irving as an early example, from the 1820s, and mentions a couple of German examples as well.[3] The most famous advocate of this view, however, was of course Karl Barth. Christ's being as man, he declared,

is not sinless in itself. The Word becomes flesh—not just man, but the bearer of our human essence, which is marked not only by its created and unlost goodness but (in self-contradiction) by sin ... He made our human essence His own even in its corruption, but He did not repeat or affirm its inward contradiction. He opposed to it a superior contradiction.[4]

On the opposite side we might mention, for example, Mackintosh himself commenting on Irving:

The oneness of our Lord with us in the moral conflict, which was for Irving the heart of all things, is indeed a great fact; yet a theory of it is not to be purchased at the price of asserting that His humanity was corrupt, with a corruption which only the Holy Spirit could hold in check ... Irving passionately repudiated the idea of Christ having *actually* sinned; but it is after all only a loose idea of sinlessness which takes it as compatible with the existence in Christ of a potential fault and strong efficacious germ of evil.[5]

The trouble is that there is no agreed doctrine of what original sin consists of for us to assert it or deny it of our Lord. Some have held that the guilt of Adam is immediately imputed to his descendants irrespective of their corruption. This appears to me

[2] Robinson (1973), p.53, cites Nestorius and Julian of Norwich as possible exceptions, though not explicit ones.
[3] Mackintosh (1913), pp. 276–7.
[4] Barth (1956–8), IV, 2 p. 92.
[5] Mackintosh (1913), pp. 277–8.

to be mistaken, the more so when we consider its implications for the person of Jesus. If He was free of original sin, it was apparently only by an arbitrary exclusion of Him from the guilt imputed to all others; if He was not, if He bore human guilt in the same way as the rest of us, it is not easy to see quite how it was defeated in Him, being not a power but an imputed guilt. An alternative is to see original sin as a tendency, a disposition to do wrong even when we realize that we ought not to. This can itself be taken in more than one way. It may mean that there is a tendency to do wrong for its own sake, or simply out of the pleasure that evil-doing gives, irrespective of any gain or other pleasure for ourselves, an almost disinterested evil like that of the men some years back who were caught breaking glass into a children's paddling-pool. This sort of tendency was surely quite absent from Jesus; with this kind of sin Schleiermacher would be right to see even the temptation as evil. It is, by God's mercy, rare even in most of us. (There was of course no need, on any theological theory, for our Lord to be tempted to each and every individual kind of sin!) Or it can mean the weakness of any tendency to do good, so that when we do do good it is with motives so mixed that we should not have done it without the bad or merely indifferent motives. This again I see no need or reason to ascribe to our Lord, and very strong reason indeed to deny it of Him. But it can also mean simply a disposition to do something (in itself good or morally neutral) despite the fact that to do it would, because of some other aspect of the deed, be wrong. And whether this might be attributed to our Lord requires further thought.

An analogy might help us to consider what our attitude should be to something with an undesirable disposition. A sheet of glass, being fragile, is unsuitable as part of the wall round a cricket-pitch. Of course, it may happen that no ball is ever hit so as to come near the particular stretch that has been built of glass, and in that case, though fragile, it will not be broken (at least, not by a ball from the cricket-field). But it would still be unsuitable for its purpose; the builder who put glass there would be rightly condemned as a fool. Similarly, someone with a tendency to sin who by some chance has not so far committed any actual sin (an infant, for example) cannot be regarded as a wholly 'suitable' human being. (I recall a character in a book by Martin Buber, whom Satan carefully refrained from tempting for twenty-eight years in order to make his eventual lapse into a malicious lie the more devastating.[6]) But if the glass is *protected*, so that no ball can hit or break it, then its fragility no longer matters, and if it is suitable in other ways, there is no reason why it should not be left standing. Similarly, one in whom there is a tendency or pressure to sin, which however is at all times counteracted and overcome by a stronger tendency or pressure not to sin (Barth's 'superior contradiction'), has no real defect. A 'corruption' which is never actual and which never had any real chance of becoming actual is no corruption. In Christ the pressures, inner and outer, which in the rest of us lead to sin, were present but utterly defeated by a greater pressure towards holiness. And if those pressures are what in theology is called 'original sin', then it was the strength of original sin which in Jesus Christ was defeated.

[6] Buber (1966), p. 182.

Excursus V

Incarnation and Fall

IT may be objected that we are separated from God by a 'barrier of nature' quite apart from our sins. Adam and Eve, even unfallen, were not divine, and indeed it was a temptation of the serpent to suggest that they might *become* divine: 'You will become like God, knowing good and evil'.[1] If, then, the Incarnation was meant, in part at least, to overcome this barrier, would it not have been needed even apart from the Fall? Is it not something independent of our fallen and sinful condition?

Of course, unfallen humanity would be in fellowship with God from the start. It would not need the Incarnation to teach it that fellowship with Him was possible. But it would still not know the extraordinary possibility latent in human nature—that of becoming one with the divine; nor the extraordinary range of God's love for His creation—to the extent of becoming part of it.

There has in fact been a strand in Christian theology, albeit a minority one, which has held precisely this: that the Incarnation *was* independent of the Fall. It seems to have appeared first in the twelfth century;[2] it was discussed as a possibility by several of the Schoolmen, including Albert the Great, who inclined on the whole to favour it, and Bonaventura and Aquinas, who decided against it, feeling that the biblical linking of Incarnation and Redemption told too strongly the other way. Duns Scotus, however, argued for it with vigour. 'Predestination of anyone to glory', he said, 'precedes foreknowledge of that person's sin ... Much more so is this the case with the predestination of that soul which was predestined to the highest glory of all ... Therefore God desired the glory of Christ before He foresaw the fall of Adam.'[3] Had there been no Fall, Christ would not have come as Redeemer, perhaps

---

[1] Gen. 3: 4.
[2] In Abbot Rupert of Deutz, cited by Westcott (1883), pp. 273ff.
[3] *Opus Oxoniense (Ordinatio)*, I. 3, dist. 7, q. 3, n. 3.

would have come in a form incapable of suffering, as there would
have been no need for Him to suffer; but He would have come
just the same. A few Renaissance and Reformation thinkers
took a similar line; but its real revival dates from the nineteenth
century onwards. Dorner placed a discussion of the Incarnation
in his treatment of Creation: 'The world is created for perfection.
In the God-man this is given. Therefore is the God-man destined
for the world by God's love.'[4] Bishop Westcott not only described
the history of the view but defended it with sincere eloquence in
his commentary on the Johannine Epistles. Dean Inge wrote: 'The
taking of the manhood into God was from the first the intention
with which the human race was created.'[5] And Charles Williams
summed it up in almost epigrammatic form: 'The world exists for
the Incarnation rather than the Incarnation for the world. But the
Incarnation became the Redemption for the sake of the world.'[6]

A strong tradition in the Eastern Church (and to a lesser extent
the Western as well) holds that the ultimate destiny of redeemed
humanity is properly to be called 'deification' (quoting above all
2 Peter 1: 4).[7] But as far as I can make out theologians in this
tradition have usually held that God's original plan was to have
this destiny achieved by unfallen man, through Adam, and that
therefore though the Incarnation was indeed to overcome the barrier
of nature, this barrier was itself the result of the fall. Had there
been no fall, the human race, being created in the image and likeness
of God, could have united heaven and earth by goodness, and
created and uncreated by love.[8] As far as unfallen humanity is
concerned, this kind of thinking would perhaps have agreed with
the passage we have already quoted from Young, that 'a real son
is not needed to produce adopted sons. Since we only receive an
adopted sonship and a derived divinity, the essential Godhead and
sonship of the one who passes it on is not logically required.'[9]

Actually, we have several interrelated questions here, which need
to be sorted out. (1) 'Is the destiny of redeemed humanity properly
described as "deification"?' The word itself is not Scriptural, but

---

[4] Dorner (1880), ii. 216.   [5] Inge (1924), p. 74.
[6] Review in *Time and Tide*, 21/46 (1940), 1122. Cf. Williams (1950), p. 119.
[7] See e.g. Lossky (1957), ch. 6, or Meyendorff (1975), ch. 7.
[8] Maximus the Confessor (PG 91, 1305–8), cited by Meyendorff (1975), pp. 139–40.
[9] In Hick (1977b), p. 37. (Young, however, applies this to fallen humanity as
well as unfallen.)

is the idea? 2 Peter 1: 4 is an obscure verse, and perhaps not too much weight should be put on it. What is it to be 'partakers of the divine nature'? Calvin, for instance, took it to mean 'partakers of the divine immortality and the glory of blessedness', so that we should be 'in a way one with God, so far as our capacity allows';[10] and more recently, I gather, the idea that immortality is what the passage is about has been defended by T. Fornberg.[11] I should have thought it possible that we should understand it in the light of 2 Corinthians 3: 18 and 1 John 3: 2, that we share the Lord's nature by seeing and reflecting His glory. (2 Peter has in fact just mentioned that we are called to God's own 'glory and excellence'; the alternative reading '*by* his own glory and excellence' seems less likely, though the whole sentence is admittedly oddly expressed and hard to follow.) In that case Calvin's 'one with God, so far as our capacity allows' seems fair enough, and the word 'deification' might be accepted, though with some hesitation (as likely to give a false impression, though rightly stressing the fact that in the end 'God has only Himself to give').

(2) 'Was this destiny intended in the creation of the human race?' There is no way of telling for certain, as far as I can see; but the imagination may help. I should refer the reader to the pictures of unfallen life in C. S. Lewis's novels *Out of the Silent Planet* and *Perelandra*.[12] In the former, the inhabitants of Malacandra (Mars) are intelligent and innocent; in the latter, those of Perelandra (Venus) end up well on the way to being 'glorious'. Both are no doubt destined to be 'one with God as far as their capacity allows', but the capacity is different, and which is nearer what might have happened without a fall on *this* planet one cannot say.

(3) 'Supposing that "deification", at least in the moderate sense suggested above, *was* God's intention in creating humankind, could this have been achieved without Incarnation?' Is Young right about 'adopted sonship and derived divinity'? I am not sure what the proper answer here ought to be. One natural retort is that unless real sonship exists there cannot be adoptive sonship either, any more than there can be imitation pearls unless there are or have been real pearls to be imitated. Yet this is not decisive. If some genetic

[10] Calvin (1963), p. 330.
[11] *An Early Church in a Pluralistic Society* (Lund, 1977), p. 88, cited by Guthrie (1981), p. 636.
[12] Lewis (1938, 1953).

engineer were to succeed in breeding a horse with wings, we might quite reasonably call it an 'imitation Pegasus' even though no real Pegasus ever existed. If there is a positive relationship to God, describable in its own right, which might be called 'adoptive sonship', then that relationship could exist without there having to be a 'real' Son of God as well—though it would never have acquired the *name* 'adoptive sonship' if it had not been supposed that there was a real Son. We might perhaps note that there is no Incarnation in either of Lewis's novels (apart from that on this planet, that is). On the other hand, if the relationship of the redeemed to God, is best described by the metaphor of 'reflecting', as in 2 Corinthians 3: 18, and this reflecting is of the incarnate Christ, might it not be that there had to be a real Son in order for there to be 'reflecting sons' as well? You cannot have the reflection of a face in a mirror without there being a real-world face for the mirror to reflect. Yet the right translation of 2 Corinthians 3: 18 is debated; many versions take κατοπτριζόμενοι to mean '*seeing* in a mirror', not 'reflecting'— presumably seeing the glory of God in the face of Jesus Christ (cf. ch. 4: 6). And, just to confuse things further, 'Lord' in the immediately preceding verse, and again at the end of this very sentence of Paul's, refers to the Holy Spirit, so that perhaps it is He whom we see or reflect! On the whole, I am myself inclined to think that 'deification' would not have required an Incarnation for an unfallen humanity, but more strongly inclined to doubt the value of speculation.

We should note that as far as the suggestion made earlier is concerned, that the Incarnation was needed to restore hope to humankind, and in *that* sense to 'overcome the barrier of nature', not only is this probably based on a fallen humanity, but it requires a real Sonship as well as an adoptive. It is the *marring* of our nature that makes this first barrier so dreadful. If human nature had never been marred, the gap between finite and infinite would still have been there, but would it have been a *barrier*? However, fall or no fall, if the barrier does need to be overcome, only God can cross it.

Excursus VI

πρόσωπον, φύσις, οὐσία, and ὑπόστασις

WHAT follows is not intended as an exhaustive survey of the use of Christological terms by the Fathers. Its aim is merely negative, to suggest that the Fathers were not as tied to Platonic or Aristotelian terminology as is sometimes supposed, which may be of some use.

'The term "nature"', wrote Forsyth in an unguarded moment, 'is a purely metaphysical term, and one which characterizes a scholastic metaphysic of being rather than a modern [1909] metaphysic of ethic.'[1] With respect to a great theologian, this will not do. The word φύσις and its cognates occur a dozen or more times in the New Testament; and by a satisfying irony which might have been deliberately designed to upset critics of the old terminology, these include reference both to human nature, ἀνθρωπίνη φύσις,[2] and to divine nature, θεία φύσις.[3] (In honesty I should add that in the former passage the phrase really means 'human kind'. Yet even there I suspect that St James had the idea of different 'natures' of different creatures in the back of his mind.) In classical Greek the word can be used for an almost incredible variety of purposes, from lofty speculations about the universe to a bawdy pun. It is not a metaphysical term unless one wants it to be: to say that an object has or participates in X-ly nature is to say that that object is an X, and the choice between the two is determined more by grammar than by metaphysics. Thus in the definition of Chalcedon the Fathers began by asserting the one Son, our Lord Jesus Christ, then used the abstract nouns 'Godhead' and 'humanity',[4] then the concrete ones 'God' and 'Man', interchanging freely; and for the final section, where they wanted to say that all this came together

---

[1] Forsyth (1909), p. 229.   [2] Jas 3: 7.   [3] 2 Pet. 1: 4.
[4] Thus perhaps meeting Pannenberg's demand that one begin with describing 'one and the same person, the man Jesus of Nazareth, from different points of view'?

in one Person, they were obliged to use the word 'natures' because
of the sheer difficulty of saying the same thing using only the concrete
nouns 'God' and 'Man'. It is like saying of a dancer that her tech-
nique is greater than her musicality; it is almost impossible to say
this without using abstract nouns, and yet no one would accuse
a ballet critic who said it of doing metaphysics (let alone 'a metaphysic of being rather than of movement'), nor deny that he was
talking about a concrete human being.

πρόσωπον is also a New Testament word. It normally means
'face' there (which of course is not its meaning in later Christological
debate!); but sometimes it has the straightforward one of 'person'.[5]
This is certainly its meaning in the formula of Chalcedon and the
Thirty-Nine Articles; God the Word and Jesus the son of Mary
are one and the same person. There is however the complication
that πρόσωπον can also mean 'appearance' or even 'mask'; and,
as we have seen, it is likely that Nestorius himself meant 'appearance'
when he used it, though not in the sense in which 'appearance'
is contrasted with 'reality', but rather in that in which (outward)
'appearance' is contrasted with (inner) 'structure'.

Dr A. R. Vine, in his history of *The Nestorian Churches*,[6] said
that it seemed safe to assume that in the later Nestorians' formula
'one *parsufa*' (the Syriac equivalent of πρόσωπον) 'means no more
than the appearance of unity presented externally by the fact of
Jesus Christ ... having one physical presence, a mere mask (a frequent meaning of πρόσωπον) of unification to cover the two person-
alities' (*qnume*, ὑποστάσεις). But it is not clear why we should
assume this; and on the other side we find Dr W. A. Wigram saying
that though the Syriac word *can* mean 'appearance', this is unusual,
and the normal sense is simply 'person', as in such phrases as 'the
person chosen as patriarch'.[7] In fact 'appearance' in the sense of
'mask' is surely impossible: in *that* sense Christ has clearly *two*
πρόσωπα which He presents to the world, the 'mask' or 'face' of
God the Son and the 'mask' or 'face' of Jesus the son of Mary.
If the word in the later Nestorian formula does mean 'appearance'
it must be in the sense Hodgson ascribes to Nestorius himself, and

---

[5] e.g. 2 Cor. 1: 11; 1 Thess. 2: 17.

[6] Vine (1937), p. 54. In his later book (Vine (1948)), he held that Nestorius himself
certainly meant more than 'appearance'—'the self-manifestation of a natural unity'
comes closest (p. 100).

[7] Wigram (1910), p. 279.

not in the weaker one that Dr Vine at first suggested. But all this
need not be settled. It is quite clear that πρόσωπον and its equivalents[8] can be used in a variety of different ways, and that therefore
their use in Christological formulae cannot be taken as evidence
of Platonic or Aristotelian metaphysics at work, or of too close
a link with Hellenistic concepts.

οὐσία, 'substance' or 'being', is another matter. Here we have
a word that really does have a technical philosophical use (or rather
uses), and is rather unusual except in such a use. (Elsewhere it usually
means one's 'property', and is found in that sense in the New Testament.[9]) It is found in Chalcedon only in the compound ὁμοούσιος,
'of one substance', 'consubstantial'; Christ is consubstantial with
the Father as far as Godhead is concerned and with us as far as
humanity is concerned. The word is of course copied from the Nicene
Creed, but is perhaps used in a less technical sense than there. For
here it clearly refers to the universals or qualities of Godhead and
humanity, being in fact identical in meaning with φύσις, whereas
in the Nicene Creed it could also be taken to refer to the fundamental
unity of the three Divine Persons, which is more than the unity
there is between three human beings in virtue of their common
humanity. In the latter case οὐσία would approximate to the Aristotelian 'material cause',[10] except of course that the Divine persons
are not material. Some of the Fathers of Nicaea may have had
this second sense in mind.[11] But in the Chalcedonian formula it
is only the weaker sense that can be meant. And though this sense
is certainly used by Plato and Aristotle, it is not a technical term
confined to their philosophies. The idea of a nature held in common
by more than one instance is surely inescapable—not, of course,
because we cannot get through life without using it, but in the sense
that it is implied every time we use the same word for two different
things. Until people stop asking 'What do X and Y have in common?'—indeed, until they stop using plurals—οὐσία will continue
to make sense.

ὑπόστασις is the most plausible example of Greek metaphysics
at work. In the New Testament it normally means 'confidence',[12]

---

[8] Including the English 'person'!   [9] Luke 15: 12, 13.
[10] Cf. *Metaphysics*, 7. 2. 5: 'since substance (οὐσία) is the cause of a thing's being'.
[11] Cf. Kelly (1960), pp. 234-7.
[12] 2 Cor. 9: 4, 11: 17; Heb. 3: 14, 11: 1.

though there is one case where it does seem to have a more 'metaphysical' meaning, Hebrews 1: 3, where the Son is said to be the 'shining out of God's glory and the stamp of His ὑπόστασις'. It is unlikely that it has any technical meaning there; the writer probably just wanted a word to emphasize the eternal being of God who is the foundation of all things. ('Foundation' is in fact another sense of ὑπόστασις.) By a follower of Aristotle it is used in contrast to 'appearance',[13] and the verb ὑφίστημι is used for 'to exist',[14] but it is not a typically Aristotelian word. It does occur in a number of later philosophers like Plutarch and Sextus Empiricus, and the Church historian Socrates says it was used as an equivalent of οὐσία by 'more recent philosophers'.

If one had to pick out what is central to the idea of ὑπόστασις as most of the Fathers seem to use it, I *think* it would be this: The ὑπόστασις is that whereby two individual entities *are* two individual entities, whether their qualities are the same or different. Thus St John of Damascus writes 'Sometimes it means plain "existence" (τὴν ἁπλῶς ὕπαρξιν)'. . . but sometimes it means an existence in itself, subsisting by itself' (τὴν καθ' αὐτὸ καὶ ἰδιοσύστατον ὕπαρξιν); 'by this an individual is indicated, differing in number from others—Paul, for instance, or Peter, or a specific horse.'[15] But there are possible variations on this. As John goes on to say a little later, 'the holy fathers used ὑπόστασις, πρόσωπον, and ἄτομος (individual) 'for the same thing'.[16] (He himself wants to use πρόσωπον for that which is *perceived* and distinguished from others of the same nature—'thus Paul speaking on the steps, being as he is one of mankind, is distinguished from others by his qualities and actions.'[17]) Bar-Hebraeus, using of course the Syriac equivalent *qnuma*, defines it as 'an individual nature',[18] which might suggest that he was distinguishing between 'nature' as in 'It's not in human nature to be so patient' and in 'It's not in my (individual) nature to be so patient'. (In the latter sense Christ, being one person, had only one nature—and Bar-Hebraeus was a Monophysite!) But he goes on to say 'Several *qnume* can subsist in one universal nature

---

[13] Pseudo-Aristotle, *De Mundo*, 4. 21 (395a).   [14] Fragment 183 (1509b).
[15] *Dialectica*, 42 (PG 94, 612).   [16] *Dialectica*, 43 (PG 94, 614).   [17] Ibid.
[18] *The Candelabrum of the Sanctuary*, 4. 4. 1 (PO XXXI, 1, p. 124).

which includes them all', which could make the word stand more for the individual itself than for the individual's nature.

Leontius of Jerusalem says that the most proper sense of ὑπόστασις is 'that which marks out the underlying' (ὑποκείμενος) 'individual',[19] but elsewhere that it 'signifies for Person and Nature that which underlies both these different concepts'.[20] The former looks like the 'individual nature', but may well be simply another way of putting the second definition, which is interestingly close to the sort of thing suggested in Chapter 10 of the present work. This is unusual, I think; though there is a passage in Leontius of Byzantium[21] where, apparently tiring of subtle distinctions, he declares 'One entity is produced out of these' (divinity and humanity); 'I do not care whether you call it Person or Hypostasis or Indivisible Being or Underlying Reality or anything else you may prefer', which suggests that others were in fact using this 'underlying' idea (one which, by the way, undoubtedly *is* Aristotelian[22] in origin, though he only uses it of material objects).

The Nestorian theologian Babai (seventh century) seems to take a line in some ways similar: the *qnuma* (ὑπόστασις) is 'the particular substance which subsists in its own single being, numerically one and separate from the rest, not in so far as it is individualized but in so far as (if it is a created thing) . . . it receives various properties . . . It is distinguished from other *qnume* that are like it by the individual attributes which the person possesses.'[23] Thus Peter's and Paul's are different *qnume*, although the *qnume* are only distinguished by the characteristics which make up the person. If we see two people approaching at a distance we know there are two *qnume* involved, even though we do not know what qualities either has. (One may have doubts about the illustration.)

In general, though, ὑπόστασις seems most often to refer to the whole entity. The Definition of Chalcedon speaks of the natures as 'concurring in one person and one hypostasis' (εἰς ἕν πρόσωπον καὶ μίαν ὑπόστασιν συντρεχούης); Leontius of Byzantium holds that two ὑποστάσεις can combine to form a single one, as happens at the resurrection, when soul and body become a single entity once

---

[19] *Contra Nestorianos*, 2 (PG 86, 1529d).   [20] Ibid. (PG 86, 1532b).
[21] *Contra Nestorianos et Eutychianos*, 1 (PG 86, 1304).
[22] *Metaphysics*, 6. 3 (1029a).
[23] *De Unione*, 17 (quoted by Labourt (1904), pp. 283–5).

more. Hence he concludes that the Word could have been united with an already existing complete human being (Leontius had Origenist sympathies) and formed a single compound ὑπόστασις, though he agrees that this did not in fact happen, as 'it would not be fitting for the Lord's humanity to be alone and without divinity for a time'.[24] And John of Damascus, while rejecting this position (soul and body do not, he thinks, have different ὑποστάσεις), can still speak of a 'compound ὑπόστασις'.[25]

The total impression that I gain—apart from a general sense of confusion—seems to be that ὑπόστασις was not used as a technical term with a fixed meaning given to it by secular philosophy; it was used primarily as a 'stronger' word than πρόσωπον.[26] The latter did leave open the possibility that there was a serious separation between God and Man within the one Christ. By insisting that there could not be two ὑποστάσεις in Him, the Fathers were not committing themselves or the Church to any theory about what sort of metaphysical entities there are in the world, nor about how the union should be analysed.

[24] *Epilysis* (PG 86, 1944a–c).
[25] *Dialectica*, 66 (PG 95, 668a); cf. *De Fide Orthodoxa*, 1097b.
[26] Post-Chalcedonian Antiochenes treated the two as equivalent (Meyendorff (1975), pp. 32–3), but only by taking πρόσωπον itself in a fairly strong sense.

Excursus VII

Methodology and the Gospel Tradition

By no means all New Testament critics give any rationale of the methods they use. Some do, however, and it could be instructive to look at one and see the kind of reasoning contained in it. It is taken simply as an illustration; the author is no longer with us; and I have ventured to leave him anonymous, lest I should seem to be conducting a vendetta against someone who cannot reply. I shall call him simply 'N'.

N's aim is to lead us up to the 'criterion of dissimilarity'; and he begins with two basic propositions about the early Church. First, she 'identified the risen Lord of her experience with the earthly Jesus of Nazareth'. So far, of course, no one could disagree; but N goes on to claim that in the written gospel 'words and deeds ascribed in her consciousness to both the earthly Jesus and the risen Lord were set down in terms of the former'. Specifically, the early Church did not distinguish 'between the words the earthly Jesus had spoken and those spoken by the risen Lord through a prophet in the community'. Secondly, 'the gospel form was created to serve the purpose of the early Church, but historical reminiscence was not one of those purposes'.

If by 'historical reminiscence' is meant the recording of an incident simply because somebody remembered that it had happened, without other reason, then the second of these propositions is correct. There is little or nothing in the Synoptic Gospels which looks as if it were reminiscence of that sort, except perhaps for a few incidental details attached to some of the narratives (and even these are regarded by many with suspicion). The catch is that someone whose purposes do not include historical *reminiscence* may still have some interest in historical *accuracy*. Imagine a Marxist historian discussing the French Revolution. He may well not be interested in reporting the exact sequence of events; he may be concerned only to show that the Revolution can be fitted into a Marxist view of history, and may therefore only mention events that seem evidence for this; and yet he may easily mention only events that actually happened. N's second point is quite useless to him without the first, which suggests that the early Church was quite prepared, in all good faith, to mention 'events' that did not happen.

Now this first point needs evidence, of course. Here N is inevitably selective: no blame to him, he could not in one chapter give an account of all the work by various scholars that led him to his conclusion. He has to summarize. 'Contemporary scholarship has [explained] pericope after pericope on the basis of the needs and concerns of the early Church', he says. Here there is a certain ambiguity. The 'explanation' may explain the present form and appearance of the pericope, as with Jeremias's work on the parables (which is in fact one of N's examples a little later on). But Jeremias did not think he had explained the *existence* of the parables by the needs and concerns of the early Church; nor, I should add, does N. The parables were not originally the work of the risen Lord in His Church but of the earthly Jesus. We need evidence that contemporary scholarship has explained the coming into existence of ostensibly dominical material that is actually later in origin. And the 'explanation' must not be just an explanation, showing how it *might* have happened, but *the* explanation, showing that it could not have happened differently. Otherwise we have the old logical fallacy of Affirming the Consequent: 'if P, then Q; but Q; therefore P'—which obviously does not follow in the slightest. ('If the sun went round the earth, it would rise and set; but it does rise and set; therefore ...') From the fact that if X,Y, and Z had happened in the early Church a passage W would have taken on a certain form, and the fact that W does have this form, it does not follow that X,Y, and Z ever happened, We need to show that there is no other explanation; that *only* if X, Y and Z happened could W have taken on this form.

N cites three examples of the creation of material. One is Mark 9: 1; 'There are some standing here who will not taste death before they see the Kingdom of God come with power.' This appears in slightly different form in Matthew 16: 28 and Luke 9: 27, and the differences are readily explicable by the theological interests of Matthew and Luke. But the Marcan version, N believes (having been convinced by an essay of Haenchen's), is Mark's own composition. He discusses the verse in two places. In one, the only reason given for regarding it as inauthentic is the 'artistic nature of the scene'; the last verse of the passage beginning with the question 'Who do men say that I am?', it forms, with 8: 38, a 'climactic combination of warning and promise'.

We may agree that Mark tells his story well; but it simply does not follow that he made the climax up. Perhaps *Jesus* combined warning and promise. N agrees that 8: 38 was only adapted by Mark, not invented; the same might equally be true of 9: 1. We are told, however, here and in the second discussion of the verse, that it has some 'distinctly Markan characteristics: the concept of "seeing" the parousia, and the use of "power" and "glory" in this connection.' But what is a 'distinctively Markan characteristic'? Presumably one which no one except Mark (and the other Synoptists where they are following Mark) uses, or which he uses far more often than others. Well, St John the Divine certainly uses 'see' in an apocalyptic context, over and over again (see especially Rev. 19: 11, perhaps the nearest to Mark 9: 1 in content). More relevantly, so does Luke in a passage with no Marcan parallel (Luke 17: 22, not discussed by N). And since Mark himself only uses it twice in the whole of the rest of his Gospel, it seems hardly strong enough to serve as evidence that Mark composed this verse himself. Still less does the reference to 'power', which only appears in one other Marcan reference to the parousia (13: 26; 14: 62 is of course a different use of the word altogether). 'Glory' does not occur in 9: 1 at all, but in 8: 38; it may be a Marcan addition there, as N believes (it is not in the Matthaean or Lucan parallels), but this tells us nothing about 9: 1. It could possibly suggest that Mark has added 'with power' there as well as 'in the glory' in the previous verse; not that Mark composed the whole verse himself.

This is followed by a return to the theme of 9: 1 as the climax of the pericope, and evidence (quite convincing) that it always followed 8: 38 and was never an isolated saying. But this of course says nothing about its authenticity one way or the other. (The fact that 9: 1 never circulated without 8: 38 does not mean that 8: 38 might not have circulated without 9: 1.) Finally, we have a suggestion as to how Mark might have composed 9: 1. He wished to end the pericope with a note of promise as well as warning, and composed the verse on the basis of 8: 38 and 13: 30. This is fair enough provided that we already know the verse to be Mark's work; but it is not *evidence* that it *is* his. To show that if the burglar climbed in through a first-floor window he must surely have climbed on to the garden wall first does not prove that he did come in by a first-floor window. Perhaps he came in by the door and never climbed on to the wall at all. N's discussion of Mark 9: 1, in short, interesting though it is, has not merely failed to prove that the verse is not dominical; it has failed to provide *any evidence at all* for that theory.

We move on to the other examples N uses. One is Käsemann's 'sacred law' sayings. These have a recognizable form (found in e.g. 1 Cor. 3: 17 and 14: 38), with the first part referring to the activity of man and the second to the eschatological activity of God, a form which Käsemann attributes to early Christian prophets. Let us suppose (though it is in fact debated) that Käsemann is right. What follows when we find a similar form in the Gospels? (See Mark 8: 38 again, or Matt. 6: 14f.) 'We must accept the fact that in their present form the two gospel sayings come from an early Christian tradition and not from the teaching of Jesus', says N. If he had said 'We must accept this as a possibility', he would have had some justice in his claim. But what has actually happened is that the 'criterion of dissimilarity' has ben treated as if it yielded, not a minimum core of material that has to be ascribed to Jesus, but the maximum possible that can be ascribed to Him. (N is, in reflective moments, aware of this vital distinction; it is a shame he did not keep it more constantly in mind.) There are of course other possible explanations for the occurrence of this form in the Gospels as well as the Epistles, besides the one that the Gospel instances are the work of Christian prophets after the time of Christ Himself. One is that the form was not confined to *later* prophets but was also used by 'the prophet Jesus of Nazareth', and imitated by His followers later. Another, and perhaps an even more likely one, is that the form is based on one found more than once in the Old Testament prophets (e.g. Isaiah 1: 19–20; Jer. 4: 1–2),[1] which either Jesus or a later Christian prophet could have used. One thing is certain, we do not have to accept the 'fact' that these Gospel sayings are not dominical. Indeed N, to his credit, has doubts himself: Matthew 6: 14 he thinks a 'legalizing' of the central petition of the Lord's Prayer, while Mark 8: 38 is derived from a more primitive form which quite probably goes back to Jesus Himself. Maybe their present form does come from early Christian tradition; but what N is trying to show is not that the wording of Jesus' sayings was

---

[1] The roots of the form are of course grounded in law, as Käsemann's designation recognizes; cf. e.g. Deut. 28: 1 ff.

affected by transmission in the early Church, but that new prophetic sayings were incorrectly ascribed to His earthly teaching; and this even he himself evidently does not think has been done.

His last example is taken from Barnabas Lindars's *New Testament Apologetic*.[2] The speech of Peter in Acts 2: 14–36 is based, Lindars (rightly) says, on Joel 2: 28–32 and Psalm 16: 8–11, with the use also of Psalm 110: 1. But, he continues, Mark 12: 35–7 parr., Jesus' question about the Messiah as David's Son, turns on the same point as the one Peter makes in Acts 2: 34. 'The whole pericope is evidently derived from the exegesis preserved in Acts 2'.[3] 'In other words', comments N, 'the pericope ... is not a historical reminiscence of the ministry of Jesus.'

In order to reach this conclusion, however, we should have to have shown, not just that the pericope in Mark makes sense in the light of the Acts exegesis, but that it is unintelligible without it; and also, one might add, that the exegesis was not first on the lips of Jesus and then taken over by Peter (or Luke, or the early Church generally, if it is supposed that Acts 2: 14–36 is a later composition and not Peter's own). In actual fact, of course, all three Synoptists clearly thought that the pericope made sense on its own without the more elaborate exegesis preserved in Acts, that obviously David's Lord had to be greater than David's Son. The Acts exegesis (which is actually designed to make the rather different point that a descendant of David could be greater than David himself) could at best reinforce the argument in Mark; more likely it would only complicate it. A case could even be made out for saying that the two exegeses are incompatible with one another. Certainly the *Sitzen in Leben* are different in the two: one is a proclamation that Jesus is Lord, the other a debate within the Jewish exegetical tradition.[4] But if for the sake of argument we assume that the Marcan exegesis *is* an abbreviated form of the Acts one, we have said nothing about their order in time—*unless* we are already presupposing the 'criterion of dissimilarity' in its illegitimate form. On Lindars's hypothesis, the Marcan version has been abbreviated at some point in its history; why not on its way from the lips of Jesus rather than on its way to be ascribed to them? We are only entitled to reject this if we already know that where the same idea occurs

---

[2] Lindars (1961), pp. 36ff.   [3] p. 47.
[4] I owe this point to my friend the Revd Alan Padgett.

ascribed to Jesus and to the early Church the latter is always the
true ascription, or if we have some special reason for thinking this
to be so in this particular case; and no such special reason has
been given.

We are faced with what is looking very like a large-scale case
of *petitio principii* or 'begging the question', purporting to prove
a conclusion with an argument which covertly assumes that conclusion and cannot get off the ground without it. For at this stage,
remember, N has not yet introduced the criterion of dissimilarity
as a principle of method; he is supposedly showing why we cannot
take the Synoptic material at face value, and then moving on to
suggest the criterion as a way of unearthing material on which we
can rely. But in order to show this he has in both these latter examples
assumed the criterion in advance—in all good faith, it need hardly
be said; it is so much a part of his approach that he does not notice
his own use of it.

We may conclude this excursus with a brief glance at N's reply
to three objections sometimes raised against this sort of form-critical
approach: that it ascribes too great a creative power to the early
Christian community; that the New Testament itself appeals to eyewitnesses (Luke 1: 2); and that the continued existence of Jesus'
own disciples while the tradition was taking shape would have been
a check on misattributions and distortions.

The first need not detain us long. N's reply is obviously correct:
it is not a nebulous 'community' that was creative, but individual
prophets, exegetes, and evangelists, classes which certainly existed
in the early Church. The third is met by the argument that there
is no reason to suppose that James, Peter, John, and the rest were
any more interested in biographical accuracy than (say) Paul or
Luke. Now there are writings in the New Testament ascribed to
Peter, James, and John; yet it would be hard to find any evidence
in these writings of their conflating the risen Lord and the earthly
Jesus. Indeed, the Book of Revelation, which ascribes a number
of sayings to the Lord, makes it clear that it is the *risen* Lord who
is referred to, nor do these sayings appear elsewhere ascribed to
the earthly Jesus. Still, we may concede that if Paul and Luke did
blur the earthly Jesus and the Lord of the Church, then perhaps
James, Peter, and John did too. One might wonder about the
premiss, though, especially in the light of Luke 1: 2, and possibly
of 1 Corinthians 7: 10 ff. as well. What does N have to say about

Luke's reference to eyewitnesses? That when Luke says 'eyewitnesses' he includes even people like Paul. We must 'ban from our
minds what a modern writer would mean by an "eyewitness", he
says. The trouble is, an ancient writer would mean exactly the same
as a modern one—somebody who had seen a thing with his or her
own eyes. δι' ἀκοῆς αἰσθανόμενος ἢ καὶ παντάπασιν αὐτὸς
αὐτόπτης, says Plato, 'either learning of it by hearsay or being
himself an eyewitness'.[5] Ah, says N, but Paul was 'appointed to
be a witness' (Acts 22: 14f., 26: 16), and says of himself 'Have I
not seen the Lord?' (1 Cor. 9: 1, to which we may add 15: 8). Paul
was, to himself and to Luke, as much an 'eyewitness' as Peter or
John.

Were it not for the fact that N is aware that αὐτόπτης, 'eyewitness', is not found in Luke's writings except at Luke 1: 2, the horrid
suspicion would creep into one's mind that N had been using an
English Bible rather than a Greek, and had overlooked the fact
that in Greek the words for 'witness' and 'eyewitness' are unrelated.
Acts 22: 15 and 26: 16 use μάρτυς, 'witness', not αὐτόπτης, 'eyewitness'. μάρτυς is an active word, referring to what one says, a witness
in the sense of someone testifying; αὐτόπτης is more passive in
flavour, referring to what one has seen. Hence one can be a *false*
or *lying* μάρτυς, but not a false αὐτόπτης. In Acts 1: 21–2 the
two qualities are at once united and distinguished: in Judas's place
someone is to be chosen who had accompanied the Apostles from
the baptism of John till the Ascension (i.e. an αὐτόπτης, though
the word itself is not used), who is now also to be a witness (μάρτυς)
to tell of the Resurrection. It is this last kind of witness that Paul
is to be. He does claim to have seen the Lord, of course; but this
refers to his vision on the Damascus Road, and as far as that was
concerned he was an 'eyewitness' in the so-called 'modern' sense
of the word.

What we have here is no failure of industry, or learning, or
ingenuity; it is fundamentally failure to reason carefully enough,
failure to see what evidence actually goes to establish a position
and what is merely consistent with it. In effect, it is as a rule failure
in logic. There may well be other 'radical' critics who have a better
grasp of method, and maybe if N had had more space to give examples we should have formed a more favourable impression

---

[5] *Laws*, 10, 900a.

(though presumably he chose his best examples); but an outsider
to biblical criticism like myself cannot help wondering how much
of the edifice of contemporary New Testament scepticism may be
a lot more rickety and unreliable than is realized.[6]

[6] For interesting essays by other 'outsiders', see Lewis (1967), pp. 152–66; Sherwin-
White (1963), pp. 186–93; Palmer (1968), pp. 175–92. For a similar complaint by
a definite 'insider' see Hooker (1970–1), pp. 480–7.

References

APPASAMY, A. J. (1942), *The Gospel and India's Heritage* (London and Madras).

ATHANASIUS, St (1944), *The Incarnation*, introd. C. S. Lewis (London).

BAILLIE, D. (1961), *God was in Christ* (p/b London).

BAKER, J. A. (1975), *The Foolishness of God* (p/b London).

BARBOUR, R. S. (1972), *Traditio-Historical Criticism of the Gospels* (London).

BARCLAY, W. (1962), *Jesus as They Saw Him* (London).

BARROW, J., and TIPLER, F. (1986), *The Anthropic Cosmological Principle* (Oxford).

BARTH, K. (1956–8), *Church Dogmatics*, part iv (ET Edinburgh).

BARTHOLOMEW, D. J. (1984), *God of Chance* (London).

BARTSCH, H. (1953) (ed.), *Kerygma and Myth*, i (ET London).

Bhagavad-Gītā, The (1969), ed. and trans. R.C. Zaehner (Oxford).

BONHOEFFER, D. (1978), *Christology* (ET p/b London).

BORGES, J. L. (1962), *Ficciones* (ET New York).

BORNKAMM, G. (1973), *Jesus of Nazareth* (ET 2nd edn., London).

BOYD, R. (1969), *Introduction to Indian Christian Theology* (Madras).

BROWN, R. (1968), *Jesus, God and Man* (London).

BUBER, M. (1966), *For the Sake of Heaven* (ET New York).

BULTMANN, R. (1955), *Theology of the New Testament* (ET London).

—— (1960), *Jesus Christ and Mythology* (ET London).

—— (1964), *Existence and Faith* (ET p/b London).

—— (1971), *The Gospel of John* (ET Oxford).

BURI, F. (1966), *Christian Faith in Our Time* (ET London).

CAIRD, J. (1899), *The Fundamental Ideas of Christianity* (Glasgow).

CALVIN, J. (1963), *Commentary on Hebrews, etc.* (ET Edinburgh).

CAMPBELL, C. A. (1957), *On Selfhood and Godhood* (London).

CARTER, S. (1969), *Songs of Sydney Carter in the Present Tense*, book 3 (London).

CHESTERTON, G. K. (1955), *The Everlasting Man* (p/b New York).

CHEYNE, T. K., and BLACK, J. S. (1899–1903), (eds.), *Encyclopaedia Biblica* (London).

CONZELMANN, H. (1969), *Outline of the Theology of the New Testament* (ET London).

CUPITT, D. (1976), *The Leap of Reason* (London).

—— (1979), *The Debate about Christ* (London).

DAVENPORT, S. F. (1925), *Immanence and Incarnation* (Cambridge).

DODD, C. H. (1963), *Historical Tradition in the Fourth Gospel* (Cambridge).

DONNE, J. (1953–62), *Sermons*, ed. G. R. Potter and E. M. Simpson (Berkeley).

DORNER, I. (1880–2), *System of Christian Doctrine* (ET Edinburgh).

DOYLE, A. C. (1981), *The Final Adventures of Sherlock Holmes* (London).

DRIVER, T. F. (1981), *Christ for a Changing World* (London).

DYSON, A. O. (1969), *Who is Jesus Christ?* (London).

—— (1974), *The Immortality of the Past* (London).

EDWARDS, J. (1754), *A Careful and Strict Inquiry into the Prevailing Notions of the Freedom of Will* (Boston).

FARQUHAR, J. N. (1915), *The Crown of Hinduism* (Madras).

FARRER, A. M. (1972), *Reflective Faith* (London).

—— (1976), *Interpretation and Belief* (London).

FLEW, A., and MACINTYRE, A. (1955) (eds.), *New Essays in Philosophical Theology* (London).

FORSYTH, P. T. (1909), *The Person and Place of Jesus Christ* (London).

—— (1916), *The Justification of God* (London).

FRANCKS, R. (1979), 'Omniscience, Omnipotence, and Pantheism', in *Philosophy*, 54, pp. 395ff.

FULLER, R. (1963), *The New Testament in Current Study* (London).

GALOT, J. (1969), *La Personne du Christ* (Gembloux and Paris).

—— (1971), *La Conscience de Jésus* (Gembloux and Paris).

—— (1980), *Who is Christ?* (ET Rome).

GODET, J. (1876), *The Gospel of Saint John* (ET Edinburgh).

GORE, C. (1889), *Belief in Christ* (London).

—— (1891), *The Incarnation of the Son of God* (London).

—— (1895), *Dissertations on Subjects Related to the Incarnation* (London).

—— (1922), *Belief in Christ* (London).

GOULDER, M. (1979) (ed.), *Incarnation and Myth* (London).

GREEN, M. (1977) (ed.), *The Truth of God Incarnate* (London).

GUTHRIE, D. (1981), *New Testament Theology* (Leicester).

HAGIN, J. (1972), *I Believe in Visions* (Old Tappan).

HANSON, A. (1975), *Grace and Truth* (London).

HARVEY, V. A. (1967), *The Historian and the Believer* (London).

HENDRY, G. S. (1959), *The Gospel of the Incarnation* (London).

HENGEL, M. (1976), *The Son of God* (ET London).

HERBERT, R. T. (1979), *Paradox and Identity in Theology* (Ithaca).

HICK, J. (1964) (ed.), *The Existence of God* (London).

—— (1977a), *God and the Universe of Faiths* (p/b London).

—— (1977*b*) (ed.), *The Myth of God Incarnate* (London).

—— (1989), 'The Logic of God Incarnate', *Religious Studies*, 25, pp. 409–23.

HODGSON, L. (1943), *The Doctrine of the Trinity* (Welwyn).

HOOKER, M. D. (1967), *The Son of Man in Mark* (London).

—— (1970–1), 'Christology and Methodology', *New Testament Studies*, 17, pp. 480–7.

HOULDEN, J. L. (1977), *Patterns of Faith* (London).

HUME, D. (1738), *A Treatise of Human Nature* (London).

ILLINGWORTH, J. (1900), *Divine Immanence* (2nd edn., London).

INGE, W. R. (1924), *Personal Idealism and Mysticism* (3rd edn., London).

JEREMIAS, J. (1966), *Rediscovering the Parables* 1 (ET London).

—— *New Testament Theology*, vol. 1 (ET London).

KELLY, J. N. D. (1960), *Early Christian Doctrines* (2nd edn., London).

KIERKEGAARD, S. (1967), *Philosophical Fragments* (ET Princeton).

KLOSTERMAIER, J. (1969), *Hindu and Christian in Vrindaban* (London).

KNOX, J. (1963), *The Church and the Reality of Christ* (London).

—— (1967), *The Humanity and Divinity of Christ* (Cambridge).

KULANDRAN, S. (1964), *Grace: A Comparative Study of the Doctrine in Christianity and Hinduism* (London).

KÜNG, H. (1976), *On Being a Christian* (ET p/b London).

LABOURT, J. (1904), *Le Christianisme dans l'empire perse* (Paris).

LAMPE, G. W. H. (1977), *God as Spirit* (Oxford).

LEWIS, C. S. (1938), *Out of the Silent Planet* (London).

—— (1946), *The Great Divorce* (London).

—— (1953), *Perelandra* [Voyage to Venus] (p/b London).

—— (1955), *Mere Christianity* (p/b London).

—— (1959), *Shall We Lose God in Outer Space?* (London).

—— (1961), *An Experiment In Criticism* (p/b Cambridge).

—— (1964), *Poems* (London).

—— (1967), *Christian Reflections* (London).

LIDDON, H. P. (1891), *The Divinity of our Lord* (14th edn., London).

LINDARS, B. (1961), *New Testament Apologetic* (London).

—— (1971), *Behind the Fourth Gospel* (London).

—— (1972), *The Gospel of John* (London).

LONERGAN, B. (1974), *A Second Collection* (London).

LOSSKY, V. (1957), *The Mystical Theology of the Eastern Church* (ET London).

LUCAS, J. (1970), *The Freedom of the Will* (Oxford).

MacDONALD, G. (1976), *Creation in Christ*, ed. R. Hein (Wheaton).

McINTYRE, J. (1966), *The Shape of Christology* (London).

MACKEY, J. (1979), *Jesus, the Man and the Myth* (London).

MACKINTOSH, H. R. (1913), *The Person of Jesus Christ* (2nd edn., Edinburgh).

MACQUARRIE, J. (1973), *Thinking about God* (London).

MCTAGGART, J. M. E. (1906), *Some Dogmas of Religion* (London).

—— (1918), *Studies in Hegelian Cosmology* (2nd edn., Oxford).

—— (1934), *Philosophical Studies* (London).

MARTENSEN, H. (1874), *Christian Dogmatics* (ET Edinburgh).

MARTIN, C. B. (1959), *Religious Belief* (Cornell).

MASCALL, E. L. (1946), *Christ, the Christian and the Church* (London).

—— (1956*a*), *Christian Theology and Natural Science* (London).

—— (1956*b*), *Via Media* (London).

—— (1977), *Theology and the Gospel of Christ* (London).

—— (1980), *Whatever Happened to the Human Mind?* (London).

MATTHEWS, W. R. (1950), *The Problem of Christ in the Twentieth Century* (London).

MEYENDORFF, J. (1975), *Christ in Eastern Christian Thought* (New York).

MOORE, G. E. (1912), *Ethics* (London).

MOORE, S. (1980), *The Fire and the Rose are One* (London).

MORRIS, L. (1972), *The Gospel according to John* (London).

MORRIS, T. V. (1986), *The Logic of God Incarnate* (Ithaca).

NESTORIUS (1925), *The Bazaar of Heraclides*, ed. G. R. Driver and L. Hodgson (Oxford).

NINEHAM, D. (1963), *The Gospel of St Mark* (Harmondsworth).

NOWELL-SMITH, P. H. (1954), *Ethics* (Harmondsworth).

OGDEN, S. (1962), *Christ without Myth* (London).

—— (1982), *The Point of Christology* (London).

OPPENHEIMER, H. (1973), *Incarnation and Immanence* (London).

PALMER, H. (1968), *The Logic of Gospel Criticism* (London).

PANIKKAR, R. (1964), *The Unknown Christ of Hinduism* (London).

PANNENBERG, W. (1968), *Jesus, God and Man* (ET London).

PERRIN, N. (1959), *Rediscovering the Teaching of Jesus* (London).

PITTENGER, W. N. (1959), *The Word Incarnate* (Welwyn).

—— (1970), *Christology Reconsidered* (London).

—— (1978) (ed.), *Christ for Us Today* (London).

PLANTINGA, A. (1975), *God, Freedom and Evil* (London).

PUCCETTI, R. (1968), *Persons* (London).

RAHNER, K. (1961), *Theological Investigations*, i (ET London).

—— (1988), *Foundations of Christian Faith* (ET London).

RASHDALL, H. (1919), *The Idea of the Atonement* (London).

RELTON, H. M. (1917), *A Study in Christology* (London).

REUTHER, R. R. (1983), *Sexism and God-Talk* (London).

RITSCHL, A. (1900), *The Christian Doctrine of Justification and Reconciliation* (ET Edinburgh).

ROBINSON, J. A. T. (1963), *Honest to God* (London).

—— (1973), *The Human Face of God* (London).

ROWDON, H. H. (1982) (ed.), *Christ the Lord* (Leicester).

SALMON, G. (1952), *The Infallibility of the Church* (5th, abridged, edn., London).

SAMUEL, V., and SUGDEN, C. (1983) (eds.), *Sharing Christ in the Two-Thirds World* (Bangalore).

SAMUEL, V. C. (1973), 'The Christology of Severus of Antioch', *Abba Salama*, 4, pp. 126–90.

SANDAY, W. (1910), *Christologies Ancient and Modern* (Oxford).

SARTRE, J.-P. (1969), *Being and Nothingness* (ET London).

SCHILLEBEECKX, E., *Jesus: An Experiment in Christology* (ET London).

SCHILPP, P. (1944) (ed.), *The Philosophy of Bertrand Russell* (Evanston).

—— (1952) (ed.), *The Philosophy of G. E. Moore* (2nd edn., New York).

SCHLEIERMACHER, F. (1928), *The Christian Faith* (ET Edinburgh).

SCHMITHALS, W. (1968), *Introduction to the Theology of Rudolf Bultmann* (ET London).

SCHOONENBERG, P. (1972), *The Christ* (ET London).

SCHWEIZER, E. (1971), *The Good News according to Mark* (ET London).

SELLERS, R. (1940), *Two Ancient Christologies* (London).

SHERWIN-WHITE, A. N. (1963), *Roman Society and Roman Law in the New Testament* (Oxford).

SMART, N. (1960), *A Dialogue of Religions* (London).

SOBRINO, J. (1978), *Christology at the Crossroads* (ET London).

SONG, C.-S. (1979), *Third Eye Theology* (London).

STRANGE, R. (1981), *Newman and the Gospel of Christ* (Oxford).

STRAWSON, P. (1952), *Introduction to Logical Theory* (London).

STREETER, B., and APPASAMY, A. J. (1921), *The Sadhu* (London).

SWINBURNE, R. (1979), *The Existence of God* (Oxford, 1979).

SYKES, S., and CLAYTON, J. (1972) (eds.), *Christ, Faith and History* (Cambridge).

TEMPLE, W. (1924), *Christus Veritas* (London).

THORNTON, L. S. (1928), *The Incarnate Lord* (London).

TOAL, M. (1957–63)(ed.), *Sunday Sermons of the Great Fathers* (London).

TOLKIEN, J. R. R. (1964), *Tree and Leaf* (London).

TOULMIN, S., *et al.* (1957), *Metaphysical Beliefs* (London).

VAN BUREN, P. (1963), *The Secular Meaning of the Gospel* (London).

VERMES, G. (1976), *Jesus the Jew* (p/b London).

VICEDOM, G. (1972) (ed.), *Christ and the Younger Churches* (London).

VIDLER, A. (1962) (ed.), *Soundings* (Cambridge).

VINE, A. R. (1937), *The Nestorian Churches* (London).

—— (1948), *An Approach to Christology* (London).

WACE, H., and SCHAFF, P. (1890) (eds.), *Select Library of Nicene and Post-Nicene Fathers*, series 2, vol. xiv (Oxford).

WELCH, C. (1965) (ed.), *God and Incarnation in Mid-Nineteenth Century German Theology* (New York).

WESTCOTT, B. F. (1883), *The Epistles of Saint John* (London).

WESTON, F. (1907), *The One Christ* (London).

—— (1920), *The Revelation of Eternal Love* (London).

WIGRAM, W. A. (1910), *History of the Assyrian Church* (London).

WILES, M. F. (1970), 'Does Christology Rest on a Mistake?', *Religious Studies*, 6, pp. 75ff.

—— (1974), *The Remaking of Christian Doctrine* (London).

WILLIAMS, C. (1943), *The Figure of Beatrice* (London).

—— (1950), *He Came Down from Heaven* (London).

—— (1954), *The Greater Trumps* (London).

—— (1958), *The Image of the City*, ed. A. Ridler (Oxford).

WITTGENSTEIN, L. (1953), *Philosophical Investigations* (Oxford).

ZAEHNER, R. C. (1958), *At Sundry Times* (London).

Index of Names